D1447073

THE TROUBLE
WITH EMPIRE

THE TROUBLE WITH EMPIRE

Challenges to Modern British Imperialism

Antoinette Burton

OXFORD
UNIVERSITY PRESS

OXFORD
UNIVERSITY PRESS

Oxford University Press is a department of the University of
Oxford. It furthers the University's objective of excellence in research,
scholarship, and education by publishing worldwide.

Oxford   New York
Auckland   Cape Town   Dar es Salaam   Hong Kong   Karachi
Kuala Lumpur   Madrid   Melbourne   Mexico City   Nairobi
New Delhi   Shanghai   Taipei   Toronto

With offices in
Argentina   Austria   Brazil   Chile   Czech Republic   France   Greece
Guatemala   Hungary   Italy   Japan   Poland   Portugal   Singapore
South Korea   Switzerland   Thailand   Turkey   Ukraine   Vietnam

Oxford is a registered trademark of Oxford University Press
in the UK and certain other countries.

Published in the United States of America by
Oxford University Press
198 Madison Avenue, New York, NY 10016

© Oxford University Press 2015

Library of Congress Cataloging-in-Publication Data
Burton, Antoinette M., 1961–
The trouble with empire : challenges to modern British imperialism /
Antoinette Burton.
pages cm
Includes bibliographical references and index.
ISBN 978-0-19-993660-1 (hardcover : alk. paper)
1. Great Britain—Colonies—History.   2. Imperialism—History—19th century.
3. Imperialism—History—20th century.   4. Anti-imperialist movements—
Great Britain—History—19th century.   5. Anti-imperialist movements—
Great Britain—History—20th century.   I. Title.   II. Title: Challenges to
modern British imperialism.
DA16.B863 2015
325′.320941—dc23
2015009994

1 3 5 7 9 8 6 4 2
Printed in the United States of America
on acid-free paper

For Catherine

with admiration, respect, and love

Small things matter, and that's where the leakage begins.
VIRGINIA WOOLF, *Night and Day, 1919*

The little bird forgets the trap, but the trap does not forget the bird.
AIMÉ CÉSAIRE, *A Season in the Congo, 1966*

CONTENTS

ACKNOWLEDGMENTS

The problem of how to write the kind of British empire history I can live with has troubled me for quite some time. Many people have helped me figure it out, and for that I am deeply grateful. In Philippa Levine and Dane Kennedy I have invaluable interlocutors who push me out of my comfort zones and offer knowledgeable, committed critique. Philippa has been there from the start: our journeys to and from the Fawcett Library have diverged and converged again in ways that keep our friendship vigorous. Jean Allman read early drafts of the book and offered detailed, thoughtful comments I have taken to heart. Minnie Sinha and Caroline Bressey did the same, for which I am also grateful. George Robb has been there since our Fulbright days. His expert eye and acerbic wit have long been indispensable. Isabel Hofmeyr knows her way around a book, and she read parts of this one with verve and enthusiasm. I feel really lucky to be in conversation with her. Peter Fritzsche, Herman Bennett, Onni Gust, Augusto Espiritu, John Lynn, Lara Kriegel, Poshek Fu, Kristin Hoganson, Srirupa Prasad, Scott Harrison and Fred Hoxie gave me invaluable feedback at various stages, while Ken Cuno and Siobhan Lambert-Hurley generously fed me key sources on empire and

Islam. Heather Streets-Salter also provided me with work that was hot off the press. Zarena Aslami has been uncommonly generous in spite of the fact that we have never met. Asef Bayat's "politics of the ordinary" is an inspiration, and his feedback on the chapter he read was most welcome. Dave Roediger read with characteristic care; he sent me toward George Padmore and economic hegemony and so much more. Tony Ballantyne is always one step ahead of me. The effects of his work, his friendship, and our collaborations can be seen and felt on every page of this book.

The intellectual community I live in on a daily basis has left an indelible mark on my research, writing, teaching, and thinking. Thanks to Dana Rabin for encouraging me on many fronts and helping me stay abreast of the latest work via our "Britain, Empire Knowledge" reading group. Three years of "World Histories from Below" have also left their mark, thanks to the intellectual sodality of Kathy Oberdeck and the labor, intellectual and otherwise, of Zach Sell and Stephanie Seawell. Parts of this manuscript were presented at the Center for South Asia and Middle East Studies brown bag lectures, the History Workshop, and the Labor and Working Class Reading Group at the University of Illinois. The epilogue started as a piece for the Illinois Program for Research in the Humanities, for which I thank Dianne Harris. Such intellectually rigorous opportunities are a dime a dozen at Illinois, but the department's long-standing History Workshop provides the kind of tough-love feedback you just can't get anywhere else. I thank Jim Barrett, Diane Koenker, Tamara Chaplin, Ken Cuno, Kathy Oberdeck, Tariq Ali, Terri Barnes, Jim Brennan, Clare Crowston, and Bob Morrissey for many stimulating sessions beyond my own.

Jim Barrett, for his part, seems to have always thought I could do this, and his brotherly love—as well as his line-editing devotion—has meant the world to me. Behroozala is, quiet simply, a brother of the heart. Sam Frost read every sentence with a fine-tooth comb. It's been a true joy and privilege to share my work with her, and I am profoundly grateful for all she has done for and been to me these last few years. Siobhan Somerville has also been there every step of the way. I could not ask for a more generous, caring friend: a comrade faithful and true in all struggles, and the keenest of minds as well. Tom Bedwell is so indispensable to our lives in History at Illinois that it's hard to know how to properly thank him; I am so happy we are in the same orbit. Although she was not involved in this project, Miriam Angress is so special to me and I treasure our friendship, as I hope and trust she knows.

Students in my graduate seminar in spring 2014—a veritable laboratory of dissent and disruption—helped me work through the final stages of the book in ways too meaningful to fully capture here. Profound thanks are due to Ben Bamberger, Utathya Chattopadhyaya, Beth Eby, Heather Freund, Anna Harbaugh, Liz Matsushita, Umair Rasheed, Zachary Riebeling, Mark Sanchez, and Esti Ezkerra Vegas. Utathya is inimitable: he's an eager reader of every single thing and always helps me clarify my thinking. Mark is one of my favorite interlocutors, and I thank him for what is always thought provoking intellectual company. T. J. Tallie, now a colleague, has shared many a chai and a vent and has shaped my thinking in more ways than he knows. He has a sharp eye for Indo-centricity, Cetshwayo, and that's not all. To Julie Laut, Irina Spector-Marks, Zack Poppel, Anna Jacobs, Zach Sell, Devin Smart, Ryan Jones, Brandon Mills, Ian Hartman, Mike Staudenmaier, Emily Skidmore, and Karen Rodriguez'G, I am also grateful for letting me share in their growth as historians and for shaping my own. Julie's hard work in the last stretch was invaluable and has made this book much the better. As for Susan Ferber, her editing is brutally honest, but it makes all the difference. She believes in my work when I am not sure. The

same has long been true of my parents as well. Thanks too to
Vicki and Monica for all their love and support. Bastian funds
made research trips possible. To the John Simon Guggenheim
Foundation I owe an incomparable debt. My 2010 fellowship
was a real boon, giving me a badly needed opportunity to
rethink and recharge after some years of administrative work.

Colleagues and friends near and far were supportive while
I was writing this book, in ways witting and unwitting. I thank
Eileen Ford, Ann Curthoys, Jed Esty, Fiona Paisley, Chantal
Nadeau, Barbara Ramusack, Gerry Forbes, Karen Flynn, Renisa
Mawani, Jessica Millward, Sanjam Ahluwalia, Nancy Abelmann,
Hannah Rosen, Ania Loomba, Suvir Kaul, Samia Khatun, and
Madhavi Kale. In friendship I am far richer than I deserve.
Jennifer Morgan has been there through thick and thin, and
the warmth of her embrace is like no other. Laura Mayhall is a
gem. Her friendship sustains me in so many ways. Our weeks in
London both with and without Isabel have been precious beyond
words and I will always cherish them. I owe Laura Welle a huge
debt for the loving care she showed all of us for three years. Nick
and Olivia are what gets me up in the morning, even if they are
still sleeping. And Paul is the sine qua non, now for a quarter of
a century.

The late, beloved Stuart Hall was a powerful influence on
me, and his death remains cataclysmic for all who knew him,
whether as a teacher or a friend. I hope he knew how deeply
I admired him and how much I valued those quiet talks in the
living room before dinner. Catherine knows, because she made
them happen. I have labored in the ambit of her work and love
for many years, and I dedicate this book to her humbly and
with deep appreciation.

THE TROUBLE
WITH EMPIRE

Introduction

The Troubled Ground of Empire

What are the roots that clutch, what branches grow
Out of this stony rubbish?

T. S. ELIOT, *The Waste Land*, 1922

The trouble with British imperial histories is that they are not written with dissent and disruption in the lead. Even when they concede that agents of resistance shaped the end of empire, historians of its long life rarely write as if trouble, rather than extension and hegemony, was the characteristic feature of imperial power on the ground. Yet the very character of imperial power was shaped by its challengers and by the trouble they made for its stewards. Empire arguably has no history outside these struggles. Whether on imperial battlefields, where the British were deemed victorious, or in the colonial marketplace of labor and consumption, where capital was said to be settled, or in the realm of transnational politics, where colonial subjects were thought to have acquiesced in the endless deferral of independence and self-rule—in all these domains antagonists continually challenged the narrative of Pax Britannica and breached the security of empire's defenses. Those who lived through the realities of modern British imperialism, whether as colonized or colonizer, settler or native, witnessed firsthand the combination of resistance and insecurity that characterized the daily life of empire on the ground. Those who live in the shadow of the British empire and continue to draw so much from its legacy ought, therefore, to have a keener understanding of how and why the trouble with empire was so apparent to those in its grasp.

If there is no comprehensive history dedicated to insecurity in the nineteenth- and twentieth-century British empire, this is not for want of attention to the enemies of imperialism or challenges to it. There are accounts of the nature and character of colonial discourse and of the role of discrete nationalist figures and organizations in disrupting the colonial state. There are narratives of episodic political rebellion and economic uprising and diagnoses of imperial fatigue and decline. There are even a few choice histories of metropolitan anti-imperialism and, increasingly, a literature on the imperial police and intelligence systems that developed to combat conspiracies and plots against British representatives and outposts of empire. But while imperial blockbusters fly off the shelves, wide-ranging accounts of those who struggled with and against imperial power across its many holdings, whether by weakening its hold on local economic and political structures or outright challenging its claims to hegemony, have failed to materialize. Such an absence is particularly striking in an era of spectacular and empire-humbling insurgency like our own. The legacy of Pax Britannica is not simply an ornamental trace of a Victorian optimism that guaranteed the benefits of the civilizing mission. In the absence of grand synthetic counter-narratives of protest, resistance and revolution, the presumption of basic stability remains the working premise of British imperial history in its grand narrative forms, especially as it is popularly consumed and understood. This study offers a short, focused account of the British empire's turbulence by foregrounding the frictions that marked its limits and the tenuous hold it had on colonial subjects during its troubled life.

Arguing for a keener sense of empire's instabilities does not mean that empire was powerless or that, in the face of successive military, economic, and political crises, it obtained merely "meager" sovereignty or dominion.[1] In many respects, British imperialism was indubitably successful; its global reach was a key metric of that success. As many British schoolchildren knew, the map of the world was either red or pink, with imperial influence and British capital and commercial activity extended across an impressive range of global territory. Indigenous populations were variously contained, displaced, or decimated as their labor and resources were appropriated. The authority of traditional leaders was undercut, often significantly, and the legitimacy of their culture was subject not simply to critique but to reform and "uplift" and unending scrutiny as well. Land was confiscated, alienated, or absorbed into markets that were geared toward the interests of the colonizers. Taxes were levied and extracted, resources were identified and extracted with a ruthless hunger, economic patterns and physical landscapes were fundamentally transformed to serve the interests of imperial moneymen and markets. Not least, settlers were settled, railways were built, and terrible violence was done to try to guarantee all those projects. Empire was certainly durable, and its wherewithal cannot be gainsaid.

But there were always dangers lurking at the edges—dangers that could give settlement a semi-permanent feel, make occupation look precarious, and cast a dubious light on the promise of explorer David Livingstone's three Cs: commerce, civilization, and Christianity. Despite the abstract appeal of the upward arc of imperial progress and even the concrete reality of empire's global reach, imperialism on the spot was downright rocky, its realities grimmer and more alarming than the tuneful imperative of *Rule, Britannia!* allows. The turbulence of empire deserves more attention in comprehensive narrative accounts of British imperial history not because it is the whole story, but because it was a regular, everyday feature of imperial experience for colonized and colonizer alike. Such insecurity was sponsored by the very global ambition of British imperialism and is one powerful index of its aspiration. As such, the trouble with empire—its perpetual insecurity—should drive big histories of modern British imperialism rather than serve merely as backdrop to the story of its rise and fall.

Despite the many varieties of British imperial history made available by new archival evidence and innovative methods in the last twenty-five years, that rise-and-fall narrative of British imperial power has proven amazingly resilient. An inheritance from western histories of Rome solidified by Edward Gibbon and Thomas Babington Macaulay and undergirded by the political promise of liberalism, that particular narrative arc—a kind of "great arch" model—has persisted, both directly and more subtly, as the schematic underpinning of the great majority of narratives produced about British imperialism since the nineteenth century.[2] The subtitle of Niall Ferguson's *Empire*—"The Rise and Demise of the British World Order and the Lessons for Global Power"—may not be representative of the kind of scholarly approach most empire historians take today, yet traces of its contours remain in the catchphrase "empire on which the sun never set" and in the general preoccupation of imperial histories with "twilight" or "endgame" (whether as romantic ebbing or dramatic reversal). This book-ended notion of imperial power, with its confident punctuations of rise and fall and its tendency to spotlight conditions of British expansion and consolidation, continues to dominate understandings of the British empire and of empires writ large and to support a Pax Britannica story—one in which imperial peace and stability were the normative order of the day.

Yet this model of imperial history has real limits. For one thing, the ebb and flow it invokes tends to foreclose the possibility that imperial power was neither so grandly cyclical nor so incontrovertibly successful until it, inevitably, "fell." Just because mutinies were suppressed, strikes broken, pass laws created, and assassins hanged, social and political order was not necessarily secured. Indeed, the rise-and-fall pattern assumes that histories of dramatic events such as the Indian uprising of 1857, or of longer-term conflicts like the South African war of 1899–1902, tell the whole story of imperial disorder on the ground. Understanding war and labor agitation and revolutionary activity as routine rather than exceptional offers a more accurate assessment of empire's practical limits. Big narrative history need not be set aside in order to appreciate the trouble that empire had, and took, to maintain its grip on power. Imperial history at whatever scale must do more than admit the fragility or tensions of empire.[3] It must account for the ordinary actors, everyday practices, and low-level movements that made uncertainty the standard experience, rather than the exception that made the rule.

The preeminence of the rise-and-fall paradigm in traditional narrative histories of empire has had important consequences for how British imperial history is received and read. Its recurrence in titles and arguments, from scholarly monographs to popular accounts, suggests that neither studies of resistance nor comprehensive imperial histories that center colonial dissent and disruption have made their way into commonsense perceptions of the British empire.[4] Colonial unrest is thought of as the exception to an overall story of dominance and hegemony, and even historians interested in colonial rebellion tend to focus on the sporadic event or the transgressive individual—examples that, more often than not, end up being the case of resistance that proves the rule of hegemony. As significantly, classic imperial theories such as V. I. Lenin's or Joseph Schumpeter's are more consonant with the "inner logics" of extension and consolidation than with

a recurrently turbulent, disorderly model of the nature of imperial rule.[5] In contrast, "perpetual ferment" has been the working definition of many scholars of colonialism in situ, whether
they have written about politics, labor, commerce, or nationalism. Unlike imperial historians, Africanists, South Asianists,
and students of the white settler colonies have understood that
disrupting imperial authority was a workaday practice for many
ordinary colonized peoples.[6]

   This is not a new trend. Over a quarter of a century ago, historian Ranajit Guha argued that the history of peasant insurgency
in South Asia was as old as British colonialism itself. He did so by
tracking the way that colonial administrative concerns became
imperial historiographical ones over the course of a century or
more of the Raj: a move that is best understood as "the cunning
of imperialist reason."[7] In Guha's wake have followed subaltern
and postcolonial histories that foreground the role of protest,
whether via micro aggressions and evasions or more spectacular
forms of contest."[8] The imperial turn in British history grew in
part out of convictions about the urgency of critiquing conventional extension-and-consolidation narratives that privileged
imperial actors. Yet even when scholars have investigated colonial
histories and indigenous actors for their own sake, negotiation
and encounter, rather than trouble per se, have predominated.
If this is because many historians of empire now assume indigenous pushback to be the norm, that has not prevented older narrative forms of rise and fall from persisting in synthetic accounts
of British imperialism. Were we to follow more closely the patterns of struggle as they unfolded in the Victorian empire and
after, we might write differently. Nineteenth-century crises in
liberal imperialism were managed in literary form, whether in
poetry or novels, even as the progress narrative remained key
to staving off the nightmares at the periphery. It is this fragility
and its accompanying pessimism that underlines a work like T. B.

Macaulay's *History*, which is, among other things, an exercise in archiving the chaotic incidents of misgovernment and disruption at the heart of imperial ambition—all under the banner of a forward-looking English history.[9] Beginning from a skepticism about the ability of hegemons to rule unchallenged—and about the power of narratives to finally or fully contain subversive subjects—produces a richly varied history of insecurity and limitation. That troubled and troubling history is indispensable to understanding the British imperial project as a whole, even and especially if we concede that it succeeded.

When scholars have engaged with the limits of empire, they have tended to focus on the law as the litmus test of imperial power in practice precisely because "it was everywhere breached and compromised."[10] As historian Philippa Levine has shown for prostitution, legislation that prescribed regulation was a sign that the lines between colonizer and colonized needed constant vigilance. The work that the imperial state had to do across multiple sites to prevent sexual disorder was a defensive response to the complicated business of rule, and to the possibilities of sexual and racial crisis it always entailed. [11] Colonial legal authority was extended fitfully and through fractious engagements with colonial subjects in ways that did not block its impact but, arguably, slowed it down and thwarted official attempts to "settle" indigenous peoples seeking a share in the protocols of imperial governance. That fitfulness, as well as the decelerated tempo that a combination of state failure and indigenous resistance might produce, is more characteristic than not of how imperial power unfurled, even if we concede that colonized subjects were indubitably coerced, and, indeed, even if we acknowledge that native intentions of all kinds were compromised, deflected, and defeated.[12] Such short-circuits in the history of imperial power are hardly legible in the rhetorical arc of rise and fall, which produces an uncanny kind of methodological imperialism. That is to say, empire is a given in grand narratives of ascendancy—the flatland upon which power unfolds until decolonization finally happens, rather than an uneven terrain routinely subject from the start to the response of a variety of actors, as well as to the unforeseen contingency of historical circumstance. In fact, of course, empire was not merely a surfaced traveled across or easily trampled over. It was kinetic and volatile and protean; it was as reactive and defensive as it was prohibitive or belligerent.[13] Or, it was prohibitive and belligerent because these were the affective registers in which its representatives responded to dissent and disruption.

How can this dynamism be captured in narrative terms? One way is to track how, why, and under what conditions hegemony obtained; when it did not; how it did not; and how it was scripted as ascendant at the very moment when it was not. What's needed, in short, are wide-ranging accounts of the limits as well as the possibilities of empire's method on the ground, whenever and wherever it met local responses and was compelled to deal with them. For this reason, a strictly linear approach is part of the narrative problem British empire history faces. As typically plotted out, imperial history is more amenable to a political grammar of progress and loss than it is to plotlines that tell a more routinely fractured and fragmented story.[14] The chapters that follow deliberately tack back and forth across time and space to try to conjure the dynamic field of empire as colonial officials and colonial subjects would likely have understood it—that is, as an assemblage of territories and interests stitched together unevenly and informally, vulnerable on a daily basis to local subversion and disruption. Moving across a variety of geopolitical sites and across the whole of the period under consideration reveals both the commonalities among different forms of agitation and the structural weaknesses of imperial formations in situ. In fact, when understood kinetically—in perpetual motion in all dimensions—imperial order looks regularly, properly nominal, even fugitive: subject to setback, interruption, and insurgency on a routine basis. To make this case is not only to insist, as historian John Newsinger has, that "the blood never dried," but also to show how and under what conditions that blood made noise.[15]

An emphasis on the power of protest not only highlights indigenous agency, but illuminates the limits of imperial power, official and unofficial, as well. What's more, framing modern British imperialism between 1830s through the 1930s decenters large and well-known events, such as the Indian Mutiny of 1857, and moves smaller-scale insurrections before and after mid-century to the foreground. While large-scale transformations undoubtedly impacted the direction of imperial policy and history, they have often been considered at the expense of ordinary challenges to imperial rule in ostensibly out-of-the-way places. *The Trouble with Empire* notes broad patterns of rupture and change, but it views the entire century under consideration as an extended moment of discord and protest. Not all protest was technically anticolonial, of course, and not all who contested imperial power directed their disruptions at the seat of empire in Whitehall. Nor were all those in its ambit necessarily native to the place or uninterested in collaborating with its agents and structures, though collaboration might well mean both cooptation and a disruption of imperial power on the ground.[16] White settlers could be colonial subjects as well as agents of colonial rule, whether as entrepreneurs or landlords or oppressors of indigenous people, in several dimensions. And mixed-race people occupied complex positions vis à vis the local imperial state or municipal formations, throwing allegiances and classification systems into question. To be sure, deeply local and contingent conditions shaped the character of dissent and disruption, making generalization difficult, if not impossible. The way protest happened, even the degree of its frequency and intensity, means that South Asian and African and Irish anticolonial histories, for example, are distinctive, even when they are linked by broadly shared conditions and imaginaries. Yet there was a perennial, familiar character to disruption and dissent that made it as common a feature of imperial experience as the flying of the Union Jack. It is the normative disorder of empire on the ground that this book aims to register as the condition of British imperial history.

Colonial disorder was often transnational, sponsored either by individuals who moved across supposedly discrete spaces or by deterritorialized movements creating the kinds of trouble that were hard for colonial officials to keep up with, let alone contain. Irish nationalism, with its North American networks and its Indian sympathies, is one such example. These horizontal histories are germane because they help to challenge, both empirically and methodologically, a vertical approach to British imperial history—the promontory view, the insular vantage point that privileges the colonizer over the colonized. Yet the aim of this study is not to suggest that all histories of colonial resistance and imperial insecurity must be filtered through a transcolonial lens or that imperial history is an exclusively interconnected story. Some of the histories recounted here did exceed the territorial bounds of, say, Ireland or India, while others did so only aspirationally. Noting the simultaneity of eruptions across multiple spaces reminds us of shared temporalities—and repertoires—of disruption even when people or movements were not actively coordinated, which they most often were not in the period under consideration here. In any case, this book is not a brief for the worth or validity of one kind of dissent over another. Whether singular or interdependent, individual and collective forms of contest and challenge signal a field of power that was as striated as it was smooth; as caught up in and by impediments as it was shaped by the juggernaut of metropolitan power; as contoured by frictions as it was by the certainties of the civilizing mission and its capitalist or military envoys.

Turbulence and trouble may look at first glance like rather old-fashioned explanatory models. They echo mid-twentieth-century postwar calls for attention to the instability of various frontiers, from Cape Town to Singapore. John Darwin's notion of "chaotic pluralism" is also resonant with a fractious conception of empire.[17] Indeed, there are concessions to the fragility and challenges that colonial subjects posed to imperial security in some of the deepest recesses of postwar empire history writing, though they are typically handily dismissed as comparatively insignificant when compared with role of metropolitan policy and the impact of economic factors narraowly conceived. So for, example, John Gallagher, the don of the official mind theory, granted that the cause of empire's ultimate breakdown in the twentieth century "had its origins in small sparks eating their way through long historical fuses before the detonations began."[18] Yet even though chaotic circumstances certainly did help to produce impediments to the exercise of imperial power and fractious contests around the question of imperial legitimacy, the case for trouble is not exactly the same as arguing that empire was messy and contingent, or even that it was on a long fuse. Nor is it to make a simple claim for imperial over-reach, though hyperextension over already unstable ground is certainly a conditional factor. Nor is it, finally, to gesture vaguely toward anxiety as a condition of the imperial psyche—except insofar as anxiety is related to a sense of threat, whether direct or indirect.[19] To make the case for trouble is, rather, to argue that empire was shaped as much by the repeated assertion of colonial subjects as by the footprint of imperial agents; it is to argue that empire was made—as in, constituted by—the very trouble its efforts and practices provoked.

Such trouble was not limited to colonizer-colonized relation-ships. Indeed, local assertions might cause fractures between indigenous communities that, in turn, produced multisited trouble for the colonial state.[20] The frictions that ensued were often random, unanticipated, and unmanageable, producing unpredictable and troubling effects for British imperialism as a local, regional, or global system. And when they were pre-dictable effects of, say, the opportunities imperial expansion offered—in the form of lucrative commercial possibilities, new resource expropriations, or enhanced labor reserves—they cre-ated ruptures in preexisting economic and social life that, in turn, made for turbulence and pushback. For those who ran it, it was, in effect, an impossibly contentious empire.[21] The key is recognizing those frictions and their agents as legitimate and consequential makers of empire's history and markers of its vul-nerabilities, whether they occurred in one place or were linked across multiple polities, or were motivated by the knowledge of far-flung kinships forged by political affinities. These fractious forces were not simply incidental to how empire worked. They were the very manufacturers of the modern colonial state and the diverse forms it took—often, if not most often, in response to local agitation and turbulence and disorder on the ground.[22]

Systems of race, class, and gender and sexuality were among the most powerful brakes on the ambition of imperial power in situ, and they remain utterly indispensable for appreciating the variety of drags on a full-fledged hegemony across British pos-sessions. Interestingly, recognition of these historical forces has not necessarily entailed a critical take on the rise-and-fall nar-rative of imperial history. Feminist historians of empire, myself included, have tended to work inside or alongside a rise-and-fall paradigm, taking aim at other questions (agency, intimacy, mobility, reproduction, violence) while leaving the narrative problems posed by a linear imperial history narrative relatively

underexposed.[23] Given western feminism's historical entangle-
ments with empire, this is perhaps not surprising, though it
raises important questions about the tenacity of the rise-and-fall
narrative as a framing device. Do narratives that turn on dissent
and disruption by women, workers, and other "others" count as
imperial history? What does a methodologically anti-imperial
empire history, one that does not take extension and hegemony
at face value but presumes turbulence and tension, look like in
practice? Where does imperial history leave off and anticolonial
history begin? Needless to say, these questions warrant the full
attention of anyone who wants to understand what the British
empire was and how it actually worked from the ground up.

Upending top-down narratives of empire is a priority for
students of anti-imperial empire history, as it was for empire's
enemies themselves. But the horizontal view is just as important as the vertical. It is imperative to recognize the field of
empire—historical *and* historiographical—not as a place where
power rose and fell but as a choppy, irregular terrain on which multiple historical actors assembled and collided with each other and
with forces both of their making and beyond their control. This is
not simply a move away from a rise-and-fall arc toward a lateral
plain. It is a call for a more profoundly skeptical view of the inevitability of imperial power. And it requires an interpretive reorien-
tation: an acknowledgment of the boundaries of state power and
the role of colonial subjects, not just in resisting, but also in mark-
ing out the limits of imperial supremacy in an age of global mobility, whether forced or chosen. Far from secure in their proconsular
aeries, British leaders across the whole of the century dealt with
here struggled both to manage *and* to stay ahead of the unrest
generated by imperial capital and governmentality, and to contain the spillover of anticolonial sentiment in its most subversive
forms "at home."[24] They were confronted daily with their own mismanagement, in the form of both ordinary operations and states

of emergency—and of internal disagreements between imperial managers as well. Despite the variety of administrative and legal remedies that were mobilized in such situations—from the passport to police presence to state-sponsored execution—resistance in its most overt forms could often not be quelled. Even in the hallowed halls of Parliament, interracial alliances between enemies of empire were formed out of ideological solidarity and via travel, legal and illegal. Those solidarities did not themselves bring down the empire. Indeed, empire persisted in spite of them. Its agents were compelled to develop what were essentially defensive security complexes to counter the threats posed by them, both perceived and real. Meanwhile, imperial confidence was perpetually aspirant, and the imperial project itself was perpetually on the backfoot. "Perishable empire" may be an overconfident diagnosis, but it begins to capture the precarious vulnerabilities of imperial power nonetheless.[25]

Moving away from a rise-and-fall schema also requires that grand narratives of imperial history answer more responsibly to the disruptive work of the colonial subject than they typically do, when they account for colonials at all.[26] It is not just that those living under imperial rule exhibited defiance by dodging, adapting to, and resisting the juggernaut of imperial power and its insidious, quotidian incursions into their ways of life. Colonized people did not simply wait to see how imperial modernity, in all its guises, would work on them. Nor did they fail to see it coming. Many of the subjects featured here anticipated the forces of empire as they were happening and refused them as their unequivocal destiny, via a preemptive posture that might be called protest, resistance, rebellion, insurgency, or evasion.[27] Colonial subjects across the British empire displayed an appreciation of how history was being made at their expense, and they worked mightily to prevent it from taking total hold of their polities and their lives.[28] This sense of anticipation—tense, vigilant, and no doubt exhausting—was arguably one mode of being pro-actively colonial: that is, it was one mode of being colonial in an anti-imperial way.[29]

To observe these preemptive postures through the variet-ies of evidence that the imperial archive has left behind is not to embrace a heroic history of "the native" or, for that matter, to stage a Manichean contest between colonizer and colonized. To the contrary. Placing boycotters and strikers and guerilla fighters on and off official fields of battle in the same frame of analysis highlights their accumulated responses to the imperial project in all its variety. Doing so helps us to appreciate that colonial subjects saw the theater of imperial modernity for what it was: a valoriza-tion of progress over "the primitive" that masked the realities of land theft, capital accumulation, and a desire for world domina-tion in the language of patronage, paternalism, "civilization," and above all peace. This fantasy is what W. E. B. Du Bois called the quest to be the "white masters of the world."[30] Tracing the history of the kinds of principled skepticism articulated by colonial peo-ple about the legitimacy of such global-imperial ambition recap-tures their often-unflinching assessment of colonial modernity's violences, even when they chose collaboration, coexistence, and cooperation. Colonial people, as individuals or as a community, were not simply subordinates. If and when they used the "mas-ter's tools" to dismantle the master's arguments, they did so pur-posefully, enhancing those arguments with the master's own logic (limits and all) and opening up new spaces through which to man-age the expropriative violence directed at them. And when they refused the master narrative—of the civilizing mission, of racial superiority, of the postcolonial dream deferred—they did so with a ferocity that could be devastating, whether to the machinery of empire or to their own personal security and freedom. This is more than colonial agency or the work of "native informants." This is eyes-wide-open realpolitik.

This is not an argument that even Gallagher, who saw break-down coming along the long fuse of empire's detonators, would likely concede. Indeed, most rise-and-fall narratives tend to rest on this denial or to downplay the impact, let alone the role, of anticolonial movements and people on the imperial frame-work.[31] The goal of *The Trouble with Empire* is not to recover or recuperate traces of colonial subjectivity in order to write some kind of politically correct British imperial history. There is no natural or necessary connection between colonial subjectivity and dissent or disruption. In any case, the archive is notoriously limited when it comes to indigenous intention; this book cites colonial skepticism and contest where it surfaces. When avail-able, protest voices and actions are treated here as the articu-lations of perfectly, uncannily, rational interlocutors of British imperialism—people with typically trenchant readings of the precolonial past and frankly prophetic takes on histories yet to come. Nor were indigenous modes without their own forms of violence. Recourse to "tradition" could be punitive when it came to the question of women's social mobility and economic freedom; it could serve, in other words, as a pretext for reform and restraint by colonized and colonizers alike. Invocations of the precolonial past could be indicative of demotic hopes in an authoritarian imperial age: evidence, among other things, of vernacular politics in the context of the scramble for imperial power.[32] Such politics are hypervisible when coercive state for-mations like empire are at their most ambitious, and they return us to the historical dynamism and local contingency at the heart of contest and rebellion.

Whether in the gorges of Afghanistan, the gold fields of South Africa, or the bomb-making facilities of Bengal, people subject to imperial conquest and rule refused to stand still or settle down in the face of military economic and political onslaught. They refused to concede, in short, that the consequences of encounters set in motion by colonial modernity were givens, let alone inevitabilities. In the process, they throw us back, not onto the rising ground of imperial ascendancy as a prelude to imperial decline, but onto "shifting relations of violence"—the very shapeshiftings that fuel modern imperial power and make the imperial project challenging and practically impossible.[33] Again, this is not to say that protestors and insurgents "won" in any simple sense, especially if winning means defeating empire in a single blow, or even in a set of accumulated strikes. Labor protests failed; wars were lost; and radical agitation did not itself produce decolonization in any simple sense of the term. Nor was all such dissent and disruption necessarily anti-imperial in intention, though it typically caused disorder nonetheless. To foreground the trouble with empire is, rather, to contend that histories of the colonized are not easily folded into paradigms of rise and fall. Colonial subjects strained, and continue to strain, against that framework, built as it was partly to contain them and to limit the impact of their often undisciplined, anarchic work on dominant narratives of empire history practically since its beginnings.

And yet, if the colonial subjects in this book challenged the projects of imperial power that aimed to deform them, resistance seems too narrow an explanation for their criticism; criticism, in turn, seems too anodyne a category through which to understand and, ultimately, to historicize them. The concept of dissent, as the Osage scholar-teacher-activist Robert Warrior has mobilized it when grappling with the uses of postcolonial studies for "native critics in the world," is most helpful in this context. Here, dissent is not about the truth of indigenous perspectives or the authenticity of colonial voices, though Warrior acknowledges the geopolitics, local and global, as well as the urgency, of those standpoints. He is as concerned with dissent's capacity to rematerialize "an historical line of Native writers and scholars" whose work has been marginalized, dismissed, obscured, and otherwise deemed irrecoverable or negligible, sometimes as much in local communities as in mainstream modes of inquiry.[34] This genealogical enterprise—this history making—is the function of criticism.[35] Dissent, it follows, is the history that criticism materializes. If this is what a methodology of the oppressed looks like, it is also one form that the practice of decolonizing methodologies might take in British imperial history, whether old or new.[36] The trouble with empire is, then, a dissenters' history.

The decolonization of the British empire, arguably, began in 1776, with the eruption of the American Revolution—and with it, of successful anticolonial agitation—into world-historical consciousness.[37] Yet a close examination of British imperialism in its heyday shows that decolonizing efforts were hardly limited to phenomenal events. During the century or so between the onset of the First Afghan War and the emergence of full-court press Gandhian nationalism (c. 1830s–1930s), discontented subjects of empire made their unhappiness felt across the globe, from Ireland to Canada to India to Africa to Australasia, in direct response to incursions of military might and the market-governance model of imperial capitalism.[38] Examples of military pushback, such as the Indian Mutiny and the Anglo-Zulu War, are well known. Those deemed "lesser"—the First and Second Afghan Wars and the Opium War, for example—have also gained notoriety as Queen Victoria's "little wars."[39] Yet as chapter 1, "Subject to Setback," details, the certainty of victory over contesting forces or of stability tout court remained open to question on a wide variety of battlefields. A series of wars technically won but badly bungled in military terms, combined with successive "Kaffir," Maori, Ashanti, and Afghan campaigns, are evidence of the fitful, halting character of imperial supremacy even in its heyday. Historians have noted the global convergence of multiple imperial crises at particular moments, such as 1879, when the Zulu War and second Afghan campaign were underway and Egypt and the Sudan were heading toward uprising, or 1919, which witnessed a variety of conflagrations, political, economic, and epidemiological that followed on from the Great War. As important as these convergences were for the making of British imperial insecurity, so, too, were regular, local eruptions of protest and resistance at the edges of formal battle. This kind of guerilla fighting meant that military victory was often partial and that contests for territorial possession were ongoing. Security remained elusive, in short, and maintaining the peace was an ongoing task.

If empire was always on insecure terrain, its troubles cannot be dismissed as a handful of dramatic challenges to hegemony thwarted by military might. Opposition to empire's various modes of intrusion was a nearly constant feature of the modern British imperial experience—making day-to-day empire an array of multiple chaotic sites rather than a space of either settledness or settlement, broadly conceived.[40] Sites of capital investment—from plantations to coal and diamond mines, from factories to the railway—that enabled the conversion of raw materials into profit and the creation of globally linked market economies were, like military barracks and garrisons, vulnerable to defiance and destruction. A focus on contested work disciplines and regimes of labor (chapter 2, "Subject to Interruption") underscores the comparative constancy of such activities and the precariousness of the economic power of empire in the grip of disruptions large and small. The *hartal* (work stoppage) that eventuated in the massacre at Jallianwallah Bagh in Amritsar in 1919 and precipitated a new phase of Gandhian nonviolent resistance is among the most celebrated examples of work-related protest—protest that routinely interrupted the business as usual that Whitehall officials and local district commissioners alike were dedicated to preserving as the foundation of imperial capital. Yet Jallianwallah Bagh is just one of the most globally apparent examples of the kind of common protest across a wide variety of Britain's possessions that regu-larly interrupted the daily business of empire. Whether striking in factories, deserting plantation work regimes. or choosing pros-titution in lieu of other conscripted labor options, colonized men and women registered their unwillingness to be incorporated into dominant forms of political economy. They thereby disrupted the everyday work of empire as a matter of course.

While marketplace rebellion and labor agitation put imperial interests continually at risk, there were other forms of insubor-dination that were of considerable concern to officials, whether on the spot or in the Colonial Office. Some of these may be found in the history of anticolonial nationalism in its multidimensional forms. Chapter 3, "Subject to Insurgency," focuses on upris-ings and attempts at armed rebellion and sedition, rather than on nationalism per se, tracking what, by the later nineteenth century, the British state called terrorism by any other name. Assassinations, bombings, and transnational plots against the empire were a common feature of late-Victorian anticolonial activ-ity from Dublin to Delhi to the Sudan—conspiracies that may not have succeeded in bringing the empire down but that vexed the imperial agents, officials, and sympathizers whose job it was to ensure routine order and security. Only by historicizing how and when such efforts failed—by thinking about whether these were actually grand conspiratorial plots or were simply labeled such in an effort to rationalize repression and counterinsurgency—can the validity of claims to a mainly peaceful, basically secure impe-rium be tested. And only by making the trouble with empire the foreground of the story, the driver of imperial history, rather than the backdrop to the drum-and-trumpet version of colonial power and ascendancy, can we test the contradiction at the heart of Kipling's "savage wars of peace."[41]

Kipling's phrase is a clever conceit, bound up with his sardonic take on empire. But along with the notion of Pax Britannica, it remains shorthand for the presumption of order for which British imperialism remains a model. Taken together, the cases in this book point to the insecurity of everyday affairs in Britain's modern, would-be global imperium. At the same time, *The Trouble with Empire* is not intended to be a complete counterhistory of British imperialism. Wide-ranging in scope and recuperative in spirit, it serves as an interpretive essay, a contrapuntal narrative that illustrates how and why empire is best understood not as a trumpet call but as a drumbeat of resistance and insecurity in three specific domains of imperial order: military, economic, and political. Clearly, these are overlapping fields; and they are not the only ones upon which a troubled history of empire might be written. This book could certainly have explored, say, famine as state failure or conversion as resistance, or censorious press laws as evidence of a defensive posture against sedition and other kinds of "trouble." It might even have sought to elaborate the signal failure of imperial policy in one locale in a targeted time frame, as historians have done with success.[42] In the pages that follow, the focus is instead on recurrent challenges to peace, prosperity, and "good government" across a century or so of the imperial project. This is the trifecta: the three pillars of a Pax Britannica model of modern imperial power, the objectives to which it aspired historically, and the major categorical imperatives through which scholars have narrated its accomplishment for two centuries. Inside the capitalist world system in which the British empire functioned, these are the bases of hegemony as well.[43] If the global-order model that the historiography of the British empire still projects is something more than a powerful fiction, and if its pretensions as the foundations for twentieth- and twenty-first-century geopolitical security remain largely in place, claims about its historical stability deserve to be tested on their own terms. And if dominion was in fact intermittent, that not only means that imperial power was uneven, but also that it was not everywhere continuous or secure either. It follows that dissent says as much about the historical character of empire's power as it does about dissenters themselves, if not more so. So much has been made of "the incomplete liberationist project" of Third World nationalisms—that contrary work undertaken by the sons and daughters of the troublemakers of empire. It seems past time to talk about the project of empire as equally imperfect, equally inhibited, equally unrealized.[44]

Meanwhile, convictions about the overall "success" of British imperialism shape not just history writing about empire but popular perceptions of what a successful Anglo-imperial world power looks like in historical terms as well. As long as the British empire is a touchstone for current global events, imperial histories that do not take the hegemony of western empires for granted as a starting point are arguably crucial. We are urgently in need of histories that are as amenable to considering empire's limits as its reach and as antagonistic to empire itself as recent historians of many stripes have been antagonistic to the nation or the state.[45] The view from empire's troubled, disrupted terrains might recalibrate readings of global imperial power in the last two centuries in ways that are useful for understanding how empires have actually managed the task of imperial security and survival—and how they have not. In this sense, the rise-and-fall and Pax Britannica paradigm creates binds with ramifications far beyond the study of British imperial history. Its limitations arise, certainly, from the fact that the ascendency and decline it models plots an apparently predictable outcome. But the rise-and-fall arc allows us to imagine a definitive endgame without accounting sufficiently for the struggles, stumbles, blunders, defeats, losses, failures, and general turbulence produced by dissenters and disrupters of all kinds, and with more regularity than has been allowed in big narratives of nineteenth- and twentieth-century British imperialism. Tracking how empire worked or didn't work through the trouble it faced, rather than from its presumed success, begins to recast the framework though which we apprehend, not success or failure, but imperial viability in all its iterations across the uneven plane of quotidian power. Whether all this adds up to hegemony and peace—or makes the British empire "the greatest disturber of peace [in] the world" in its time—remains to be seen.[46]

Chapter 1

Subject to Setback

Pax Britannica and the Question
of Military Victory

Violence appears where power is in jeopardy.
HANNAH ARENDT, *On Violence, 1970*

They were the victors, but they were out of breath.
WINSTON CHURCHILL, *The Story of the Malakand Field Force, 1897*

In an imperial context, military victory is critical to claims of dominance, if not hegemony. Indeed, victory in war or in battle is indispensable to rationales for post-conquest occupation, including claims to technological, civilizational, and even racial superiority over the populations subdued, suppressed, and otherwise defeated.[1] The power of this long-standing link between military success and imperial legitimacy can perhaps be best appreciated at the moment of its globally apparent rupture—that is, in the aftermath of World War I. As the English writer Philip Gibb observed, Europeans had been taught to believe that "the whole object" of European civilization "was to reach out to beauty and love, and that mankind, in its progress to perfection, had killed the beast instinct, cruelty, bloodlust, the primitive, savage law of survival by tooth and claw and club and ax. All poetry, all art, all religion had preached this gospel and this promise."[2] The Somme,

with its "sad scrawl of broken earth and murdered men," was certainly instrumental to the sense of civilizational failure brought
on by the Great War.[3] As significantly, the combination of unprecedented carnage and prolonged combat in the European trenches
made a mockery of nineteenth-century western imperial claims
to difference from, let alone tutelage over, those indigenous
peoples they sought to rule. Sigmund Freud remarked that "the
savagery that the war unleashed within Europe ... should caution the Europeans against assuming that their 'fellow-citizens'
of the world had 'sunk so low' as they had once believed, because
the conflict had made it clear that the Europeans themselves
had 'never risen as high.'"[4] The firsthand experience of Indian
and African soldiers on the western front—their exposure to the
atrocities of combat, and to the barbarities of modern European
warfare more generally—is routinely credited with fueling anticolonial nationalism and of accelerating, indirectly but powerfully nonetheless, the end of European colonialism in the first
half of the twentieth century.[5] The early failures of the "trog-
lodyte war" not only brought Europe to its knees; its military
failures and battlefield quagmires put paid to fantasies of white
supremacy in ways that rang the death knell of modern Western
imperialism.[6]

Yet across the long nineteenth century, British victory
in imperial wars had been by no means self-evident. From
Afghanistan to Zululand, from the suppression of the Indian
Mutiny to the campaigns on the northwest frontier, British
troops struggled for decisive wins in battle. More often than
not, they had to resort to extramilitary tactics to meet the challenges that the enemy posed. What's more, because they fought
alongside native soldiers or with the help of local communities,
these qualified victories were highly visible to the alien populations whom soldiers and officers sought to subject to their
command. The Somme was not the first time British colonial

subjects witnessed imperial military failure. The halting, fitful methods by which the British army secured its tenuous hold on territory deemed indispensable to imperial security were a regular feature of local and regional military campaigns. Evidence of native resistance to military campaigns is also everywhere to be found in soldiers' accounts, officers' memoirs, and the wider world of print culture through which Victorians and their successors consumed the vagaries of imperial war. Paramountcy may have been a commonplace, found as easily in the average soldier's field pocketbook as in the war plans emanating from Whitehall, but it had to be fought for over and over again. For the thousands of readers of the daily paper or the boys' adventure novel, the struggle for military victory and the impressive pushback that tribal leaders, mutineers, and other indigenous opponents mounted in the face of British invasion and takeover were readily apparent.

But the real weight of the white man's burden was not simply that he had to labor to win. It was that his victories were often hollow and impermanent, and his supremacy, always open to new challenges on the ground. This chapter examines the mud and sweat of major nineteenth- and twentieth-century battlefronts in order to explore the link between victory in military operations on the ground and imperial security writ large. Scrutinizing the way that stories of British imperial victory have been told helps to clarify when decisive victory actually obtained in nineteenth-century imperial war, when it did not, and what that might mean for histories concerned with the limits of imperial security. Though the rough terrain and impassable landscapes of the empire's northwest frontier make it look untypical of the British imperial military experience, it is, in fact, the best place to begin. The site of two Afghan wars in the space of forty years, this frontier region was in perpetual ferment, subject to successive military operations yet never finally or fully settled.

Snipers at the Periphery

Because of Afghanistan's proximity to India, it was of the highest strategic importance from the beginning of the nineteenth century until its independence in 1919 and, of course, beyond. The stakes of pacification in this region were consequently high. At a speech at the Guildhall in 1892, Lord Salisbury observed that the frontier wars "are but the surf that marks the edge and advance of the wave of civilization."[7] Writing about his experiences with the Malakand Field Force—which was responsible for taking and holding the Swat Valley region in the late summer and fall of 1897 -- young Winston Churchill agreed.

> The year 1897, in the annals of the British people, was marked by a declaration to the whole world of their faith in the higher destinies of their race . . . unborn arbiters, with a wide knowledge and more developed brains, may trace in recent events the influence of that mysterious Power which, directing the progress of our species, and regulating the rise and fall of Empires, has afforded that opportunity to a people, of whom at least it maybe said, that they have added to the happiness, the learning and the liberties of mankind.[8]

Churchill's account, which began as a series of letters for the London *Daily Telegraph* and ended up as his book *The Story of the Malakand Field Force*, did not, by his own admission, "pretend to deal with the complications of the frontier question" or to be "a party political pamphlet on a great Imperial question."[9] Rather, he intended it to be a straightforward narrative, designed to illustrate the "bravest deeds and finest characters" of the Malakand Field Force and "all the incidences of conduct and courage which occurred."[10]

Churchill should not be taken at his word. The battle narrative that takes up the majority of his account is full of reflections, both oblique and direct, that suggest how difficult it was to bring the question of frontier policy before the British public and, more generally, before the court of imperial public opinion, without revealing the recurrent challenges to it. Though he does chronicle acts of individual and collective heroism on the part of British and Indian soldiers alike, he devotes considerable space to questions of strategic vulnerability, ranging from topics as specific as the need for increased application of the cavalry to the problem of Indian border protection to those as general as the threat of Russian aggression to regional stability in the British zone of influence (the strongholds of Gilgit, Chitral, Jellalabad, and Kandahar) in which the Malakand battles took place. Ever the historian, Churchill saw 1897 as a pivotal moment in the saga of Raj security that he, like generations before him, viewed as central to the viability of British imperial power in geopolitical terms. He readily acknowledged the controversies surrounding a renewed commitment to the "forward policy" even as he chronicled the impediments that tribal fighters threw up in its way.

That policy had developed in the 1830s in response to the perceived threat to the Raj from Russia, and by the 1890s it was directed at advancing further into tribal sovereignty to stabilize India's border against Pathans and their regional allies.[11] But Churchill declared that the moment for discussion about the pros and cons of the forward policy had passed, especially given the resources just invested in the Swat Valley operations.

> We are at present in a transition stage, nor is the manner nor occasion of the end in sight. Still this is no time to despair. I have often noticed in these Afghan valleys that they seem to be entirely surrounded by hills and to have no exit. But as the column has advanced, a gap gradually becomes visible

and a pass appears. Sometimes it is steep and difficult, sometimes it is held by the enemy and must be forced, but I have
never seen a valley that had not a way out. That way we shall
ultimately find, if we match with the firm, but prudent step
of men who know the dangers; but conscious of their skills
and discipline, do not doubt their ability to deal with them
as they shall arise.[12]

What Salisbury proclaimed by way of generalization, then,
Churchill intended to support by way of detailed empirical example, offering the battle for the Swat Valley and its environs both
as testimony to the fact of the empire's capacity for civilizational
advance at its borders *and* as evidence of the ongoing urgency of
pressing that advance at the turn of the imperial century, if not
before.

The rhetoric of imperial expansion through which he frames
his story is, on the face of it, supremely self-confident, echoing
several decades of conviction about the power of the civilizing
mission to rationalize forward movement into new imperial possessions for the greater glory of the nation and the race. The
British exercise a "firm but prudent step," and their confidence
stems from their consciousness of their "skills and discipline,"
twin attributes of a racial superiority that the Victorians believed
equipped them with the technological, scientific, and organizational capacity to best primitive enemies and stake a territorial and ideological claim to global dominance. But Churchill's
account betrays a significant degree of apprehension about the
possibility of long- and short-term success based on the experience of battle that he himself had witnessed and that he narrates
in great detail. That battle experience was not only less than
triumphal; it also did serious damage to the claims of civilizational superiority, technical advantage, and, especially, military
prowess that undergirded Victorian imperial rhetoric and helped

to motivate contemporary imperial policy in both military and political terms. Events in the Swat Valley in 1897 revealed an enemy whose "primitive" cunning, "tribal" mentality, and "savage" fighting methods raised a formidable, ongoing challenge to British imperial forces and their Indian contingents. So great was this challenge that Churchill had to acknowledge its disintegrative power. He downplayed the significance of native successes by scripting the "peace" that eventuated from the conflict as definitive even though his own reportage showed how poorly the British performed and how elusive the "settlement" of the war actually was.

The area in and around the Malakand Pass had been a site of imperial defense since the Mughals had first established a presence at Chakdara in the Lower Swat Valley in the late sixteenth century. British troops were stationed in the remains of the Mughal fort until they built their own in 1895. Churchill described the Malakand as a great cup,

> of which the rim is broken into numerous clefts and jagged points. At the bottom of this cup is the 'crater' camp. The deepest cleft is the Malakand Pass. The highest of the jagged points is Guides Hill, on a spur of which the fort stands. It needs no technical knowledge to see that to defend such a place, the rim of the cup must be held. But in the Malakand, the bottom of the cup is too small to contain the necessary garrison. The whole position is therefore, from the military point of view, bad and indefensible.[13]

Indefensible though it may have been, the Malakand was pivotal to the future of the northwest frontier as an effective bulwark for India against tribal leaders resentful of the British attempts to bring them under imperial control.[14] Holding the

Malakand secured a chain of locations that had been under pressure since the early 1890s, as result of which Chitral—a protectorate of the Maharaja of Kashmir and thus technically in the British sphere of influence—had been seriously imperiled in 1895 by an enemy force that reportedly numbered 4,000.[15] In the aftermath of that siege, Chitral fell foul of political debates taking place at the end of Lord Roseberry's government over the wisdom of the forward policy on the northwest frontier. Reports of imperial bravery were matched by harrowing accounts of tribal resistance and of local determination to prevent the Chitral Road from being used as a throughway for the Raj troops—indications that local leaders were fully cognizant of the ramifications of the forward policy for their territorial sovereignty, with all its economic and symbolic meaning for tribal power.

Among the leaders of frontier pushback was Saidullah Khan, dubbed the Mad Fakir or Mad Mullah of Swat by the British. An inveterate anti-imperialist, Saidullah had lived in India in his youth and had returned to Boner in 1895, where he gained a reputation for "sanctity and piety" and even for "miraculous powers." Churchill deemed him and his followers fanatics, champions of "insulted and threatened Islam" who were awaiting the day when they would rise up and restore the Mughal empire at Delhi.[16] Though a number of regional mullahs tried to coordinate uprisings along the border in the spring of 1897, Saidullah was allegedly impatient with these and raised the standard of jihad himself in the Malakand. A. H. McMahon, the political agent, and his assistant, A. D. G. Ramsay, acknowledged that the "Sartor Fakir provided some of the hardest and sternest fighting we have known on the North-west Frontier." Wounded but still alive, Saidullah fled to Indus Kohistan, returning briefly in 1898 to try to effect another uprising.[17] The practice of jihad as an expression

of anticolonial nationalism was not born on the northwest frontier, nor can it be dismissed as fanaticism. It was part of a history of Islamic response to British imperialism that had globally
significant ramifications for twentieth- and twenty-first-century
empires. As historian Ayesha Jalal as argued, jihad was one prag-
matic response to the "growing encirclement of Muslim countries" over the course of the nineteenth century—and it was a
persistent challenge to imperial security as well.[18]

This tumultuous recent history notwithstanding, there was
little or no anticipation of the initial attack against the Malakand
encampment. Indeed, despite the attempts of the political agent,
Major Deane, to convey the "daily progress of the fanatical movement," there appears to have been a belated realization on the
part of the military officers that local sentiment was alienated
and that the "whispers of war" by the "priests of the Afghan
border" had jihadist undertones carrying the promise of deliver-
ance by a "Great Fakir." The element of surprise was undoubtedly a tactical advantage on the part of the enemy, but it was
equally a stunning failure of intelligence—or of the capacity to
take the threat seriously—on the part of the British.[19] Although
the locals on the edges of the British camp were cognizant of the
danger, the military and political officers who read the reports
did so indifferently, "privately scout[ing] the idea that any serious events were pending."[20] They played polo well into the after-
noon of the onslaught, unaware or careless of the fact that their
syces (grooms) had heard from the locals watching the match
"that there was going to be a fight."[21]

The response to the initial attack hardly showed the British
forces at their best. Overwhelmed by "the mass of the enemy,
nearly one thousand strong," the imperial troops engaged in
"desperate fighting," and even the Sikhs, normally considered indefatigable, were killed and wounded in unusually large
numbers. Bullets flew in all directions, but even so, when the

tribesmen prevailed, they often did so with swords and rocks; rarely, if ever, fully outflanked, they scrambled up the rim of the "cup" and shot their weapons around corners as well as directly at the enemy. During two initial attempts to regain their stronghold, Lieutenant Manley and his Quarter Guard in charge of the garrison were felled. Three officers were killed outright or died of their wounds, and twenty-one sepoys perished in the first stage of the fighting. The assault on the Malakand was not quickly or decisively repulsed. Sniping continued into the night, and another attack was soon underway.[22] The north camp had to be evacuated, and the enemy burned everything that was left behind, leaving some soldiers with nothing but the clothes on their backs. "Severe fighting" recommenced, but not before the tribesmen mounted an attack on the 31st Panjaub Infantry, the only unit that was left to protect the troops who had fled camp. In the second major attack, the tribesmen "held their ground and maintained a continual fire from Martini-Henry rifles. They also rolled down great stones upon the companies."[23] And the fighters appeared to have had plenty of ammunition well into the second night, when at 2 a.m. "the great attack was delivered. Along the whole front and from every side enormous numbers swarmed to the assault. On the right and left, hand-to-hand fighting took place . . . the enemy succeeded in breaking into the breastworks, and close fighting ensued, in which Lieutenant Costello was again severely wounded." But "the fire of the troops was too hot for anything to live in their front." A leading Mullah was killed, and with "several hundreds of tribesmen slain, the whole attack collapsed . . . The enemy recognized that their chance of taking the Malakand had passed."[24]

Or did they? The tribesmen dragged their dead off the field, but they got reinforcements and continued the fight, charging on the 45th Sikhs' position. They kept firing into the morning and turned with renewed vigor on Chakdara, "which they believed must fall into their hands." Speaking of Malakand specifically, Churchill neatly summarized this back and forth: "a surprise, followed by a sustained attack, has been resisted. The enemy, repulsed at every point, have abandoned the attempt, but surround and closely watch the defences. The troops will now assume the offensive, and the hour of reprisals will commence."[25] His assessment here is quite accurate: attack, resistance, "repulsion," and another attack—with moments of lull and "reprisals" in between—was the way the entire fitful campaign unfolded. The defense of Chakdara—which Churchill elsewhere called "the Lilliputian Gibraltar"—is a case in point, repeating in tactical terms the initial assault almost exactly, from start to finish.[26] Warnings from Major Herbert about the possibility of a "tribal rising" notwithstanding, the garrison officers did not "cease from their amusements"; on returning from his polo match Lieutenant Rattray got word that Pathans were approaching, and the alarm was sounded. This was on July 26, and the firing did not fall silent until August 2. The enemy mounted "vigorous attacks"; their "numbers were enormous," and they "swarmed" the neighboring villages and *nullahs* (steep narrow valleys), all the while maintaining a formidable "continual fire."[27]

Churchill's take on Pathan savagery, superstition, and rapacity is as virulent as it is unsurprising. The first chapter of his book, entitled "Theatre of War," lays out his view of the region, characterizing its inhabitants as preternaturally warlike ("khan assails khan"), committed to blood feud. and impelled by the "spirit of murder."[28] Though he concedes that this "strong aboriginal propensity to kill" is present in all humans, he links the violence of Pathans and their allies to all "races of such development."[29] Contemporary reviewers tend to critique Churchill's florid prose, which is on full display in his first published work. "To the ferocity of the Zulu are added the craft of the Redskin and the marksmanship of the Boer," he writes, engaging effortlessly in a comparative imperial ethnography. "The world is presented with that grim spectacle, 'the strength of civilization without its mercy.'"[30]

Churchill's account of the campaign gives an edge to the British imperial forces, but only just. As a counterpoint to the putative fanaticism of the enemy, he offers a story of disorganization, failed intelligence, and tragicomic blunders on the British side in which tactics fail, the lads have to fight for it, and the Field Force is pretty much continually pinned down by the insurgents. One "misadventure" is notable. After the initial march into the Mamund Valley through the pass at Nawagai, General Jeffreys—along with battery, sappers, and four infantry companies—was inadvertently left unprotected and was subject to a blistering attack.[31] Churchill's account in 1897 is much more condensed than the one he gave in 1930 in his memoir, where he reported that Jeffreys was wounded in the head, overtaken by the darkness, and forced to create a makeshift fort to keep the Mamunds (a Pashtun clan) at bay. "It was a fight," he recalled, "in a rabbit warren," and, as was so often the case, the British were more lost than in control of the terrain or even their troops.[32] This is one of a number of command blunders from which officers and soldiers were eventually rescued after being hammered by the enemy. Even those rescues, such as the one that retrieved Jeffreys, were the result of luck rather than intention. Churchill says as much: "Had not the luck of the British army led them to the village, it can hardly be doubted . . . that the guns would have been captured and the General killed. Fortune, especially in war, uses tiny fulcra for her powerful lever."[33]

The Pathans, meanwhile, had fulcra of their own. They attacked in the heat of the day, took advantage of their knowledge of the challenging local terrain, and made Captain Wright's squadron work "painfully" just to keep its ground. The officers scrambled to fortify the besieged garrison; to Churchill's evident shock and amazement, some of the enemy fighters "actually got across the tangled barbed wire and were destroyed in the enclosure."[34] Although he deemed the attempt "recklessness," he had to acknowledge its audacity: "One man climbed into the barbed wire and fired three shots at the defenders at close quarters before he was killed." Indeed, "so bold were the enemy in their efforts," he recorded, "that they rushed in under the musketry of the defense, and lighted a great heap of grass about three yards from the doorway."[35] The Brits were exhausted, the men literally falling asleep at the loopholes, as the siege of Chakdara went into its ninety-sixth hour. Communication with the base camp was constantly interrupted. Churchill gives credit to the sepoy signaler Prem Singh for keeping a heliograph going so that it could "flash urgent messages to the main force."[36] The tribesmen continued, meanwhile, to lay siege to the garrison by any means possible: they carried scaling ladders and bundles of grass; they fired relentlessly. "In spite of the cover of the garrison several men were killed and wounded by the hail of bullets which was directed against the fort, and which splashed and scarred the walls in every direction." The enemy succeeded in capturing the hospital, the first section of Chakdara to be liberated. In the end, it was the cavalry that saved the day, roaring in on their horses, killing the tribesmen who were inside, and routing the rest. But not before "the last man to leave . . . shot Lieutenant Rattray in the neck." Rattray finished, in turn, by "cut[ting] him down." In Churchill's view, it was "not possible to think of a more fitting conclusion."[37]

Conscious of the fact that the British were caught unawares—that is, that the battle was fought in defense of the fort—and that the attack was by no means handily dispensed with, Churchill all but apologized for the back-and-forth nature of the battle, and of his narrative of it:

Perhaps the reader is tired of the long recital of monotonous succession of assaults and repulses. What must the garrison have been by the reality? . . .

Like men in a leaking ship, who toil at the pumps ceaselessly and find their fatigues increasing and the ship sinking hour by hour, they cast anxious weary eyes in the direction whence help might be expected. But none came. And there are worse deaths than by drowning.[38]

Churchill unquestionably saw the ultimate relief of Chakdara as a huge success for the security of the frontier, and hence, the empire. He dwells on the enormous losses sustained by the enemy and the bravery and heroism of all the soldiers, British and Indian alike. He also concedes that the garrison had held out, but "stubbornly and desperately," throughout the siege. It did not quite "hold out," of course, insofar as the enemy had penetrated and had taken at least the hospital quarters—though, thanks to Churchill's sleight of hand, this is not clear until the moment they are being driven out. In fact, as Churchill himself notes, this is not an uncommon phenomenon "on the out-post line of civilization."[39] He compares Chakdara to the infamous siege at Rorke's Drift in the 1879 Anglo-Zulu War, where "the courage and equipment of the garrison enable them to hold out until a relieving force arrives." But he also conjures the spectacle of the siege of Khartoum (1884), when "the defenders are overwhelmed . . . [and] none are left to tell the tale."[40] The Khartoum parallel is more apt, especially given the fact that that siege took place during the eruption of the Mahdist holy war. Tellingly, it also evokes an imperial stalemate and a crisis of confidence of the kind commonly provoked by Muslim insurgency across the eastern empire.

Churchill's frontier bravado in the face of such precedents can be read as an echo of the hypermasculine melodrama of

the adventure hero who dwells on the burdens of empire, only
to better trumpet the glorious triumphs of imperial soldiers
and the greater providence of the civilizing race. Needless to
say, soldier and officer did not necessarily share the frontier a
burden equally.[41] The young Churchill does claim that such circumstances "make a coward valorous, and affords to brave men
opportunities for the most sublime forms of heritage and devotion." But a downbeat tone dominates. Such men, he says, "hold
the dykes of social progress against a rising deluge of barbarism,
which threatens every moment to overflow the banks and drown
them all." The timing and pace of that defense—the threat at
every moment and the impossibility of holding ground in every
moment—are especially notable. For as Churchill's narrative
reveals, even and especially in battle, the domination of imperial
troops was rarely, if ever, a given; positions had to be fought and
held, often against a determined and "ruthless" enemy. Take the
debacle at Inayat Kila, "the entrenched camp . . . at the entrance
of the Mamund Valley," which by any reckoning was an utter
disaster for the British, whose total casualties reached almost
150.[42] This figure was larger, according to Churchill, than virtually any other in the long history of Indian border defense. Once
again, intelligence was bad: "the valley appeared deserted. The
villages looked insignificant and defenseless. It was everywhere
asserted that the enemy could not stand." In part because the
resistance was unlooked for, in part because the strategy of moving regiments out of the camp to deal the enemy (who "came on
in great strength at the northwest end of the valley") proved a
huge mistake, the tribesmen were able to press forward with considerable success.[43] Matters were "grave," there were any number
of "horrible sights," a "black tragedy burst upon the scene" as
a party led by Lieutenant Cassells was ambushed, and half of
them killed. "The enemy had worked round both flanks and had
also the command."[44] The fallen British men were even buried

on site—a very rare occurrence. The enemy, having rushed the fort, "promptly" seized it and blew it up. "A great cloud of thick brown-red dust sprang suddenly into the air, bulging out in all directions. The tower broke in half and toppled over. A series of muffled bangs followed. The dust-cloud cleared away, and nothing but a few ruins remained."[45]

News of the frontier debacle spread quickly to Britons at home. The *Pall Mall Gazette* called it "an ugly little business," and the papers were full of accounts of "the 'Mad Mullah' on the warpath."[46] In the House of Lords, Lord Reay questioned the undersecretary of state, the Earl of Selbourne, about the rising, "which seemed [to him] to be on a considerable scale."[47] The negative attention in the press—via headlines like "the Chitral Disaster"—clearly rattled Churchill; he was particularly eager to counter the notion that the events of September 16 had been in any way a reversal.[48] He did so by a variety of means: by confining the military failure to the fate of one unit; by pumping up the heroism of a few good men, the Sikhs included; and by declaring the fighting over and the battle won when the tribesmen clearly did not acknowledge the end of the skirmish. The question of "retirement"—which might be withdrawal or retreat—is key here. British troops often pulled out or back, signaling the end of fighting for the day, or a break for the purpose of collecting the dead and wounded, an operation granted by custom to both sides. But "retirement" was apparently not recognized by the enemy in this campaign, prompting Churchill to remark that "while it is usually easy to advance against an Asiatic, all retirements are matters of danger." At Inayat Kila, British attempts to retire were routinely thwarted by sniping and even by outright attack—an attack that was not insignificant insofar as it wounded a number of officers, some to within an inch of their lives. "Those who know the range and power of the Martini-Henry rifle," Churchill observed, "will appreciate the skill and marksmanship which can inflict loss, even at so great a range."[49] The gap in firepower between colonizer and colonized could be closed in an instant and was not an ironclad guarantee of military success, especially in the chaotic series of small, intensely fought skirmishes that typically made up the imperial war.[50]

Churchill used the proximity of the Afghan frontier and the presumed support of the Amir of Afghanistan, Abdur Rahman Khan, for the tribesman as an additional excuse for why the British had been so clearly out maneuvered in these engagements—to explain, in his words, "how it was that defenders of obscure villages were numbered by the thousands, and why the weapons of poverty-stricken agriculturalists were excellent Martini-Henry rifles."[51] Though there was not a general agreement about the Amir's direct involvement, in Churchill's view the Mamunds themselves were ready for peace; it was their allies who insisted on keeping up the struggle.[52] That peace got off to an uneven start, in part because in peace as in war, the "victors" made a series of unforced errors. In this case, the British had expected the Mamunds to surrender all their weapons, including those they had taken off of dead British soldiers on the sixteenth. The tribesmen indicated that they had no intention of giving them up.

> It was obvious that the British Raj could not afford to be defied in this matter. We had insisted on the rifles being surrendered, and that expensive factor, Imperial prestige, demanded that we should prosecute operations till we got them, no matter what the cost might be. The rifles were worth little . . . It was unsound economics, but Imperialism and economics clash as often as honesty and self-interest. We were therefore committed to the policy of throwing good money after bad, in order to keep up our credit; as a man who cannot pay his tradesmen sends them fresh

orders in lieu of settlement. Under these unsatisfactory conditions, the negotiations opened. They did not, however, interfere with the military situation, and the troops continued to forage daily in the valley, and the tribesmen to fire nightly into camp.[53]

Churchill does not admit the possibility of tribal honor, let alone its equivalence to sovereignty, and in not doing so unwittingly gives credence to the idea that imperial prestige is a greater factor the more vulnerable imperial security becomes.[54] Edgar Sanderson, writing his multivolume history of the British empire in the nineteenth century, pronounced the whole operation a "splendid defence" and determined that "after this success the tribesmen in the Lower Swat Valley gave in unconditionally to British authority."[55] Churchill's simpler chapter heading is "Submission."

Was victory a matter of interpretation? In many ways, it was. That interpretation mattered very much to Churchill and, of course, to those charged with both running Her Majesty's government and making the case for a vigorous forward policy. The troops received a message from the Queen, published in Brigade orders, "expressing sympathy with the sufferings of the wounded and satisfaction at the conduct of the troops." Whether Indian soldiers were particularly pleased by this, as Churchill insisted, is difficult to know with any degree of certainty, but securing their loyalty and ongoing willingness to fight was critical to imperial security, as the disasters in the Malakand campaign made plain. Spinning the way the peace settlement unfolded was also of concern to Churchill and says much about the way imperial "victory" was achieved. The surrender of weapons was no easy gambit. A jirgah delegation from the Mamunds offered 4,000 rupees "as a token of submission" and a mere fifty weapons, which were clearly "antiquated" and not the ones from the recent battle.

They claimed that this is all they had, since their allies across the border had taken the rest. The political officer in charge told them in no uncertain terms that the British would burn their villages if they did not comply. What ensues is a discussion about the very rationale for the attack on Malakand, which those representatives claimed was in response to the burning of a village, and thus a matter of honor:

> All this showed a most unsatisfactory spirit from the Government point of view, and it was evident that the brigade could not leave the valley until the tribesmen adopted a more submissive attitude. The matter reverted to the crucial point. Would they give up their rifles or not? To this they replied evasively that they would consult their fellow-tribesmen and return an answer the next day. This practically amounted to a refusal, and as no reply was received on the 27th, the negotiations ceased.[56]

In the aftermath of this failure, the 2nd brigade destroyed all the villages in the center of the valley by setting them on fire. The valley was filled with smoke, "which hung like a cloud over the scene of destruction."[57] The tribesmen sniped from afar. Not only was "retirement" disputed, peace negotiations, too, produced ongoing skirmishes, if not the continuation of war *tout court*.

Victory, then, was hardly either final or secure. As for peace, it was achieved not by military superiority or technological skill per se but by fire. Churchill had all but sneered at this tactic when the tribesmen used it during the official battle, but here he calls it a kind of "bombardment," bringing it into the lexicon of late-Victorian military terminology.[58] It might be read as one of what Churchill calls "methods of offence," a legitimate military tactic in the context of "fair war."[59] Nonetheless, Churchill is clearly uneasy about the entire process whereby peace has been accomplished. He spends the better part of a chapter defending the peace-by-fire policy, knowing readers will see it as questionable, if not indefensible. He cites a question asked by member of the House of Commons to the secretary of state about limiting the damages in such an exercise to the properties of the guilty and to fortifications, as opposed to villages per se. Churchill protests the naiveté of such a question, arguing that it is impossible to make such a distinction on the Afghan border. Villages are fortifications, and vice versa, and "every inhabitant is a soldier from the first day he is old enough to hurl a stone, till the last day that he has the strength to pull the trigger." Given these circumstances, he continues,

> I invite the reader to examine the question of the legitimacy of village-burning for himself. A camp of a British brigade, moving at the order of the Indian Government and under the acquiescence of the people of the United Kingdom, is attacked at night. Several valuable and expensive officers, soldiers and transport animals are killed and wounded. The assailants retire to the hills. Thither it is impossible to follow them. They cannot be caught. They cannot be punished. Only one remedy remains—their property must be destroyed. Their villages are made hostages for their good behavior. They are fully aware of this, and when they make an attack on a camp or convoy, they do it because they have considered the cost and think it worth while. Of course, it is cruel and barbarous, as is everything else in war, but it is only an unphilosophic mind that will hold it legitimate to take a man's life and illegitimate to destroy his property. The burning of mud hovels cannot at any rate be condemned by nations whose customs of war justify the bombardment of

the dwelling-houses of a city like Paris, to induce the garrison
to surrender by the sufferings of the non-combatants.[60]

They cannot be caught? They cannot be brought to justice?
Churchill well knew that Saidullah had escaped and was untouch-
able in the mountain fastnesses. His successful evasion of military justice seems a pretty plain admission that the British were
not able to defeat the enemy on terms that Victorians would
have recognized as not just legitimate but also as the prerogative
of a civilized and civilizing empire.

🔸 The rationale is that the tribesmen know this is what they
are getting in for, so that in addition to deserving it, they expect
it as well—a compact that Britons, by virtue of the trust they
place in their democracy, have already acquiesced to. Admitting
as he does that the practice is undoubtedly barbarous and that
European wars have long been so would seem to further blur the
line between the wildly "primitive" Pathans and the advocates of
a civilized forward policy.

Churchill elaborated and defended this policy as follows:

> In official parlance the burning of villages is usually expressed
> euphemistically as "so many villages were visited and pun-
> ished," or, again, "the fortifications were demolished." I do
> not believe in all this circumlocution. The lack of confidence
> in the good sense of the British democracy, which the Indian
> Government displays, is one of its least admirable character-
> istics. Exeter Hall is not all England; and the people of our
> islands only require to have the matter put fairly before them
> to arrive at sound, practical conclusions. If this were not so,
> we should not occupy our present position in the world.[61]

By Churchill's lights, imperial security across the globe depended
on the unflinching execution of the burn-villages tactic; it was,

in short, the leading edge of the civilizing wave of the forward policy. Military men who came back to the scene ten years later shared his assessment. Major-General Sir James Willcocks, who led operations against the Zakka Khel Afridis in 1908, claimed that the expeditions of 1897–98 had taught the tribes a critical, if not enduring, lesson "that their secluded villages and mountain fastnesses ... could no longer be regarded as inaccessible if the country were invaded by a determined and well-equipped force." The ongoing unrest, in his view, was the result of "lenient and liberal terms" and by "sinister influences" in the tribal territory and in Afghanistan that refused to desist, regularly raided Peshawar, and thus required the presence of the Bazar Valley Field Force in 1908.[62]

If, as Churchill suggested, modern civilization was a sensitive organism "which thrills and quivers in every part of its vast system at the slightest touch," the Malakand campaign exemplifies the regular, continuous, and quotidian insecurities of that quivering system in both war and "peace."[63] Churchill wrote his book in part because he feared that the attack on the Malakand might be a shot heard round the world, a signal to rivals and others that the Raj was on its last legs.

> The noise of firing echoed among the hills. Its echoes are ringing still. One valley caught the waves of sound and passed them ... till the whole wide mountain region rocked with the confusion of the tumult. Slender wires and long-drawn cables carried the vibrations to the far-off countries of the West. Distant populations on the Continent of Europe thought that in them they detected the dull, discordant tones of decline and fall.[64]

In order to refute this downward slope, and even though the imperial troops were perforce on the defensive all along the frontier for decades; the losses were downplayed; the small victories pumped up; and the approximate victories constructed, if not outright fabricated, from the accumulation of military failures and the shards of postwar settlement—often while the bullets were still flying. The British did not govern by winning, and the enemy, while resistant, did not contest only by fighting, and certainly did not do so by the rules of the game.[65] Though he consigned them to the dustbin of history and spoke of them only in the most orientalist of terms, Churchill could not but acknowledge that "the border peoples resist the advance" of both civilization and the forward policy in its fin-de-siècle manifestations. Significantly, he did recognize the Afghans and their allies as men, though he pathologized them as primitive, murderous, and ruthless: they were an unstable, racialized other in the teeth of a struggle over territory that ought to have thrown British superiority into bold relief but instead showed British men of all ranks on the defensive. In the war of competitive masculinity on the northwest frontier, who would ultimately win was not a given.

Indeed, if British claims to imperial supremacy have rested, even tenuously, on the presumption of definitive imperial victory on the ground, Churchill is a faithful, confessional witness to the fantasy of that narrative. Inadvertently perhaps, he vividly illustrates that the limits of empire came not just from British incapacity but also, in a very real sense, from native resistance. In the Malakand campaign the enemy resisted by fighting and refusing to give ground, by fleeing and remaining at large, and by refusing to turn in their arms as well as by negotiating how the settlement would end the strife. Although the world at large may not have witnessed their challenges to British claims to civilizational difference and racial and technological superiority, the tribesmen of the Swat Valley got an eyeful at Malakand and throughout the decades that preceded it. Given the indispensability of Indian troops to British fighting forces in this, as in most if not all imperial battles, Indian soldiers were also routinely privy to the limits of imperial military power and its correlative political objectives across much of Britain's imperial century. What military historian John Lynn calls the "victories of the conquered" have, in fact, a long and respectable history stemming at least from the second Maratha War of 1803.[66] Well past Waterloo, and certainly well into the nineteenth century, Britain was an imperial state at war, though not exactly as it had been in the period 1689–1815, when it was weak at home and strong abroad.[67] Nor was it simply a matter of native response to imperial conquest in the form of various episodes of local rebellion, though such instances were undoubtedly significant in terms of the long-term instability of a variety of imperial frontiers. What is at issue here is whether, and by what methods, imperial forces may be said to have won (or lost) the day and, having won the day, under what conditions imperial security was then assured.

Empire on the Ground: The Limits and Possibilities of Military Victory

In many respects, the northwest frontier is the most obvious place to make the case for a British empire perpetually insecure in military terms. As a border region, it remains a flashpoint with high stakes, a weak spot in a perennially contested region that had been beset by attacks, sabotage, and anti-imperial currents at least since the onset of the Great Game—that "tournament of shadows" between Britain and Russia that cast such a long shadow over the history of the Raj. Though the British officially won both Afghan Wars (1839–42 and 1878–80), they had done so defensively, and not without some humiliating defeats and equally parlous alliances. Officials from Whitehall to Peshawar feared Russia's ambition along the northwest frontier, viewed by both parties as the gateway to India. But they were also wary of the Persians, who in 1834 had their eye on Herat—one of a number of strongholds they had lost after the collapse of the Safavid dynasty in the second half of the eighteenth century and had been striving to recover ever since.[68] In that sense, the Great Game involved more than two players; in fact, it had many dimensions, only some of which depended on the mutual suspicions of two European powers. Indeed, like Churchill in the Malakand region, earlier Victorians representing the war exhibited some respect, albeit often grudging, for the power, impact, and historical significance of regional dynastic regimes, even as they often relished seeing them caught in the crosshairs of a wider global-imperial struggle for hegemony.[69]

The key to British stability on this fraught frontier at the beginning of the nineteenth century was the emir of Afghanistan, Dost Mohammed, scion of the Barakzai tribe and a man at the very intersection of several imperial gambols.[70] Though he had pledged fealty to the British, his relationship with the Russians was a cause for concern; once he was perceived as a double-crosser, his reputation as a duplicitous warlord was sealed in British imperial history, only negligibly revised when he became an ally again after the end of the war. This is not to say that the British did not try to play the emir against Ranjit Singh or the Russians. They were attuned to the regional stakes of their diplomatic mission and divided on the prospect of an alliance with Dost Mohammed. Lord Auckland, the governor general, was less well disposed toward him than was his political agent on the ground, Sir Alexander Burnes. Neither man appreciated the fact that their quest to bind Dost Mohammed fully to them was not to be. Dost Mohammed's main concern was securing East India Company support against the Sikhs for the recapture of Peshawar, something the British were not prepared to offer.[71] Auckland's "Simla Manifesto" of 1838—which stated that to secure India, the British needed a reliable ally on the northwestern frontier—was not exactly a declaration of war, though it

was a pretext for intervention. Failing Dost Mohammed's cooperation, in March 1839 Sir Willoughby Cotton advanced through
the Bolan Pass, installed Shah Shuja as the new emir, and occupied Kabul. Dost Mohammed obtained a *fatwa* and declared *jihad*,
but the local histories of Barakzai aggression meant that his natural base in southern Afghanistan was loath to support him. He
fled, later gave himself up after attempting a failed insurrection,
and ended up in exile in India.[72]

Shah Shuja, Britain's choice for emir, had been overthrown
by a rival in 1809 and living in exile in India ever since. The
singular advantage he had over Dost Mohammed was that he
was an ally of both the British and the Sikhs, with whom he had
actually brokered a treaty in 1833. The British determined, in
other words, that embracing an enemy of the Sikhs was worse
for the security of India than supporting their nominal ally.[73]
Though the march to Kabul was by no means easy, though the
countryside was not subdued until well into 1841 (if ever), and
though local tribesmen and peasants continued to attack supplies and convoys on a regular basis, the fortress of Ghazni fell
relatively quickly in summer of 1839. Eyewitness accounts testify to the stop-and-start character of the struggle on the ground
and the lack of finality, if not of victory, that characterized the
whole campaign for Afghanistan in this period. Meanwhile, the
occupation of Kabul—undertaken to stabilize Shah Shuja's early
reign—dragged on for three years, looking increasingly permanent to a variety of observers, especially Afghan residents.
A source of particular irritation to locals, both elites and commoners, was the coming and going of Afghan women into and
out of the cantonment, a common enough occurrence in British
imperial military campaigns but a flashpoint in the context of
an otherwise fragile and fractious occupation.[74]

The cost of maintaining such a large military and civilian
contingent was a drain on the Indian treasury. The danger to

supplies and to the occupiers themselves at all ranks was considerable and, in some cases, fatal. Sir Alexander Burnes was hacked to death during an uprising directed at least in part against the occupation forces.[75] The revolt spread. The Afghans bombarded the cantonment, making clear that the security of Kabul was in peril. Sir William Macnaghten, adviser to Auckland, was forced to negotiate with the new Afghan leader Akbar Khan, the son of Dost Mohammed. The terms were humiliating—total British withdrawal, safe passage, and the return of Dost Mohammed as emir—but Macnaghten was confident they would be met. Instead, Akbar Khan ambushed him and his three assistants. Macnaghten's lifeless body was dragged through the streets of Kabul and his head paraded as Akbar's prize, symbols of British defeat and humiliation and a harbinger of worse to come.

The retreat and the ensuing massacre were among the bloodiest episodes in British imperial history. One witness estimated that 3,000 men and women died trying to make an escape on January 7, 1842. As they fled through the passes they could look back and "see the glow of the fire that now consumed their cantonment."[76] Sir William Elphinstone and several other officers were taken prisoner by Akbar Khan, and this added to British demoralization and sheer despair. Any resistance that the British troops were inclined to put up, either as a fighting force or as a human collectivity, was significantly hampered by the notorious mountain gorges and the bitter cold and snow, described in vivid terms by survivors as red with the blood of men, women, and children, not to mention camels and horses. The destruction of the retreating army—what the late nineteenth-century historian Archibald Forbes called "the shock of the catastrophe in the passes"—galvanized Auckland, who authorized Field Marshall Sir George Pollock to organize an "army of retribution," even though this had not been part of the original plan.[77] Kabul was retaken by the fall of 1842, and its bazaar destroyed by the retaliating British forces; the British hostages were released via negotiations that granted their guardian, Sahel Muhammed, a pension for life. Akbar Khan was finally defeated, though his father—whose political activities had not been diminished by exile—quickly reestablished his authority in Afghanistan, where he continued to shape the fortunes of Central Asia, mostly in alliance with the British, until his death in 1863.

Despite his "relative powerlessness" during the early years of his reign, Dost Mohammed influenced Victorian Afghanistan as much as if not more than the British.[78] He should be seen as part of a long line of patrimonial state-builders, a prime example of the "empire of tribes" at the heart of Afghan state formation, and one of the region's three significant players in the Victorian period.[79] Because the war itself was only intermittently battle centric, the British perpetually braced against the possibility of sudden skirmishes and sniping in this frontier region.[80] These were the kinds of guerrilla tactics that would keep them on the defensive there at least until the end of the century. Victorian representations of the 1839–42 war conveyed a sense of the ongoing challenges to imperial security and stability that Afghans, and Afghanistan, routinely posed, both in and outside battle. Memoirs by British officers and soldier-historians exhibit a preoccupation with the natural environment—not as backdrop, but as an active, often insurgent, agent in the making and unmaking of military success on the ground and in shaping the very prospect of imperial security.

In these contexts, Afghans were fierce and formidable warriors, but they often appeared as extensions of an equally punishing terrain, throwing their very humanness into question. Henry Havelock's two-volume *Narrative of the War in Affghanistan*, for example, has all the characteristic features of imperial takeover: the trampling, the promontory view, the collection of indigenous specimens, the ascription of alien place names, the indifference to/contempt for vernacular knowledges, and the imposition of enemy-terrain language onto enemy combatants. Havelock maps the very real challenges that Afghan men and the Afghan environment, together, posed to English soldiers with an arguably picaresque ideal of war and manly valor—even as he anticipates some of Churchill's tendency to conflate alien men and alien terrain. His account demonstrates longing for a more heroic invasion and occupation of Afghanistan than the infamously difficult terrain of that region permitted.[81]

Thus, by the time Churchill recorded the failed and fitful British military responses in the Malakand, the threat to imperial victory by anticolonial tribal warfare should have been familiar to readers, if not to military men in the upper ranks. Meanwhile, in the wake of the second Afghan war, Abdur Rahman, the grandson of Dost Mohammed, whom the British installed in 1880, played the "masterful double game" his predecessors had engaged in, perhaps a bit more successfully. By the mid-1880s, he had made it clear that he was his own man, in part because he was successful not just in individuating from the superpowers but in "pacifying" rival tribes and indigenous threats to his sovereignty as well.[82] Archibald Forbes, though he had deemed Abdur Rahman's tenure "extremely precarious" at first, had to concede that within a year of his accession, the new emir was in control of the country—which was more than the British had ever managed to accomplish fully. Forbes concludes his narrative of the second Afghan war by observing that "Candahar and Herat had both come to him, and that without serious exertion. He continues to reign quietly, steadfastly and firmly; and there never has been any serious friction between him and the Government of India, whose wise policy is a studied abstinence from interference in the internal affairs of the Afghan kingdom."[83] The cost to Britain was "the lives of many gallant men[,] ... the expenditure of about twenty millions sterling," and precious little in the way of frontier territory, stability or security.[84] By 1897, one year after the publication of the third edition of Forbes's popular history, *The Afghan Wars*, Winston Churchill was in the Swat Valley and the northwest frontier was ablaze again. Remarked one observer, "Never had our frontier prestige been so menaced. Never had our authority been so daringly set aside."[85] The British technically held Afghanistan by until the third Afghan war in 1919, through which an independent Afghan nation was created, but the country remained "the weak spot of Imperial defence" well after that. British power remained precarious and vulnerable across the whole of the nineteenth and early twentieth centuries, both because of Afghan assertion and because of the weaknesses of an Indian policy that could not countenance, in the words of Edwin Montagu, secretary for India in 1920, "diplomacy which strives to accomplish something we have not got the force to accomplish."[86]

A close reading of British imperial battle literature and military accounting suggests a similar pattern of defensive engagement, local struggle, and decidedly imperfect "victory" across most of the Victorian empire. Much has been made of the Indian Mutiny in big narrative histories of British imperialism. But in the forty years before the outbreak of those hostilities in the spring and summer of 1857, the British empire faced indigenous enemies and challengers, from China to New Zealand to Burma. Some of these conflicts were, undoubtedly, wars of aggression on Britain's part, designed to secure economic interests on which the British already depended or to consolidate the kind of territorial reach required to protect the kind of short- and long-term political order such interests required. In purely strategic terms, military engagements during the reign of Queen Victoria were more often than not provoked, a reaction to defiance by local merchants and/or local leaders in the face of imperial incursions, changing economic circumstances, or even unresolved issues from earlier conflicts that had ostensibly been "settled" by previous wars. The First and Second Opium Wars are cases in point. These were unquestionably watershed defeats for Qing dynastic power, in both political and military terms. Still, the first war lasted three years; the combination of expeditionary forces, blockade capacity and firepower devastated the Chinese forces who, though superior in number, were unable to hold out. Although the Chinese had an impressive military tradition, the First Opium War was the first of many Sino-western conflicts they fought against "a steep technological gradient."[87] In fact, a refusal prompted the war itself. In a bold attempt to assert China's right to control trade in its harbors and at the behest of the Emperor himself, Lin Zexu, a Qing imperial commissioner, banned the sale of opium, demanding that all quantities be surrendered to Chinese authorities and requiring that foreign traders sign a "no opium trade" pledge, under penalty of death. Lin also closed the channel to Canton and held British traders hostage, putting local British officials in an impossible position: they had to agree to the seizure and destruction of the opium, for which they also had to promise restitution to the traders. Hence, the provocation of war.

This was not the only way the Chinese held the British empire temporarily hostage. In what became known as the "Kowloon incident" of July 1839, a Chinese man was killed by a group of British and American sailors who found themselves on shore as a result of Lin Zexu's seizure of their captain in the ongoing opium trade dispute. Lin argued that he should have jurisdiction over the guilty parties, for whom Charles Elliott, the British superintendent of trade, sought punishment under English law. Though Elliott got his way, he refused to submit to the pledges Lin demanded. The refusal escalated tensions and led to more provocations: Lin exerted pressure by cutting off supplies to British ships in Macao. Given the willingness of some English merchants and captains to submit to the opium ban, this might be viewed as a free trade-war among Englishmen. But the defiance of the Qing is not to be discounted. Lieutenant John Ouchterlony, eyewitness to the unfolding of events, described the emperor as "undisguisedly hostile" by the start of 1841: "Defiance was hurled in his own edicts against the British, and a large bounty was set upon their heads, to excite the populace along the sea-coast to expel and destroy them as noxious reptiles."[88]

The emperor's defiance was famously unsuccessful. Ouchterlony recorded the scenes that ensued in vivid detail: "Hemmed in on all sides, and crushed and overwhelmed by the fire of a complete semi-circle of musketry, the hapless Chinese rushed by hundreds into the water; and while some attempted to escape the tempest of death which roared around them . . . others appeared to drown themselves in despair."[89] If the defeat of the Chinese was a foregone conclusion, it did not occur without struggle or without considerable effort on the part of the British troops both on the water and on the ground. In addition to defying British laws of opium trading, Lin was an astute commander. At the start of the war he played cat and mouse with British warships, facing off fifteen men of war with ten fire-ships, "each pair connected by iron chains, which swept down thus with the tide. The foreign ships all made off hastily: but two sampans [wooden boats] were burnt; and from this time the English did not venture into the port."[90] Lin had good intelligence as well: in addition to having spies everywhere, he had the English newspapers translated, from which he learned that "the Europeans held the Chinese navy in utmost contempt, but were in great dread of our pirates and fisherman." He capitalized on this knowledge to create his own mercenary army from among those constituents; the better to surprise the "barbarian" enemy and ward off British attempts to crush and destroy the Qing forces with more technologically developed weapons.[91]

The war was not won by technological superiority alone, of course. In Zhengjiang it was hand-to-hand combat and a scene of "death and desolation" prompted by Manchu troops who fought furiously but unsuccessfully to the death.[92] As with Churchill's experience of the Malakand campaign, British victory was not self-evident but was, rather, the result of a series of cut and thrusts, of attack and counterattack, of subterfuge and success, of night attacks and minor gains, of peace proposals and returns to the fray—though in this context it was volleys and "stink-pots" and "fire-balls" rather than the effects of the Martini-Henry or Enfield rifle.[93]

Even Ouchterlony, so confident in his account of British triumph, records that

> the 55th regiment and Madras rifles, having observed that a large body of the enemy were escaping from this scene of indiscriminate slaughter along the opposite bank of the river from the citadel and batteries which the naval brigade had stormed, separated themselves, and pushing across the bridge of boats, severed the retreating column in two; and before the Chinese could be prevailed upon to surrender themselves prisoners, a great number were shot down or driven into the water and drowned.[94]

Though "hapless," the Chinese still exhibited, even under conditions of such hopeless siege, the will (if not, in the end, the capacity) to escape, and their flight had to be mercilessly stopped. The ferocity is telling:

> The prisoners were all set at liberty on the following day, deprived of course of their arms, and also some of their tails, which, though an accident easily remedied by the humblest of their tonsors, (by plaiting a new tail into the

root of the old one), was a mark of disgrace that did not fall
to the province of the victors to inflict, and was a wanton
outrage on the feelings of the Chinese, which could only
serve to exasperate them against their invaders. Sir Hugh
Gough, when informed by an officer of what was taking
place, sanctioned his interference, and ordered that the
prisoners should be merely disarmed, and released without
degradation of any kind. When, however, this gentleman,
who had followed Sir Hugh Gough in a boat, reached the
shore, the last man of the Chinese *detenus* was under the
hands of an operator, a tar, who, upon being hailed to cease
his proceedings, hastily drew his knife across the victimized
tail, exclaiming that it was a pity the fellow should have the
last laugh against the rest.[95]

Such ritual humiliation might readily be chalked up to the rac-
ist revenge fantasies of orientalism, so easily directed against
the body of even the prostrate enemy—in this case not once but
twice, as the tar cuts off not simply the actual tail, but its replacement too. This kind of retributive action is so common in conditions of war as to make it appear almost transhistorical, even
allowing for contingencies of time and place—and even allowing
for the gendered ferocity of a disfiguration designed to right the
imbalance of Asian men, who appeared as western women might,
with gender-inappropriate (long) hair. Yet here the revenge script
is quite historically specific: the combination of slaughter of the
arguably defeated enemy with evidence of systematic, semiof-
ficial ritual humiliation, coupled with the purposeful, individu-
ally "tailored" vengeance that Ouchterlony reports, suggests an
anxiety about finishing the job as much as a confidence in having already definitively done so—all in the name of the Victorian
scramble for China.[96] Fears about gender disorder were clearly
at work. Even in the heat of imperial victory, even in a context

in which the victor appears to have won a complete monopoly of authority and control, violence at an intimate level illustrates how imperial power remained perpetually in jeopardy—in the very midst of military success, and at the most micro of scales.

Nowhere is this more apparent than in the case of the Indian Mutiny, whose histories are so routinized around a tale of uprising, defeat, and hegemonic consolidation that it scarcely seems possible to imagine a different narrative, let alone interrupt the arc of rise and fall that tends to shape the contours of that infamous story. Though standard accounts sometimes sketch the background to the 1857 uprisings, they typically begin with the greased-cartridge conflict, a story of indigenous religious prohibition against contact with cow or pork products colliding with the development of a more efficient system of rifle loading that involved tearing the animal-fat-greased cartridge container with one's teeth—a requirement inimical to the sepoy, both Hindu and Muslim. The typical mutiny narrative tracks the spread of rumor and rebellious sentiment, fixes on the Bibighar—where British women and children were massacred during the siege of Kanpur—and moves with more or less haste to the denouement: the Queen's proclamation of 1858, which reframed the terms of imperial rule by doing away with the East India Company and bringing India under the direct control of the Crown. There are, naturally, a number of variations to this narrative arc. Some authors have attended to the aftermath of the revolt; others unpick the cartridge controversy in great detail; and subaltern historians have dwelt on the indifference of rebel leaders to the Raj and emphasized local questions and the antecedent histories of peasant discontent and resistance. Recent work has also turned to the specter of racial violence, especially at Kanpur, in an effort to settle the question of the fate of the British women and children who perished there and to understand the role of race and gender in the outcome of the siege. And there is that exemplar of gender disorder, the Rani of Jhansi, queen of the Maratha princely state. She not only organized a women's battalion and practiced pistol shooting on her palace grounds, but she also dressed in a Pathan-style outfit and died as a rebel in battle, clad as a horse soldier.[97]

These arcs remain fairly faithful to Victorians' own memorializing of the mutiny. They follow the trail of evidence laid down by multivolume histories such as J. W. Kaye's and G. B. Malleson's and even tack to contemporaries' own anxieties at home, which were undeniably focused on the acts of violence committed against British women. "I can think of nothing but these Indian massacres," novelist Charles Kingsley wrote in 1857. "I can hardly bear to look at a woman or child, even my own sometimes. They raise such horrible images, from which I can't escape."[98] Such evocations of racialized sexual violence ("mutiny atrocities," as they have come to be euphemistically known) were by no means fleeting. They have become so codified in historical narrative and popular memory that a kind of "mutiny complex" has resulted—reproduced not just in English or English-language narratives of the mutiny but in Indian and European accounts and in many histories of the events of 1857 down to the present.[99]

✱ This preoccupation with anti-English violence—so characteristic of both the Victorian narratives and the more recent histories of the mutiny—is telling, not least because it indicates the ferocity with which Indians on the ground responded, during an extended moment of social and political upheaval, to potent symbols of British "civilization" and its supposed inviolability. But it also tends to obscure the spectacle of British counterinsurgency—the reverse atrocity factor. And that counterinsurgency was vicious. Suspected rebels were shot out of cannons, and they were also rolled in pigskin and otherwise ritually humiliated as part of the Raj's formal and informal mechanisms of retributive "justice." The face of British counterinsurgency was Lt. Colonel James Neill, who had served in Burma and the Crimea by the time he arrived in Calcutta. As one member of his staff wrote about him, "he feared nobody." Shortly after the retaking of Kanpur, he was left in charge of the captured rebels. He himself recounted that

> whenever a rebel is caught he is immediately tried, and unless he can prove a defense he is sentenced to be hanged at once; but the chief rebels or ringleaders I first make clean up a certain portion of the pool of blood, still two inches deep, in the shed where the fearful murder and mutilation of women and children took place. To touch blood is most abhorrent to high-caste natives, they think that by doing so they doom their souls to perdition. Let them think so . . .
>
> The first I caught was a subadar, a native officer, a high-caste Brahmin, who tried to resist my order to clean up the very blood he had helped to shed; but I made the Provost-Marshal do his duty, and a few lashes soon made the miscreant accomplish his task. Which done, he was taken out and immediately hanged, and after death buried in a ditch at the roadside.[100]

As with the ritual violence done to Chinese prisoners of war in the 1840s, battlefield passions are clearly partly at work. But it was not simply officers who carried out these atrocities, nor was the backlash only meted out in the heat of battle. In the case of the Benares Mutiny, which Neill helped to suppress, gallows were set up in the immediate aftermath and dozens of Indians suspected of being rebels were hanged, including "some young boys, who, perhaps, in mere sport had flaunted rebel colours and gone about beating tom-toms." The perpetrators were civilian officials empowered by Act XIV, dated July 6, 1857, which

allowed for the summary execution of any Indian even suspected of consorting with the rebels. Eyewitnesses noted that
volunteer hanging parties were wandering around Benares and
environs, "with one gentleman executioner boasting of the
'artistic manner' in which he had strung up his victims 'in the
form of a figure eight.'" [101]

The specter of gentleman executioners of young Indian boys
has its own gendered dimensions, reminding us of the homosocial world of empire even and especially at moments of emergency. Brutal repression in response to collective uprisings was
a common enough feature of modern British imperialism. In
the context of 1857, Benares is a particularly instructive episode because the nature of the "mutiny" there was so confused.
The rebels were by no means in the majority and, due to chaos
in the ranks, a considerable number of loyal Sikhs were shot by
British soldiers who had conflated them with mutineers, seeing the enemy in every sepoy uniform. This uncertainty spilled
over into counterinsurgency tactics. In Benares, the reaction was
disproportionate to the local conditions of the rebellion itself, a
situation that was not uncommon across the subcontinent. The
brutality of the backlash, its patent excesses, and the incapacity
of the officers to contain it, indicates something about the character of the mutiny's suppression. It may have been activated by
battlefield fury and stoked by an annihilating racism, but it was
also far from sure-footed or deliberate: the randomness of the
violence suggests a defensive agency rather than a purposeful,
offensively "disciplined" tack. Leaving aside the tactics of counterinsurgency, very few of the pitched battles for various quarters of India where the rebels were holding out were quickly or
easily won, and each setback could readily be "magnified into a
crushing defeat of the British power."[102] While no hard-and-fast
numbers on this exist, it is quite possible that as many mutineers escaped as were captured and executed. These included

several high-profile leaders, such as the rebels Maulana Liaquat Ali and Tatya Tope, the latter repeatedly escaping before he was caught and executed in 1859 after the bitter struggle to pacify Kanpur. In many respects that struggle, and the delay it added to achieving the definitive end of the mutiny, was itself the result of those escapees, for it meant that "the flames of rebellion in Oudh and neighboring Rohilkhand were not finally extinguished for a further twelve months, and many thousands of British lives were lost as a result."[103] Nor was battle the only way British lives were lost. In 1858 alone, ten times as many British soldiers died of sunstroke, exhaustion, or disease as were killed in battle—a rate of mortality directly impacted by the time it took to put down the mutineers, hardly a image of valiant white men going out in a blaze of glory.

Victorians at home and abroad wanted to see the total annihilation of the rebel forces and viewed swift and retributive justice as indispensable to restoring imperial order and as grounds for the continual civilizational mission of the Raj. Lord Canning's attempts to call for clemency were thwarted and ridiculed; the nickname "Clemency Canning" is both a rebuke to his capacity to rule and—given conventional Victorian associations of mercy with women—a challenge to his very manhood. Public sentiment in the metropole was hardly more sympathetic. "Nothing in mainstream British culture of the complacent 1850s," literary critic Christopher Herbert has argued, "prepares one for the crazed bloodthirstiness that stamps itself ... on British responses to the rebellion."[104] By its very definition, of course, mutiny puts empire on the defensive. Atrocity fantasies and their actual execution are also reactive: a sign of revenge, perhaps, but also an index of anxiety about the ultimate insecurity of empire even in the midst of complacent certainty that victory has been secured, and Britain has survived the test of rebellion. Much like the Black Hole of Calcutta narratives that dominated eighteenth-century accounts of the Raj, when the authors of mutiny memoirs and histories talk of revenge acts, they are actually producing stories not of triumph but of "failure, abjection, and extreme fear," generating images of "terrible reversal"—in this case, of English civilizers-turned-savages—and in the process, offering "a salutary reminder of the tenuousness of colonial power."[105] The emergency moment showcases the limits of the logics of colonial sovereignty: the state of regular, quotidian lawlessless in which empire typically functions and in which peace is actually the exception rather than the rule—and in which the fantasy of peace is secured only through a monopoly of violence that is neither self-evident nor easily won, predictable, uninterrupted, or even made final by success in "battle."

If military victory was not won without a struggle, and pacification of the enemy was not accomplished easily, the British ultimately did suppress the Indian Mutiny and secure a new kind of hegemony on the subcontinent. Yet regardless of this signature success, Pax Britannica had been and remained perpetually at risk across the whole of the nineteenth century. In terms of sheer numbers, Richard Gott counts sixty-plus instances of rebellion and resistance to imperial forces across the empire from the eighteenth century up until the eve of the event of 1857.[106] The kinds of debacles the British faced on the eastern Cape were buried in dispatches but have failed to find a foothold in narratives of imperial conquest and hegemony.[107] In the 1834–35 war with the Xhosa chief Hintsa, initial Xhosa successes were followed by terrible defeats, though conquest was no guarantee of total control. Indeed, military victory—even the mutilation and execution of Hintsa himself—was insufficient for exploiting the colonial economy. By the 1840s, this necessitated forms of imperial intervention that were carried out by colonial troops but were decidedly not battle centric. British soldiers "actively set fire to Xhosa imizi [homesteads], destroyed their grain stores and gardens and captured thousands of head of cattle"—a series of events so destructive that even an observer sympathetic to settlement called it "a disgrace to the age we live in."[108] Such sentiments anticipated Churchill's unease about similar measures in the Malakand campaign—but they also underscore that British imperial wars were rarely if ever solely won via "military" superiority alone regardless of where the battles were fought.

Meanwhile, victories proliferated more wars. The First Opium War and the First Anglo-Afghan War were virtually simultaneous. If the outcomes of both were success for the British, they each resulted in a second war before the century was half finished. The two Anglo-Sikh wars, which were undertaken to secure for control of the Punjab in the wake of the death of Ranjit Singh in 1839, are an example of the costliness of serial failure—and of contemporaries' awareness of their impact in strategic terms. Here the British were on the defense from the start against the disciplined Sikh army. Even so, as in Afghanistan, they were remarkably unprepared for the level of resistance they met, and for the way their frontal attacks "precipitately hurled them into the mouth of Sikh guns." According to one eyewitness to the battle, "half-outside and half within the enemy's position, unable either to advance or retreat, regiments were mixed up with regiments, and officers with men, in the wildest confusion."[109] Tidings of victory at Sobraon were a relief, but they also led to a barrage of criticism of army leadership, not least because egregious blunders on the field ultimately left Delhi—whose security was the indirect object of the campaigns—utterly exposed.

By early 1846, the British army had occupied Lahore, but this had a short-term strategic consequence. Field Marshall Henry Hardinge (later the governor-general of India) reasoned that the troops were so winded, literally and metaphorically, that he did not have the capacity to annex the Punjab. The second war began almost immediately upon the conclusion of the treaty of the first, sparked by an insurrection at Lahore that followed on the heels of serial assassinations of Britons. More "terrible action" followed on the battlefield, with British troops outnumbered and outmaneuvered. At the battle of Chellianwala, the Sikhs exhibited greater technological capacity and lost fewer men than the British. The situation was so dire that Lord Napier was dispatched, a vote of no confidence that prompted the British officer in charge, Colonel King, to take his own life. Lest there be any question that the security of Afghanistan was at stake, Dost Mohammed supported the Sikhs against his once and future enemy; a combination of setbacks on the field resulted in General Gough becoming the object of frank criticism in Britain and India. When the time came for annexation, the rationale of the governor general, Lord Dalhousie, was not just in direct violation of the peace treaty but also effectively conceded the improbability of winning on the battlefield. "I believe in my conscience that we shall never have peace till we deprive them of the power to make war. . . . I think, we ought to subvert that government, abolish that army, and convert into a British province the Raja of the Punjab."[110]

The iconic status of the Mutiny notwithstanding, there was a lot of military pushback before its outbreak. Though in imperial histories, it is often treated as a sideshow to 1857, the Santals took up arms against British rule in eastern India a full two years before the outbreak at Meerut. They were led by two brothers, Sidhu and Kanhu Mumu, who galvanized the tribal community against the Raj with such success that it took six months and the imposition of martial law to quell the rebellion, which has lived on in the history of the Jharkandi freedom movement as foundational to twentieth-century claims for self-rule.[111] So persistent was the Santal resistance that a commanding officer was quoted as saying that "it was not war . . . they did not understand yielding. As long as their national drums beat, the whole party would stand, and allow themselves to be shot down. Their arrows often killed our men, so we had to fire on them as long as they stood."[112] Another chronicler noted that villages were sacked and several Europeans killed outright, and that even after British troops were able to subdue the country around Bhagalpur, the rebels under arms were still estimated at 30,000. The situation was considered so dire that it provoked a declaration of martial law in 1855.[113] As was typical of the rhythms of such uprisings, confidence in their quick suppression was outdone by repeated evidence of the rebels' continued determination and vigor. Fearful of fresh outbreaks, the lieutenant governor considered it "impossible to make other than a partial and incomplete defense by means of the [extant] troops" alone, prompting him to seek information on, and funding for, enhanced road works and telegraph lines—a development that strained the already tense relations between the civil and military authorities.[114]

Despite the role the Indian Mutiny tends to play in imperial history narratives as a turbulent exception to empire's normative order, in fact armed revolt was "endemic" throughout colonial India.[115] Ironically, the very importance ascribed to the Mutiny itself—and its centrality to histories that emphasize the return to order and the post-mutiny settlement over the long, drawn out, and contested nature of its suppression –– may overstate its significance for Pax Britannica writ large. This is especially the case when 1857 is seen as paradigmatic of resistance to empire in the nineteenth century, exceptional not just by virtue of its capacity to disrupt imperial business as usual but because of the comparatively swift denouement and reimposition of order (eighteen months from the outbreak at Meerut to the Queen's Proclamation) in Britain's largest colonial possession. Rather than view 1857 as sui generis, it would be just as accurate to understand it as a nodal point, at once temporal and spatial, for imperial unrest in the nineteenth century.

Indeed, elsewhere in the empire, 1856–57 was also a conflict-ridden period. The millenarian uprising led by the charismatic figure of the young girl Nongqawuse—known as the cattle-killing movement—preoccupied colonial officials in Xhosaland and London. The immediate cause of the turbulence was the governor of the Cape Colony, Sir George Grey, whose determination to co-opt the local chiefs and "civilize" the Xhosa people via what was to become the classic toolkit of colonial pacification: mission education, European medicine, colonial law, and wage labor.[116] If, as a result, southern Africa was a total war zone, this was at the instigation of local people with agendas of their own—among them deep resistance to white expansion.[117] The cattle-killing movement was led by the young prophetess, whose message was that the ancestors would come with great bounty to the Xhosa but only if they would destroy their means of livelihood (by killing cows and burning crops). As with the Indian Mutiny, this was no sudden eruption; it stemmed from long recent histories of imperial war, colonial depredation, and "calamitous dispossession," including (most proximately) the fierce and devastating War of Water (1846–47). It is worth noting that while the movement was in part a response to colonial frontier warfare, it had a cosmological dimension of its own, connected as it was with traditions of ancestor worship and beliefs about resurrection. Yet scholars call the prophecies anticolonial nonetheless, because of how their narratives were cast. Some included "invulnerability to bullets, driving whites into the sea and the return of fallen warriors," an indication of how powerfully intertwined indigenous imaginaries were with imperial histories—and how powerfully such imaginaries might motivate resistance. Here, as elsewhere under British dominion, the "spirit realm of agency," so little understood by would-be conquerors, was absolutely consequential to the trouble with empire.[118]

The cattle-killing movement lasted until 1858. As the mutiny had in India, it produced new configurations of power that curtailed Xhosa autonomy and enhanced British colonial rule. This is not to suggest that events in southern Africa can or should be subsumed into the mutiny, its causes, or its afterlives. Nor do patterns of ongoing eruption indicate with any degree of specificity what the particular local outcomes were and how they shifted or rewrote conditions of power, hegemony, or legitimacy. But they do underscore the serial wars through which the British were not simply extending their reach before 1857 and after, but actively defending extensions or would-be extensions of formal and informal empire. As historian John Darwin has observed, successive wars demonstrate that "we should not assume that the British could always exploit the advantages of discipline and technology."[119] But they also surely exemplify the tenacious, troublesome power of indigenous kingdoms and polities in the face of British will to imperial dominion. They underscore too the invocation of war as an instrument of imperial policy, especially in territories where Pax Britannica was linked to the exigencies of white settlement. Multiple wars and campaigns against the Maori in New Zealand left the certainty of imperial order in question from the 1840s at least until the beginning of the 1870s. As historian James Belich notes, by 1845, five years after the Treaty of Waitangi was signed by representatives of the British Crown and Maori chiefs, the wars ensured were "an unbroken series of British disasters." Skirmishes developed into ambushes, surprise volleys felled British soldiers left and right; "every tree contained a Maori sniper; every mass of fallen logs was a bush redoubt." Writing in his dispatches, Colonel Henry Despard had to admit that "the extraordinary strength of this place, particularly in the interior defence, far exceeded any idea that could have been formed of it."[120] Settler politicians attributed the emergence of the Kingitanga (or King movement) of

the 1850s to the weakness of the governor, Sir Thomas Gore
Browne, who was confident that a "sharp lesson" from the army
would suffice to bring the resistant to heel. But as it turned out,
"armed intervention in 1860 triggered a thirteen-year sequence
of conflicts, campaigns and rebellions through the central North
Island. The wars [in Taranaki (1860–61) and Waikato (1863–64),
and the campaigns against the prophets Titokowaru (1868–9)
and Te Kooti (1868–72)], "reflected the colonial state's commitment to crushing any explicit challenge to its authority."[121]
In fact, whether governor, settler, or colonial official, Britons
determined to colonize New Zealand "regularly butted against
the limits of their rule," and of their military capacity as well.
Though Sir George Bowen, appointed governor in 1867, thought
the King was an "insolent barbarian," he capitulated to a "modi-
fied recognition" of his sovereignty on the grounds that neither war nor taxes was sufficient to contain him, "as he was not
conquered by Generals Chute & Cameron with 10,000 regular
troops, it is absurd to suppose that he can be conquered by the
raw and scanty Colonial levies alone."[122]

As for the New Zealand (Maori) wars themselves, the
path to conflict itself was, literally, halting and full of obstacles. Maori leaders resisted road building and other forms of
communication-network extension, which in turn hindered
troop mobility and delayed invasion by months at a time.
Kingitanga established an *aukati* (boundary line) to limit the
purview of colonial law. Even after the war was so forcefully and
effectively policed, "colonists who transgressed the autaki without permission were liable to be killed."[123] The wars were "neither
an easy nor a complete success for colonial or imperial rule," and,
as significantly, representations of victory were their own turf
battles.[124] In one telling example, the defense of Turuturu Mokai
in 1868 was "a devil of a battle" from which Haowhenua and his
men eventually retreated. Though "historians have construed

this to mean that the engagement was a noble British victory," Belich suggests that they are wrong to do so. "British and Maori casualties were 16 and six respectively, and most contemporaries saw Turuturu Mokai for what it was—a sharp and embarrassing little Pakeha defeat. The Ngaruahine achievement in crippling the garrison of a fortified post with small loss to themselves was a minor triumph of tactical planning." Charles Kane, the Irishman who hoped to kill Titokowaru with his own hands, was felled by a tomahawk blow from an ancient warrior shortly thereafter, and was subsequently turned into a glorious martyr to the colonial cause.[125]

Maori achievement on the battlefield was significant. In the end, "it required 18,000 British troops, together with careful preparation and logistical operation, to defeat them—and even then they were able to delay and limit the enemy victory." Belich ascribes their success to a combination of indigenous methods, imitation of European tactics, and "adaptive innovation," what he calls "fighting fire with water."[126] Yet it was precisely the fact of victory that the British failed to admit and, more importantly, to register in the historical narrative. The expectation of victory repeatedly "overshot the evidence" and produced "fictional victories, and the still more frequent exaggeration of real ones."[127] This misreading may have been an attempt to absorb the shock of defeat at the hands of indigenous people. Such accounts of victory were embraced by contemporaries and subsequently by historians who have ended up distorting the record. These distortions have left their mark on the battlefront of sexual violence as well. Though the treatment of women is little commented on in histories of the Maori wars, indigenous women were commonly the victims of sexual violence. Few enough of these incidents made their way into court, and when they did, Maori women's virtue and respectability were what was mainly on trial. Though the white men in question were often acquitted,

Maori communities made their frustration and disgust publicly known, as when they openly harassed the governor on his visit to the Bay Islands in 1867, where just such a verdict had been delivered.[128]

  ✿ Beyond the case of the Maori wars, the quest to claim imperial victory was almost as keen as the various battles themselves. No fewer than four wars were fought against the Ashanti. "Script-writing"—that is to say, efforts to create a narrative of certain stabilization and comparatively easy conquest—was part and parcel of campaign activity.[129] Not only were the officers of governor Charles MacCarthy (governor of Sierra Leone) eager to reassure him that pacification was assured, MacCarthy himself was busy telling his bosses in London that "the Ashante tributaries [are] seeking shelter under the British flag."[130] This was 1823, and MacCarthy's agents were furiously bribing chiefs and trying to play one tribe off another. Here, as elsewhere, the standard definition of Pax Britannica as the project of preventing indigenous factions from fighting with each other is only partially true. Yes, the body commanded by Nsuttahene Yaw Sekere was dispatched by the Asante government to punish the Nkyona and Wusata "for their failure to provide contingents for the Gyaman expeditionary force in 1818." But MacCarthy's men were themselves busy "raising rebellion" in the southern provinces—with consequences they could not fully control. Unduly confident that he had little to fear from the Asante army, MacCarthy moved his troops into Wassa, in January 1824, where he was fatally beaten back. He and eight officers were killed; more than half of their 200 men did not return; MacCarthy was beheaded, his skull encased in gold and paraded annually thereafter. The narrative of total and easy military victory was not just made in the wake of big events like the mutiny; it was part of the script of every campaign and skirmish. As Ivor Wilks notes in his history of the nineteenth-century Asante, "Although in virtually every engagement the Asante forces in the south-central provinces had won the day, the British commanders nevertheless proceeded to congratulate themselves on 'the recent successes which have been obtained, with so much bravery, by His Majesty's forces, over the Ashantee tribes, and the enemy's consequent retreat to Coomassie [Kumasi]."[131] Apparently, even many years later, Asante people were still insisting they had not been defeated.[132]

This is not to say that the Asante's victories were any less partial or fitful: Osei Bonsu, the Asante king, was killed on or about the same day as MacCarthy, and the Asante troops were denied easy victories well into 1826, specifically because of the mobilization of the Congreve rocket by the British. There was disagreement among the leaders of the Asante war council, and, to be sure, there were complex and dynamic rivalries between indigenous British enemies and indigenous British allies. Even so, MacCarthy's successor, Governor Campbell, worked hard to control the story told about, for example, the all-important battle of Katamaso, where Wilkes concludes that Bonsu's successor, Osei Yaw Akoto, lost the battle but won the war.[133] Nor was peacemaking a neat affair; the treaty that finally ended the war was only officially agreed to by all the parties in 1831. This delayed "victory" scenario was by no means untypical. There were nine frontier wars in southern Africa between 1779 and 1879, each one arguably testing the limits of imperial hegemony and collectively defining the elusiveness, if not the limits, of conquest. As in New Zealand, ambush and the capacity of "unseen eyes" in the bush threw the British troops perpetually off guard and filled their dispatches with anxiety about "distressing warfare" and "no advantage of any real importance has been gained."[134] Imperial confidence was by no means totally shaken. As lieutenant general Harry Smith wrote to his sister in 1851, with what can only be called a complete want of irony, "But for this inexplicable Hottentot revolution, I would have put down the Kaffirs in six weeks."[135]

If British officers waxed confident in their ability to beat the natives decisively, Africans themselves were witnesses to the contrary. By the time Sir Garnet Wolseley was appointed to command the expedition to the Gold Coast, for example, neither the Asante nor the Fante "had any real evidence that Britain was a great military power in her own right."[136] Despite his bravado, Wolseley admitted to being unable "to exercise any general control over the course of a fight" because of a combination of dense bush, army indiscipline, and Asante military capacity. He made a grand display of showing the Gatling guns to the Asante envoys, which apparently did not impress them, possibly because the guns initially misfired. And despite Sir Garnet's ultimate victory, the British were back in the region by the 1890s because within a few years of his success, "the Ashantis had rebuilt most of Kumasi, recovered the whole of their lost territory except Kwahu and Adansi, had conveniently forgotten about paying indemnity and were again causing sleepless nights on the Gold Coast."[137]

Elsewhere on the continent, there was more evidence of indigenous military capability. The battle to subdue Natal and bring the king of the Zulus, Cetshwayo KaMpande, into line was notoriously fierce and by all accounts disastrous until the final, bloody success at Ulundi in 1879. Detailed accounts of the assaults, attacks, ambushes, and sieges that made up the Zulu war of 1879 suggest that the "debacle" at Isandlwana—often held up as the most calamitous engagement of the campaign—was just the most intense version of the recurrent micro-failures on the ground that beset the whole undertaking.[138] Even the end was delayed by Cetshwayo's flight. When Cetshwayo was caught, he expressed surprise that the British troops had proved able to come down the mountain through the forest, since their skill at managing the terrain had been so disastrous throughout the war—a fact that British military men readily admitted to themselves.[139] As significantly, how defeat and victory were scripted was an issue, not just at the moment of conflict, but in its very anticipation. According to historian Jeff Guy, the script for the battle of Ulundi, which was the basis of Zulu defeat and the end of the war, was foretold even before the hostilities commenced:

> By the time the battle was fought, the intensity of Zulu resistance had already persuaded London that the cost of ending Zulu independence by force of arms would be too high, that the officials who had brought about the war had been checked, and that orders had been given that Zululand should not be annexed. Nevertheless Isandlwana could not go unavenged; Britain's colonial peoples had to be convinced of the Queen's military superiority, and the "stain" on Britain's honor had to be wiped out. To achieve this the battle of Ulundi was promoted to the rank of major military victory. Peace was in fact attained in the weeks that followed Ulundi by promising the Zulu people that they would retain possession of their land if they laid down their arms.[140]

As was to be the case with the Malakand Field Force on the northwest frontier, the British hoped for a clear-cut military victory, but they had to settle for peace—in this case, a "peace" driven by their determination to absorb Zululand once and for all into the regime of white settler capital—by other means.

In Zululand, as elsewhere in the empire, those in charge took a shellacking in the press, adding to their resolve and to the ferocity of their determination to best a formidable enemy.[141] Defeat in battle was often quick—one historian reckons that the battle of Isandlwana was lost between 8 a.m. and 2:30 p.m.—and costly in reputational terms as well as in human lives. British casualties did add up, though they rarely matched those of the enemy. And those deaths cast doubt on the value of imperial victory in campaigns far removed from the battlefield. The metropolitan press derided Disraeli's penchant for "little wars" like the one against Cetshwayo, mocking it as a simple game of chess which might be won in three moves: occupation, rectification, and war and annexation. But others negotiating the limits of empire in the public sphere were not so sanguine. Stumping in the contest for the premiership against Disraeli, William Gladstone noted in his famous Midlothian speech of 1879, "In Africa we had the record of 10,000 Zulus slain for no other offence than their attempt to defend their hearths and homes, their wives and their children." Sir John Fortescue recounted in his Cambridge lecture in 1913 the challenges Britain faced on the ground in the Kaffir wars, declaring, "It is actually a fact that . . . the military power of England was strained almost to breaking point by 3000 naked savages."[142]

The proliferation of minor set-tos on both sides of the Queen's 1858 proclamation was so worrisome to imperial stability that the very category "small war" had to be invented. It was coined in 1896 by Major C. E. Callwell of the Royal Artillery in his book *Small Wars: Their Principles and Practice*. Both the book and the term are testimonies to the perpetual irritants facing British military officers and soldiers in outposts across the empire.[143] A 500-plus page catalogue of the causes and objectives of small wars, Callwell's chapters include discussions of "hill warfare," "bush warfare," "night operations," "surprises, raids and ambuscades," and "Guerilla warfare in General." If this sounds like a concession to the recurrent dangers facing British warriors on the ground, Callwell all but admits it, emphasizing the perils of "desultory warfare" and skirmishes versus "general engagements"—and urging commanders to "tempt the enemy into action . . . upon the battlefield" as opposed to lingering in uncertain terrain or allowing the enemy to resist being drawn into direct attack. He was not alone in his views. James Stuart, in his *History of the Zulu Rebellion* in 1906, wrote at length of indigenous military strategy, acknowledging that major and minor military successes on their part were not merely chance or random, but part of a full-fledged "Zulu military system."[144]

Callwell's fin-de-siècle book anticipated the very circumstances Churchill grappled with virtually simultaneously in the Malakand.

The evil effects which will from time to time result from ignorance of the theater of war can best be demonstrated by a few examples. A fruitful source of trouble, for instance, is that the route to be followed may not be accurately known.

This is well illustrated by Hicks Pasha's disastrous attempt to march from the Nile to El Obeid in 1883. The staff were not familiar with the position of the wells, the distances and the difficulties to be encountered. The guides were treacherous. The force lost its way, lost time, and lost heart, and when at last the Mahdists attacked it, the troops, worn out and despairing, made no fight of it and were annihilated . . .

Or again the resources of the theatre of war in supplies, in water, and in transport may not be properly estimated. It is a most serious thing if an operation has been undertaken in the belief that supplies will be found in a certain locality, and if this belief is, when too late, discovered to be unfounded. . . . Inconvenience and even disaster may be caused by doubt as to the exact position of some topographical feature or locality, or by an error in a map in which the commander of the troops is trusting. Ignorance as to the nature of a place which it has determined to capture may also cause much trouble.[145]

A veteran of several small wars (the Second Anglo-Afghan War, 1879–80 and the First Boer War, 1880–81), Callwell was particularly keen to emphasize the dangers of the alien terrain and to document examples of how such ignorance cost British lives and, in some cases, turned small battles into "major wars." Significantly, his manual is as attentive to the skill and capability of the enemy as it is to the ways the British army can beat him, if not more so. Although he relied on the frontier campaigns in India to demonstrate his point, these were by not his only examples. Callwell drew on failures big and small against the Asante, the Burmese, and the Maori in in arguing the need to pay careful attention to "savage" defense works, for example, which most often made the exception seem more like the rule. So while "irregular warriors are often very skillful in the use of obstacles, and expend much ingenuity in surrounding their defence works with stakes, pits, and so forth," on the whole they are generally unprepared for artillery fire. It turns out, however, that the real problem was that "semi-civilized races" like the Ashante and the Dahomeans "do not understand the value of a clear field of fire": they wont be drawn into "regular" battle, insisting on complex, even serial lines of defense and, in the case of Maori pas, establishing fortifications that "were by no means easy to capture." Nor was this a uniquely British imperial problem. Examples from French conflicts, from China to the Africa, were also common. In the 1899 edition of *Small Wars*, Callwell noted, in a chapter ostensibly on the routine inferiority of indigenous defense works, that "in 1898 the French had to bring quite a formidable little park of artillery against the town of Sikasso in the basin of the Upper Niger, and only captured the place after a fortnight's siege, during which the walls were breached."[146]

By Callwell's own definition, the designation "small war" did not refer expressly or even primarily to scale. Practically, he wrote, "it comprises the expeditions against savages and semi-civilized races by disciplined soldiers, campaigns undertaken to suppress rebellious and guerilla warfare in all parts of the world where organized armies are struggling against opponents who will not meet them in the open field."[147] Small wars and their regular, ongoing challenge to global imperialism were, in effect, the very conditions under which the British empire operated: the everyday, workaday, and generalized state of semi-emergency and misrule—the very unexceptional premise of Pax Britannica regardless of when or where it was believed to have been secured. Callwell's book was a cautionary tale for those who thought the acquisition or maintenance of imperial power on the ground was a given. It endures as an ethnography of imperial military psychology, offering insight into how the cumulative experiences of imperial small wars were accounted for by century's end. Not only was the enemy capable and strategic, his resistance required not just cataloguing but also an encyclopedic archive of what he could accomplish and how to prevent him from prevailing.[148] *Small Wars* went into several editions and has been taken up by recent military strategists, for whom the small war, far from "irregular," is the commonest form of threat to twenty-first-century global-imperial security on the ground.[149]

Seen in this light, the most infamously disastrous and questionably "won" campaign of the whole nineteenth century—the Anglo-Boer War of 1899–1902—appears not so much exceptional as exemplary. Though the fact is often overlooked in grand narratives of empire's rise and fall, the siege of Mafeking and its consequences were themselves legacies, direct and indirect, of two earlier wars, the Zulu war (1879) and the first Anglo-Boer War (1880–81). They were the culmination, in effect, of a series of failed attempts to secure southern Africa for Britain in what has come to be viewed as the overwhelmingly successful "scramble for Africa." The guerilla warfare for which the 1899 war is so well known is not sui generis but typical of the cut-and-thrust maneuvers British troops had experienced across the whole of empire in the Victorian period. In terms of local unrest, extensive use of imperial troops, and metropolitan anxiety about imperial constancy, the period 1895–1902—the same extended moment in which Churchill was narrating the Malakand chronicle—is possibly one of the densest moments of imperial instability in the history of the British empire, especially when one factors in the simultaneity of the Boer war and the threat of another Mad Mullah, the Somali leader Sayyīd Muhammad ʿAbd Allāh al-Hasan, and the chaotic overrun of European empires beyond just the British into the equation.[150] The fin-de-siècle struggle over the spoils of Africa, and, by extension, of the interdependent global empires for which it served as a nexus, is the story of white men trying (strenuously, if not also breathlessly) to keep up with the enemy and to keep a lid on the military conflicts they themselves unleashed in the interests of securing the foundation for global territorial sovereignty.[151]

Imperfect Victory and the History of Imperial Insecurity

Read against these narratives, *The Story of the Malakand Field Force* is not simply unoriginal. It looks positively derivative, echoing as it does a recurrent pattern of advance and retreat on numerous fields of battle upon which so-called primitive enemies did more than stand their ground: they inflicted considerable damage on the British fighting forces and threatened imperial security wherever it aimed to take root. Was the young Churchill simply fulfilling a kind of generic formula in his narrative, drawing on earlier forms and accounts in his rendition of the limits of British imperial power, not to mention of the significant indigenous challenges to hegemony via the Martini-Henry? Or was he just the last in a long line of Victorian witnesses to the successive failures of British imperial victory? The archive of soldier and officer accounts, combined with evidence from dispatches and other, more official forms of documentation, suggests a pattern of partial military success: evidence of the possibility that far from supreme, let alone total, the British imperial military exerted a tenuous, imperfect, and eminently contestable hold on the alien populations it sought to bring to heel—in war after successive war, on multiple empire-wide fronts.

Until quite recently, historians have taken Churchill to be ambivalent about the forward policy, despite the fact that contemporaries who followed his journalism or read his published account of Chakdara and the events following it would have seen his position quite clearly. His rationale stemmed from his commitment to decisions taken by past administrations and from his conviction that the fate of imperial prestige was on the line. If his views on the wisdom of going "forward" were shaped by his observations of the Malakand Field Force, this had not happened by abstraction. The nature, conditions, and outcome of battle—and specifically of the drubbing of September 16, 1897—were key to the consolidation of his views on the stakes of imperial defense. Rather than engendering supreme confidence, the events of the Malakand campaign produced a singular unease about the possibility of long-range frontier stability, and raised questions about the character of imperial expansionist rhetoric and policy in the years immediately before the Boer War. Churchill's embrace of the forward policy was, in short, a distinctly defensive mechanism, the consequence of his first-hand view of war on the ground and his eyewitness experience of seeing imperial troops defeated, even decimated, in "a savage war of peace" on the outskirts of empire.

In fact, the whole campaign was a response to a coordinated anti-imperial rising, a mini-rebellion against the forward policy, making it a notably reactionary maneuver.[152] The "forward" nomenclature tends to obscure this defensive posture, whether its object was to stall Russian aggression or contain tribal insurgency, or both. Beyond the question of the forward policy itself, the Swat Valley engagement illustrated, for Churchill no less than for his readers, how imperfectly subdued and how insecure the field of empire and its would-be subjects could be—not just in the heat of battle, but in its aftermath as well. They would have been hard-pressed to read it as victory except in the most qualified terms. Such a critical reading of imperial military operations was possible, if only long after the fact. At the very moment that the Swat Valley was in flames, for example, Lord Roberts's memoir of the second Afghan war of 1878–79 was being widely reviewed and held up as evidence that, despite the "succession of victories, it is impossible not to perceive that the war was a signal failure."[153]

A reviewer of Churchill's book for the *Saturday Review* in 1898 wrote, "We have never seen the power which fanaticism wields in the wild borderland of India better described than in this volume." He also commented on the "mismanagement and bad generalship in certain incidents," and went on to deliver a far more succinct and devastating critique of the military leadership than Churchill had offered.[154] But in the end, the British thought they had won in the Malakand campaign, and they certainly acted as if they had. Taking them at their word misses a crucial opportunity to understand what the terms of engagement and of victory were and, frankly, to assess the relationship between the claim to victory and the success of imperial dominion. The link between military success and, in this case, technological superiority is not as tight as was asserted—a gap that Churchill himself recognized and chronicled in the guise of imperial confidence, no less. The gap between "victory" in battle and both short- and long-term stability on the northwest frontier was not just considerable, it was there for contemporaries to see—revealing just what an interpretive effort went into constructing the fantasy of imperial supremacy, and racial superiority along with it. Victorians also clearly saw how fiercely indigenous populations, in this case the Pathans and their allies, resisted imperial hegemony in battle and in peace: they witnessed the empire on fire even as they heard the rhetoric about "Pax Britannica." Like Churchill himself, Victorians were capable of seeing the disaster on the northwest frontier in all its dimensions: of admitting to the strength of resistance and critiquing the military maneuvers but crediting the British with victory nonetheless. Overwhelmingly, this is what the reading public was treated to in the years following the Malakand Field Force deployment.[155]

These patterns did not end with the death of Queen Victoria. The Great War, with its recurrent disasters for the western allies, was an imperial war, and the struggles over future imperial territories at its heart were ferocious and by no means of certain outcome at the time. Charles Townshend titled his recent book on the battle for Mesopotamia *Desert Hell*, narrating with harrowing precision how desperately the British needed military success there in the wake of Gallipoli and how devastating (and demoralizing) battles like the one in November 1915 at Ctesiphon (the former imperial Persian capital) were. Townshend's analysis of this defeat, and of the raid on Baghdad that followed, does not shy away from the conclusion that the leadership was confused, and the morale of the men, at rock bottom. One general on the scene wrote that "these troops of mine are <u>tired</u> and their tails are <u>not</u> up, but slightly down."[156] Initial successes were recurrently Pyrrhic, and retreat was never far behind. As much if not more so than elsewhere across the nineteenth-century empire, these battles were shambolic and ultimate victory was the result of serial offensives, bungled negotiations, and maladministration from top to bottom.[157] In the region as a whole, victory was secured only after the use of the twentieth-century equivalent of the Maxim gun: air power. The Somme was unquestionably a disaster at an unimaginably huge scale. But it was also an echo

of a century of British imperial military debacles that had challenged the notion of an invincible white race in the eyes of colonized and colonizers alike.

British military "supremacy" was not a fiction, but it was also
not the self-evident consequence of superior skills, military or
otherwise, on the ground. Assessing the relationships between
"victory" and the claim of hegemony, between insurgency and
claims to domination, between military failure and imperial
insecurity is indispensable to a critical history of British imperial power, though as a method, the view from the ground of
battle—or more pointedly, from the perspective of indigenous
challengers—has rarely been the focus of British imperial historiography, whether old or new. This chapter has relied heavily
on imperial sources, suggesting what a counterreading of even
these archives can accomplish. Much remains to be done. Given,
for example, the way that imperial knowledge circulated across
frontiers, to what extent did enemy combatants also share or
exchange knowledge about military tactics to their advantage,
and did such knowledge spur armed resistance across empire,
as the Haitian revolution famously did?[158] A skeptical history
of empire, one that questions the scope of imperial victory and
gives credence, even centrality, to the forces that contested it, has
ramifications well beyond the particularities of Churchill in the
Swat Valley. Presumptions about the overall "success" of British
imperialism shape not just empire history writing, but common
and popular perceptions of what successful Anglo-imperial world
power looks like in historical terms as well. When scholars have
challenged the "drum-and-trumpet version" of Britain's imperial
history, they have done so in the realm of cultural representation or discourse, though recent research on the failure of the
imperial administrative apparatus to accomplish its disciplinary
ambition have begun to advance more a skeptical view of the
legal and bureaucratic reach of imperial power.[159]

Meanwhile, the drama of the frontier war—a designation that is arguably applicable to all imperial wars—models not the givenness of imperial supremacy but the "ceaseless struggle for empire," its perpetual chaos, and its ultimate ungovernability.[160] It also raises the possibility that far from being exceptional, the northwest frontier—that wilderness in which Churchill cut his journalistic teeth, and so much more—is not atypical but exemplary of the kind of insecurities that plagued empire at the moment of military conquest as well as throughout its life as a civilizational project. For some, the prospect of a continuum between counterinsurgency at moments of crisis and the coerciveness of colonial regimes in their normal operations—of reading empire as a whole as functioning in a kind of state of emergency—may not seem credible. Yet given how long "military" authorities and their representatives might take to conquer and keep the peace, this interpretation should not be beyond the realm of believability. If all of the empire was not Afghanistan, Afghanistan was not, perhaps, the state of exception either.[161]

A surprising number of those who wrote about imperial military campaigns as they happened or shortly thereafter emphasized how tenuous and negotiable military victory was across the nineteenth-century terrains the British were determined to hold via the Gatling and the Maxim guns. In contrast, where imperial war is concerned, historians taking the longer view have not given either the role of enemy combatants or Britain's own unforced errors a sufficiently explanatory role in the history of the outcomes—except as a kind of harrowing backdrop. Even an amateur like Elliott Evans Mills, whose 1905 book *The Decline and Fall of the British Empire* prophesied a world in which Japan was the future of global imperial power, blamed European rivals abroad and religious and moral decay at home for Britain's inglorious demise. The book is written as if by a Japanese observer, as an ostensibly cautionary tale for Japanese schoolchildren curious about the fall of a once great power. Apart from a few South Africans, who had "knowledge of the grave Native problems in the United States" and were armed with Martini-Henry rifles, there is hardly a colonial warrior to be seen in Mills's narrative. In his apocalyptic vision, in which the British empire is now "among those which had ceased altogether to control the future of the world," the imperial endgame is not played out through internal rebellion but eventuated from a debilitating weakness that corroded the imperial body politic while its masters, "too effete and nerve-ridden to guide the destinies of the world," appear unaware of the stakes of their own decline.[162]

By accounts both amateur and professional, then, the British empire was apparently lost as well as gained in a fit of absence of mind. Or, there was no prototype for the colonial war, except perhaps the wars in early Victorian Afghanistan, which have not been seen as anything except marginal but whose histories foretold, perhaps, the futility of frontier war and the decisive limits to British military victory on the ground.[163] (The pushback of indigenes in warfare—and their impact on the outcome of events and on the conditionality of victory—is hard to ignore, not least because contemporaries who witnessed it and sought to understand it as part of larger narratives of Britain's imperial power and its world historical destiny in the nineteenth century especially were so utterly preoccupied with it.)To recognize how and why imperial ambition foundered in military terms is not to suggest that violence was not done, that indigenous peoples were not slaughtered, or that conquest was merely a figment of the imperial imagination. It is to admit the significant resistance posed to the forward movement of imperial hegemony by indigenous environments and those who knew them and used them to their strategic advantage; it is to recognize that these were agents in the making of British imperial history rather than to simply dismiss them as the vanquished. What we need is not just a new field guide to Victoria's empire but an appreciation for the cultures of risk to which military imperial power was perpetually subject.[164] It was surely this to which Churchill referred when he declared that "the British Empire is held together by moral not by material forces." Given what he had seen on the field of battle, he knew that empire was not secured by "vulgar brag" but by the skin of its teeth; that the imperial grip was as much a recurrent adjustment to the shock of indigenous assertion as it was the confident effect of British paramountcy.[165] It seems only fitting that, following in his uneasy footsteps, we should find one pathway toward rethinking British imperial history, not as a relentlessly progressive arc of conquest, incorporation, and hegemony, but as a perpetually, precariously vulnerable enterprise in which those seeking to secure imperial sovereignty met with obstacles and impediments that served as trip wires for a larger, ongoing set of troubles once the heat and smoke of battle had disappeared.

Chapter 2

Subject to Interruption

Economic Protest and the Limits of Imperial Order

*An underdeveloped people must prove, by its fighting power,
its ability to set itself up as a nation, and by the purity of
every one of its acts, that it is, even to the smallest detail,
the most lucid, the most self-controlled people.*

FRANTZ FANON, *A Dying Colonialism*, 1965

*We must start by characterizing the commonest ways that people
handle the tangled, many-sided legacy of imperialism, not just
those who left the colonies but also those who were there in the
first place and those who remained, the natives.*

EDWARD SAID, *Culture and Imperialism*, 1994

One way of telling the history of empire is as the story of how,
why, and under what conditions the integration of agricultural
production and industrial capital into a market-based world system required both the control of labor power and a consensus
on how goods would be produced, exchanged, and consumed.
Imperial historians have debated the comparative weight of
metropolitan structures and international rivalries in determin-
ing that process, but the role of "peripheral" actors and events
does not factor in any sustained way into assessments of the

historical character of the British empire as a commercial project.[1] Though the uneven terrain of colonial economic development is scattered with evidence of the kinds of trouble colonial
subjects made in the face of settler capital and other forms of
market relations, economic protest has not been a sustained feature of narrative accounts of modern British imperialism either.
This is not because scholars have been unaware of the work of
economic rebels. Rather, the often small-scale events they spear-
headed tend to be stepping stones on the way to the enthralling
tale of empire's rise, growth, and consolidation, while decline is
attributed to large-scale structural causes like global depression
or the recalibration of financial capital. Tracking the emergence
of free-market ideology or proffering a cost-benefit analysis has
tended to sideline colonial economic protesters and the interruptions they made to capital's interests and to the work of those
imperial agents whose job it was to protect them.

Yet ordinary colonial subjects routinely disrupted the business of empire, and they did so in a variety of ways. Some withheld their economic power by boycotting goods, while others
withheld their labor power via sabotage, desertion, or the strike.
Their actions could be the effect of immediate dissatisfaction
or a response to conditions of exploitation over the course of
months or years. In some contexts anti-imperial protest was part
of larger anticapitalist efforts linked to the emergence of nationalist demands, as in the late nineteenth century Irish Land Wars.
In others, nationalist imperatives might drive economic sanction, with Gandhi's *swadeshi* (self-sufficiency) campaign the
most familiar example. Though the empire of market capitalism
developed unevenly across British territories and possessions
in the nineteenth and twentieth centuries, it was nonetheless
a provocation to colonials—whether settler or indigenous—as
both workers and consumers. They engaged in a range of expres-
sive forms to demonstrate their dissatisfaction with imperial

encroachments into local and regional economies and to interrupt the patterns and profits of global-imperial business as usual.

Many modes of protest were short-lived, and their
repression—via police violence and other forms of coercion—was
as likely to hobble fledgling collective-action cadres like unions as
it was to galvanize long-term solidarities around issues of class
and labor. The vehemence with which labor action, especially,
was suppressed was meant to forestall such possibilities, even
if it was hardly a safeguard against them. These protests were,
more typically than not, relatively minor. They were enmeshed
in big structures in ways that limited their efficacy, let alone
any permanent, radically transformative outcome. Moreover,
the intentions of those who protested economic conditions varied enormously. Some actions were manifestly anti-imperial
in a political sense as well as in an economic sense, while others were directed at the imperial face of capital with no specific
anti-imperial aim. Still others were entangled in the warp and
weft of economic self-interest that even colonial people who
profited might, if provoked, nonetheless protest. Yet the recurrence, and even the episodic nature, of such protests suggests
how skeptical colonial subjects could be about the capacity of
British capital development to realize its global ambition in their
local patch—and in some cases, how determined they were to try
to stop it. These recurrent confrontations also suggest why and
how officials and entrepreneurs with a stake in the security of
imperial power were routinely on the defensive against just such
unpredictable, micro-level challenges to their authority and to
the quotidian stability of empire on the ground.

The empire was not, in any simple sense, brought down by
common protest. The histories of comparatively small-scale defiance that follow do not explain the demise of British imperialism, but they can shed light on the economic instability at the
heart of the imperial project. The guardians of empire's longevity

were vulnerable, in other words, to the threat of short-term disruptions, and they lived with frequent disturbances as a regular feature of the lived experience of empire's daily life. To appreciate the multiple dimensions of imperial insecurity, we must acknowledge the recurrent role that economic protest—in all its commonplace variety—played in the making and unmaking of the fiscal order so indispensable to modern British imperial ambition and security.

Small Acts: Imperial Boycotts, Political Virtue, and Economic Disruption

Now are you men or cattle then, you tillers of the soil?
Would you be free, or evermore in rich men's service toil?
The shadow of the dial hangs dark that points the fatal hour
Now hold your own! Or, branded slaves, forever cringe and cower! . . .
Oh by the God who made us all, the master and the serf
Rise up and swear to hold this day your own green Irish turf!
Rise up! And plant your feet as men where now you crawl as slaves
And make your harvest fields your camps, or make of them
    your graves!

—*Fanny Parnell, "Hold the Harvest," 1880*

People across the British empire tried to thwart the colonial economic system through direct action that manifested their frustration over the administration of its fiscal policies or the larger implications of those policies for their daily livelihoods. Though the term *boycott* was not coined until the 1880s, in connection with the Irish land wars, the idea of protest centered on practices of withholding of one sort or another was practically as old as the modern British empire itself. In *The Marketplace of Revolution*, historian Timothy Breen goes so far as to call the boycott "the distinguishing mark of colonial protest."[2] Some of these actions were spectacularly public and have become emblematic of revolutionary, anticolonial fervor, such as the Boston Tea Party of the late eighteenth century. Those who participated sought to prevent the collection of the duty on tea as a direct, purposeful way of denying the colonial state its due. Similar forms of economic protest could also be used at home. Less than twenty years after tea was dumped into Boston harbor, abolitionists in Britain were calling for a sugar boycott as part of their protest against that empire of unfreedom, the slave trade. William Fox's 1791 pamphlet—which opened with a verse from Cowper's poem "Negro's Complaint"—galvanized thousands of ordinary people to forego sugar in the name of freedom from the tyranny of slavery in the British empire. Fox spoke in no uncertain terms about "the power of every individual to increase or diminish" the extent of slavery's influence in the life of the nation as well as in his or her own.[3]

Nor was this mere rhetorical flourish. Fox calculated that a family that consumed only five pounds of sugar a month could, by abstaining for twenty-one months, save the life of a slave. He urged readers to think collectively as well, suggesting that if 38,000 families boycotted, they could effectively stop the trade altogether.[4] Fox's pamphlet provided a primer of the political economy of "West Indian produce" as well as a lesson in the moral economy of protest. Some 70,000 copies sold in just four months. Fox's call to conscience was part of a larger pamphlet war against slavery that drew thousands of average Britons into a boycott of sugar grown by slaves and even led some merchants, such as James Wright of Haverhill, Suffolk, to suspend its sale on the grounds that, as Fox had suggested, to trade in sugar made him an agent of slavery.[5]

Wright was a Quaker, part of a British community of religiously inspired abolitionists for whom slavery—and the "human blood" it traded in—was an abomination that they believed all Britons should come to recognize and protest. Like a number of others who shared their political views, Quakers often had an economic stake in the trade. As Wright himself was quick to tell his customers, he would stop selling sugar "when I have disposed of the stock at hand." Those who were persuaded to boycott West Indian sugar and thus to participate in a call for the legal end of the slave trade in 1807 were happy to resort to sugar made in India. While not technically produced by slaves, it was nonetheless part of a labor-intensive, exploitative business routed through imperial interests. These factors do not diminish the significance of the sugar boycott or its impact on the larger anti-slavery movement that mushroomed in the first years of the nineteenth century, but they do underscore the highly selective nature of consumer protest. It did not necessarily entail anti-imperialism per se. On the other hand, such protest could cause trouble for the imperial state, and, as in this case, it could have significant political consequences and ramifications beyond the immediate protest act itself.

Quakers emphasized abstention and the urgency of refusing to eat sugar as well as to buy it, drawing on their beliefs about the dictates of conscience. Given white middle-class British women's role in domestic consumption, as well as their control over household expenses, they were at the heart of the revival of the sugar boycott campaign in the 1820s, a campaign that showcases the limits and possibilities of consumer protest in an imperial frame. Through ladies' associations that carried out a variety of social reform work, women such as Elizabeth Pease and Jane Smeal were at the forefront of anti-slavery radicalism. Nor was this simply a bourgeois movement. In Sheffield, where anti-slavery was a labor issue as well as a constitutional one, artisans supported the cause, and "the rich were urged to follow the example of the local poor, the majority of whom had promptly agreed to abstain."[6] Even when the links between abstinence and emancipation were clear, those between "no sugar" and racial equality were far harder to imagine. Black women in particular became emblems of victimhood whom it was fashionable to patronize. But many white Britons found it impossible to imagine them equal partners in reform or social life.[7] In this sense, much like abolition itself, the sugar boycotts were only partial victories, and they interrupt any easy equivalencies between economic protest and the end of empire in either the public or private realms.

The incompleteness of abolition as an Atlantic world emancipation project had many consequences, among them, the continuation of bonded labor in various quarters of the British empire. Important evidence of the afterlife of slavery is to be found in the shift in the commercialization of Africa's Gold Coast (now Ghana), where patterns of land and resource use changed in response to both the persistence of slaves as an export commodity and the aggressive market interventions of European companies in the region. Events in the eastern part of the Krobo-dominated Gold Coast in the late 1850s and 1860s offer a window onto how Africans in the post-1833 era might hold up production and outfox not just metropolitan merchants but the Colonial Office as well. Through a combination of migration patterns, land acquisition, and a demographic boom among the Krobo (the fourth largest ethnic group in Ghana), their leaders were able to control a much-coveted segment of the market for palm oil, deemed crucial for both machines and soap making.[8] They had control over a product that was indispensable for the twin pillars of modern western modernity: industrial production and the consumer market. The Krobo must have recognized their economic power; in any case, they were willing to test it. They resisted attempts in 1858 by a London-based merchant house to fix the palm-oil price, in the midst of a worldwide recession, by refusing to accept anything less than market price and effectively stopping the supply of oil altogether.[9] They persisted in this course of action, even in the face of the threat of government troops and a hefty fine.

The impasse created by the chiefs' defiance of the merchants' demands continued for years, despite the attempts at redress that serial colonial administrators attempted; meanwhile, the amount of oil shipped from the Gold Coast continued to drop precipitously. The situation was resolved in 1866 at a considerable financial loss for the London merchants and only because the Krobo themselves were ready to talk terms. Not only did the Krobo producers win the contest, not only did they put a brake on the metropolitan market, they experienced "unprecedented prosperity" from the new trade routes that were opened up to them. This helped them, in turn, to develop ports on the River Volta, which would have long-range implications for their livelihoods. Eighty years later, cocoa farmers in the same region would engage in similar forms of economic protest, though they were only able to hold out for one year (1937–38) as opposed to eight. If the twentieth century cocoa growers knew about what their forebears' boycott had achieved, there is little record of it. There were a variety of interim "hold-ups" on the Gold Coast, interruptions that were more or less successful as boycotts but that gave farmers the chance to air other grievances in the process.[10]

The word *boycott* itself entered the English language when the Irish Land League launched a campaign against the estate of Lord Erne, whose land agent was one Charles Boycott. Boycott was Norfolk-born and he had been Lord Erne's County Mayo land agent since the early 1870s. His name became forever associated with the tactics of Charles Parnell and the Irish Land League not only because he was a target of their agrarian protests but also because he wrote a letter to the London *Times* expressing outrage at his victimization by Irish nationalists: the nineteenth century equivalent of going viral. Boycott was well known locally as a tyrannical agent who routinely cut into the small but significant privileges (like wood cutting and gathering) customarily afforded to tenants, which may explain why Land Leaguers and other locals treated him so harshly. Leaguers drove Erne's servants away and isolated Boycott's family, harassing them in public and on the periphery of their farm. As part of the larger land war they were waging, Leaguers also withheld labor and rent; kept farms from which people had been evicted empty; and generally put a stop to the business of farming for empire.[11] Boycott, for his part, was hissed and shouted at, and denied custom and services in local shops—further indication of the collective feeling that such withholding had the capacity to galvanize. As the face of imperial economic expropriation for Catholic tenants, Boycott was the quintessential man on the spot, forced to defend his patch and with it the system of unfair rent, tenure, and sale that underpinned the political economy of colonial rule in nineteenth-century Ireland.[12]

The 1880 boycott was part of a long history of agrarian protest in rural Ireland that eventuated in an outright Land War (1879–82). Though boycotts were peaceable protests in this context, part of a call for moral law, complete with Land League courts to oversee it, they occurred alongside traditions of violence and intimidation that had loose connections with murderous secret societies and radicals linked to assassinations, both local and metropolitan, of the kind that were flashpoints for expressly nationalist and/or revolutionary unrest. The language of withholding that took root exacted a cost to the government in symbolic and real terms. Fanny Parnell's exhortation "hold the harvest" was read out by the prosecutor in court as an example of Land League radicalism in 1881, and as a result, six men were arrested for getting in the way of an eviction (one extension of boycotting practices) were released.[13] Meanwhile, Boycott's *Times* letter bemoaned his humiliation and helplessness at the hands of his Irish tenants:

> The people collected in crowds upon my farm ... and ordered off, under threats of ulterior consequences, all my farm labourers, workmen and stablemen ... The shopkeepers have been warned to stop all supplies to my house ... My farm is public property ... I can get no workmen to do anything, and my ruin is openly avowed as the object of the Land League unless I throw up everything and leave the country.[14]

Peasant women were active in the boycott campaigns as well, and fiercely focused on local protests, including against Boycott: they were part of the crowd that had assembled at his home, harassed his employees, and helped to produce the outrage that prompted his public cri de coeur.[15]

In response, fifty Orangemen from counties Cavan and Monaghan came to harvest the crops on Lord Erne's estate, armed with revolvers and supervised by one thousand members of the Royal Constabulary. The cost to the government was £10,000. Rain lashed the workers, making their tasking of lifting the potatoes doubly hard. Following the Land League's instructions ("Treat those mailed and buckshot warriors with silence and contempt ... Show the world over by your calm, but resolute demeanour, that you are worthy of your name and traditions"), the locals did not disrupt the proceedings.[16] Boycott fled, and his name was spread by the international press and used thenceforth as a rallying point for economic protest in Ireland and beyond.

Though some anti-imperial boycotts were small in scale, isolated events, many were linked to larger causes, either by design or by the momentum they gained and the galvanizing impact they had on communities far and wide. While they might erupt spontaneously or in response to long-standing conditions of hardship or impoverishment, as in Ireland, some of the boycotts in the British empire were provoked by specific episodes of anti-imperial violence. This was the case with the Canton–Hong Kong boycott and strike of 1925–26, undertaken as a direct response to the massacre of anti-imperialist protesters on May 30 in Shanghai. Indian police, under the aegis of British imperial authority, had fired on a crowd of Chinese, who were gathered to demonstrate and protest the death of a Chinese worker by a factory guard, killing nearly a dozen, wounding others, and sparking industrial action in a number of Chinese cities. Stoked initially by the Kuomintang, the Chinese fled the colony in such numbers that China's economy was driven to the brink of collapse. In this context, the anti-British-goods boycott was a powerful weapon of resistance, more so even than the strike itself. British officials were helpless in the face of the goods ban and engaged in all manner of "chicanery" to try mitigate its impact, behavior decidedly unbecoming to the supposedly superior ruling race.[17] The cost of the boycott was especially high in 1926, when Britain was facing a general strike at home and could ill afford the £3 million trade loan it issued to Hong Kong to prevent total economic collapse.[18] This "strike-cum-boycott" was organized and directed from Canton. It is an example of economic protest that was used as a vehicle for political mobilization. In this case, it brought out a quarter million workers, constituting, in the estimation of one historian, the "first ever . . . serious challenge" to the British colonial administration in Hong Kong.[19]

Significantly, the events of the 1920s were part of a tradition of economic protest and social unrest by "aliens" in Hong Kong against a variety of foreign interests: the French in 1884, the Americans in 1905–6, and the Japanese in 1908. The latter two boycotts reflected frustration on the part of merchant elites with both economic restrictions on and capitalist inroads into Hong

Kong's commercial affairs—and they reflected the larger Chinese diasporic influence in the economic and political life of this frontier settlement.[20] Kerosene oil, piece goods, and flour were the main boycotted items in the 1905–6 action, which, despite being advanced by the Chinese Commercial Union, was mainly carried out by students, teachers, journalists, some coolie laborers, and the "consumer public."[21] As with the sugar boycott in Britain in the nineteenth century, the protests here were anti-imperial, if complexly so: Chinese business managers went along with British colonial rule to such a degree that they are rightly considered a comprador elite, in socioeconomic and cultural terms. Yet their call to boycott could strategically mobilize support from workers and others in ways that galvanized the community toward political consciousness and might even exceed their capacity to control it. Such alliances were as unstable and fractious as they were opportunist, and they posed law-and-order challenges to the British colonial government, which struggled to deal with the crises on the ground on a regular basis.[22] In the case of the anti-Japan action of 1908, the boycott turned into rioting; with establishments in the Central District were looted by crowds determined to punish Chinese merchants who persisted in selling Japanese goods. The rioters—mainly laborers and vegetable hawkers—then headed toward the International Hotel, where they "hurled bricks, stones, bamboos, flowerpots" and wielded bill hooks and boat hooks as they shouted "*Ta, Ta, Ta-he*" (strike, strike, strike). Police fired on the crowd, arrests were made, and the colonial government issued banishment orders to try to restore peace.[23]

This series of Hong Kong boycotts model the disruptive potential of this protest form, for both colonial officials in charge of public order and for those who sought to use boycott as an anti-imperial weapon in the marketplace of goods. But it did not necessarily prioritize the common worker (who took his

or her opportunity to make trouble nonetheless). Though limited in its short-term success, a boycott could leverage political
sentiments and catalyze political crises having long-term consequences for imperial power and stability. Such was the case in
late nineteenth-century Iran, where a tobacco boycott played a
role in galvanizing the revolutionary movement. The shah had
secretly awarded a monopoly of all Iranian tobacco to British
subjects, an arrangement discovered by the Istanbul newspaper
Akhtar in 1890 and publicized in leaflets circulated in Iran in
1891. This publicity generated massive public protests, first in
Shiraz and then in Tabriz. What ensued was a nationwide boycott of the sale of tobacco, "observed even by the shah's wives
and by non-Muslims," provoking demonstrations in Teheran
and the shooting of protesters, followed by even-more-massive
protest. Here, the concrete political outcomes are very clear: the
British were forced to abandon their monopoly concession policy, which was personally favored by Britain's prime minister,
Lord Salisbury, and to concede that it had backfired. Not only
did the boycott help to ramp up Russian influence in Iran (the
Russians openly and actively supported the boycott), it helped
solidify links between unlikely allies—ulema (Muslim scholars),
modernists, merchants, and ordinary people—in what looked
to the British like a coordinated challenge to their policy. The
tobacco boycott is considered the first successful mass protest in
modern Iran and the cross-interest alliance it brought into being
continued to be important into the twentieth century—the very
"roots" of revolution.[24]

Iran's tobacco boycott anticipated consumerism's key role in
the theater of anticolonial politics.[25] In colonial India, the practice dated at least from the 1870s, when Bholanath Chandra
had called for Indians to resolve to "nonconsume the goods of
England" and thus to "dethrone King Cotton of Manchester." In
the 1880s and 1890s, tariff issues led to calls for boycotting in

the Bombay and Poona newspapers; even the agitation against the Age of Consent Bill in 1890s had some early swadeshi elements, specifically to do with calls to protest impurities in salt.[26] In India, the partition of Bengal, promulgated by Lord Curzon in 1905, politicized and popularized the idea of boycott as a protest weapon. The Sanskrit composite *swadeshi* is derived from two words: "self" (*swa*) and "homeland" (*desh*)—a combination designed to capture the virtue of goods made at home, by Indian workers, outside the sphere of imperial production, commerce, and market value. As an "indigenous enterprise motivated primarily by conscious patriotism," swadeshi drew on earlier ideas and practices to create a veritable swadeshi market in everything from soap to chrome.[27] Those motors of British capital—jute, tea, and coal—were largely untouched, but the boycott slogan succeeded in unifying a wide cross-section of nationalist opinion in Bengal, as local political associations (samitis) enforced the boycott through everything from picketing to social ostracism.[28] The link between economic virtue and patriotic virtue was not necessarily self-evident, and techniques of mass action were riven by class hierarchies and interests. Nonetheless, the range of impacts that swadeshi had on contemporary Indian politics in the near term was considerable; the state was effectively delegitimated as the result of organized economic protest.[29] British observers were alarmed by the cry of boycott and were moved to wonder "whether British rule itself was to endure, in Bengal, or for the matter of that, anywhere in India."[30]

Gandhi's swadeshi campaign modeled both his exhibitionary activism and the links he made between self-rule (Swaraj) and the withholding of economic power in the interests of challenging imperial power at its economic heart. The specific historical conditions that led to the initial swadeshi campaigns highlight the material and symbolic meanings of homespun cloth (khadi) would take on in the political movement that developed in the interwar period. The replacement of India-produced textiles (in places like Bombay, Sholapur, and Ahmedabad) by Lancashire-made goods over the course of the nineteenth century effectively put indigenous industry out of business.[31] Moreover, the dominance of England-made wares disrupted local ritual meanings of cloth, its textures, and its exchange values, creating a sense of urgency among Indians around the call for homemade goods that went beyond the purely economic. In the early twentieth century, modern western dress style was increasingly appropriated by Indian elites at the expense of the Indian working class and the poor. Gandhi drew explicit connections between Indian political freedom and India's liberation from dependence on foreign cloth, mobilizing Indians rich and poor to wear khadi as a sign of their aspiration to self-rule.[32]

The mass circulation of khadi objects—like the topi (hat) and the charka (spun on the wheel) flag—in public, together with the collective organization that followed, turned this anti-imperial boycott form into a mode of civil disobedience writ large. Disruptions were carried out in a variety of public spaces, from courtrooms to the streets, and the ensuing riots drew not only official attention but also the intervention of Anglo-Indian residents, some of whom literally stripped khadi from the bodies of passersby in counter-protest.[33] Crucial to the efficacy of swadeshi as a political change agent was its embrace by women. Not only did they do the work of spinning the cloth at home, but they were also indispensable to the public face of noncooperation through the wearing of homespun clothes and the picketing of shops that sold foreign cloth. Gandhi called khadi "the livery of freedom," and he used it to draw women into boycott activities and, by extension, the nationalist movement:

> In this struggle for freedom, the contribution of women will exceed that of men. Swaraj is tied to a strand of yarn. Hence,

> whether we wish to boycott foreign cloth through the means
> of Khadi or through mill-made cloth, it is women who are the
> spinners. Therefore it us women who will play a larger part in
> the non-violent struggle for swaraj.[34]

The wearing of khadi was not limited to Indian National Congress leaders or elites. As images from the Dandi salt march protest and others clearly show, by the 1930s regular people—even working-class Indians who had become disenchanted with Gandhi's politics and now sought a more radical anticolonial politics—commonly wore the topi or carried the charkha flag.[35] These included communists and Muslim Leaguers, who participated in a variety of public demonstrations across the subcontinent, even though they were subjected to police harassment that included having the hats picked off their heads with specially prepared canes and hooks.[36] Khadi and the boycotts with which it was associated succeeded in creating nationalist public spaces that were heterogeneous and subject to reprisal but challenged imperial power in material terms nonetheless.

Elsewhere in the interwar British empire, anticolonial nationalists openly challenged their rulers in the marketplace of goods. They did so by tackling the logic of western consumption and developing strategies and rhetorics to articulate a critique of western modernity that linked buying power with political power—giving birth to what has gained traction in the twenty-first century as an equivalence between political virtue and shopping—that is, political consumerism.[37] As in Ireland and India, boycotts in post–Word War I Cairo were not impersonal affairs. Members of boycott committees assailed shopkeepers and, right on the shop floor, dissuaded potential customers from buying English goods. The practices of withholding reached into urban living quarters, where store-bought cakes were substituted with homemade ones at tea, and women shopped at alternative markets that were set up to expressly compete with foreign ones. Residents of Cairo knew what had been going on in India, in part because Gandhi was a cause célèbre in the international press and offered a model of how to scale up anticolonial protest from the elite to the street. Transnational connections closer to the ground were also key. In 1925, the Arabic newspaper *Al-Ahram* interviewed a visiting Muslim physician from India who relayed the specifics of the boycott as an anticolonial strategy. In the mid-1930s, the Egyptian paper *Ruz al-usuf* ran a cartoon featuring "Misri Effendi," the icon of bourgeois Egypt, conversing with Gandhi while he sat at the spinning wheel. Significantly, the caption indicated the Egyptian's frustrations not with imperial economic policies but with those local elites who had bought into the seductions of colonial modernity via dress and other accessories.[38]

Gandhi's hiatus at the Suez Canal, in 1931, on his way to London for the second Roundtable Conference allowed Egyptians to experience his powerful inspiration firsthand. But boycotts had already spread across the Middle East at the beginning of the twentieth century, the most notable examples being the Ottoman boycott of Austrian goods on the annexation of Bosnia-Herzegovina in 1908, just two years after swadeshi had begun.[39] Whether Egyptians knew about these other boycotts or not is an interesting question. Meanwhile, in Ghana, a series of boycotts of European goods and refusals to sell cash crops to foreign firms occurred periodically between 1920 and 1937, at the height of the worldwide depression. The same was true in South Africa, where strike leaders wedded the boycott of European shops and goods to collective wage action as part of a larger call for "black self-sufficiency." [40] Here, as elsewhere, boycotts bridged the symbolic and the material, and had tangible effects on British merchants and imperial economic stability in the short and long runs.

It is important not to romanticize the boycott, or to imagine that its vectors ran simply or smoothly between colonizer to colonized, or to see economic protest as automatically equalizing, even momentarily.[41] In 1917, for example, rural women in the Transkei, Cape Province (southern Africa), boycotted European goods to protest price fixing and refused to supply basic commodities on credit. But their efforts were undermined by a combination of state pushback and threats from local loyalist chiefs.[42] What's more, the boycott is only one way of withholding economic power. Anti-tax movements—which either began with women or successfully catapulted them, often to the front of the proverbial crowd—were forms of boycott, signifying as they did a withholding and thereby a direct economic challenge to the economic demands of the local colonial state. This practice occurred in British East Africa in 1908, for example, when the administration sought to impose a hut tax. Muraa, a renowned prophetess, kindled the ire of the local young men who readily sold their cattle to obtain money for the tax by mocking them in public, sparking a minor war that brought out the King's African Rifles and, in the longer run, a millennial protest movement that kept the British on the ropes into the 1920s.[43]

In 1913–14, Mekatalili Wa Menza, a charismatic leader in coastal Kenya, also mounted an anti-tax campaign on behalf of her Giriama community, again on the grounds that the exigency of wage labor threatened heretofore successful forms of the traditional peasant economy. Not only that, she galvanized women and men in face of threats by the British agent Charles Hobley to make Giriama land tenure available to the indigenous only if they were willing to be tenants of the government. Women took oaths and brought anticolonial grievances to the elders; a women's council was formed; and a general crisis for the colonial authorities ensued. According to historian Cynthia Brantley, in the face of this widening protest, "British administration simply ground to a halt."[44] By calling for the withholding of tax, Mekatalili managed to collect money to support her campaign, an accomplishment that irritated the colonial officials who witnessed her protest. At the same time, many of them also underestimated the threat she posed to business as usual precisely because she was a woman. In the end, so effective was Mekatalili in drumming up collective resistance to the British tax policy that she was exiled to a western province of Kenya, though she did return to continue her anticolonial opposition after only five years.[45]

In 1922—when most Britons likely knew only of Gandhi's hartal (stoppage of work)—a woman named Mary Muthoni Nyanjiru joined a protest over the arrest of the Kikuyu nationalist leader Harry Thuku, who had taken a stand against the forced (wage) labor of young men and, especially, women—labor that helped to guarantee that Africans could pay taxes in specie and diminished the market potential of women's crops. If not a call to boycott in the strictest sense, Thuku's impulse was to encourage the withholding of labor, both in the interest of thwarting colonial authority and to retain control over the Kikuyu's economic livelihood. Nyanjiru was a Kikuyu; she and her step-daughter attended a public rally organized by the East African Association in support of the detainee in which Jomo Kenyatta, future president of Kenya, also participated. In a gesture of defiance that was as courageous as it was gendered, Nyanjiru disrobed in order to shame both the Kikuyu leaders and British officials into avowing their patriarchal bargain. She is reported to have said, "You take my dress and give me your trousers. You men are cowards. What are you waiting for? Our leader is in there. Let's get him!" She was shot and killed in the mayhem that ensued.[46]

These three examples from East Africa under British colonial rule point to the flexibility of a protest strategy like the boycott, as well as to the specific economic and political circumstances on the ground that might give the withholding of economic power very particular meanings. The boycott in its more conventional form remained a common resource for a wide variety of anti-imperial actors in the context of twentieth century decolonization and its twenty-first century afterlives. As Julius Nyerere, the president of Tanzania, wrote to the editor of *Africa South*, in the context of calls to boycott the apartheid regime in South Africa in 1959, boycotts might succeed where even the international court of public opinion had not:

> We in Africa hate the policies of the South African Government. We abhor the semi-slave conditions under which our brothers and sisters in South Africa live, work and produce the goods we buy. We pass resolutions against the hideous system and keep hoping that the United Nations and the governments of the whole world will one day put pressure on the South African Government to treat its non-European peoples as human beings. . ... Can we honestly condemn a system and at the same time employ it to produce goods which we buy, and then enjoy with a clear conscience? . . . Each one of us can remove his individual prop to the South African system by refusing to buy South African goods. There are millions of people in the world who support the South African Government in this way, and who can remove their support by the boycott . . . it is only in this way that we can give . . . encouragement to sympathetic governments of the world to act.[47]

In both colonial and postcolonial contexts, the withholding of consumer power was not simply a common form of protest, it was a characteristically anti-imperial strategy, even if it was not, in and of itself, always a decisive agent in structural change, economic or otherwise. But it could be an impetus to related protest actions and, as in the case of late twentieth-century South

Africa most dramatically, for historic shifts in coalition building, union-community relations, and political destabilization more generally.[48] Such actions challenge facile notions of unchallenged market imperialism and restore consumer protest and its political effects to the narrative of Pax Britannica. They suggest continuities between political virtue and boycott in the colonial and contemporary global arenas.

Empire on Fire: Strikes and the Work of Labor Protest

Though boycotts were common forms of protest across the modern British empire, the strike posed an equally powerful threat to imperial interests and to the security of British imperial capital in all its local variety. Labor action was a regular feature of twentieth-century imperial disorder, in part because economic crises the world over combined with rising nationalist movements that saw opportunity in the chaos and were determined to imagine histories for their local communities that involved working for the end of empire rather living in subordination to it. That combination of anti-imperial movement and economic upheaval meant that from the interwar period onward, the British empire was subject to perpetual ferment, buffeted by global forces it struggled to manage and challenged by subjects who understood the power of labor action. Yet despite the significance of this moment for protest, strikes and other forms of labor struggle had a long history. They were so common a feature of the economic landscape that capitalists and empire officials alike continually braced for their impact, viewing their success or failure as one index of the fiscal security of the empire as a whole.

To observers of the British imperial scene, it must have seemed as if the empire was on fire in 1919. Demobilization brought African, West Indian, and South Asian soldiers into the streets of British cities after the armistice. It also brought white soldiers and workers face to face with the prospect of having to compete for work with men of color, especially in the shipbuilding industry, where they had gained ground during the wartime boom for black labor. Tensions on the ground were inflamed by the government: the Ministry of Labour sent secret communications to the managers of the labor exchanges—those whose job it was to find employment for ex-soldiers and sailors—instructing them to keep black men of British nationality uninformed about their right to employment, presumably so that white servicemen could get priority. The first "race" riots broke out at Tyneside in February of 1919, when Arab seamen who had just paid their union dues were denied work. Unrest spread to port towns across Britain, many of which had decades-old black residential quarters, but were attacked nonetheless. Black men were attacked or shipped out to other port towns, where they ended up penniless and without community support. When they fought back, they were beaten, jailed, and caricatured in local and national newspapers. Though many had fought with valor and distinction in the theaters of war less than a year before, or had been peaceable members of their local communities for decades, the combination of their labor power and their color made them a direct threat to the fragile postwar settlement. The *Manchester Guardian* captured the frenzied anxiety of white Britons facing the specter of labor unrest by deflecting it in gothic racial terms: "The quiet, apparently inoffensive nigger becomes a demon when armed with a revolver or razor."[49]

Lest there be any doubt about the fear that there was a connection between what was happening in the street and the security of the empire, an editorial in the *Liverpool Daily Post* in June 1919 warned:

Careful and commonsense handling of the 'colour' disturbances is necessary if what at present is little more than a
local disorder is not to develop into a serious imperial problem. There would be infinite possibilities of mischief if any
idea gained ground in India and Africa that the isolated conduct of riotous mobs represented the prevailing British attitude towards the black members of the empire who are in
our midst.[50]

The press was aflame with opinion about the matter, not least
on the part of members of the black community in Britain. When
Leo Daniels, secretary of the African Races Association, wrote to
the Glasgow newspapers to protest violence against black people,
he asked a question that was surely on the minds of many: "Did
not some of these men fight on the same battlefields with white
men to defeat the enemy and secure the British Empire?"[51]

Racial disorder linked to labor action in the streets at home
was matched by unrest over work stoppages in India in 1919. That
year inaugurated two decades of economic contraction and labor
strife, exacerbated by a rampant global depression that spared
no quarter of His Majesty's dominions and brought successive
political convulsions and, eventually, the breakup of empire in its
wake. By far the most significant manifestation of the collision
between imperial crisis and colonial nationalism was Gandhi's
call for satyagraha, or peaceful protest, in the face of the Rowlatt
Acts, which granted the government a set of emergency powers,
instituted to suppress sedition in March 1919. A brilliant tactical move, satyagraha technically put Gandhi outside the ambit
of the "terror" that the acts delineated as illegal while capitalizing on popular collective antipathy to them. Gandhi's Rowlatt
satyagraha took a very particular practical form: the hartal. He
called for a day across India when Indians would cease work altogether and engage only in fasting and prayer. The success of the

1919 hartal varied—depending on region, depth of organizational support, and the popularity of Gandhi himself. But there was overwhelming participation, in Bombay and Gujerat especially. Given the far-flung nature of the protests, Gandhi was not able to control how the hartals played out in every place they were taken up. In the Punjab, where tensions ran high and conspiracy theories were rampant, Brigadier Reginald Dyer ordered his troops to shoot on a crowd of Indians engaged in a hartal in Jallianwallah Bagh; several hundred Indians were killed in what was dubbed the Amritsar massacre. The event set off a firestorm of outrage and protest that was to have a decisive effect on the nature and direction of Gandhi's nationalist campaigns for the rest of the decade.

Local histories of communalism and nationalism in the Punjab made the region particularly alive to Gandhi's call to protest.[52] Though a Congress committee was only formed there in 1917, the economic hardships of the war and the large numbers of Punjabi men who had fought in it combined to produce the overwhelming participation of urbanites in the Rowlatt Satyagraha in 1919, of which the Jallianwallah Bagh hartal was the keystone.[53] The hartal is a meaningful form of common protest because it combines a boycott and a strike. A withdrawal of labor, it was a declaration of abstinence with respect to both the workplace and the marketplace, insofar as shops were closed and economic activity related to the imperial state was ceremoniously suspended. As with the Quaker sugar boycotts, there was also a spiritual dimension and an ethic of self-care at the heart of the act, in concept and in practice, though the commitment to self-denial was more pronounced in the Gandhian context. Women and men, children and elderly people were all in the enclosure at Jallianwallah Bagh and made up some of the dead as well. Satyagraha called on all Indians to take up economic protest in the name of the dead.

Both the massacre at Jallianwallah Bagh and the anticolonial outrage the event provoked have tended to overshadow the hartal in imperial history narratives. A very particular mode of protest, the hartal was designed to impose economic sanctions on the regular business of imperial commerce—not just to withhold colonial buying power or to thwart the everyday workings of economic life but to interrupt the exchange nexus at the heart of imperial political economy. While boycotts and strikes are often seen as reactive, the events at Jallianwallah Bagh demonstrate how mindful of quotidian forms of power anticolonial protesters could be and, of course, how proactive "passive" resistance was. As a robust challenge *and* an alternative to emergent forms of market governmentality, such action is best read as a weapon of the strong, not the weak. It short-circuited the machinery of state, demanding recognition of the dependence of the colonizer on the colonized for economic power and profit, however temporarily and unsuccessfully the interruption ended up being.[54] In this sense the hartal, like other instances of anti-imperial boycott and strike, backlit the fragility of the Pax Britannica and focused international attention on the high cost of normalizing imperial security in its wake.

The interwar period was rife with labor action and indiscipline across the length and breadth of the British empire. The infamy of Jallianwallah Bagh has overshadowed some of these, such as the combination of tax, boycott, and anti-landlord riots among the Bhils, led by Motilal Tejawat on the border of Gujarat and Rajasthan in 1921–22. The Bhils were fired on by British troops, who killed 1,200 tribals, more than twice than were killed at Jallianwallah Bagh.[55] Coverage of colonial protest was a regular feature of metropolitan newspaper fare, appearing side by side with headlines about metropolitan labor unrest, including the General Strike of 1926 and the Jarrow March a decade later. These eruptions suggested the unraveling of imperial order on the factory floor, in the townships, and on the streets, from Kanpur to Cape Town. The year 1919 was undoubtedly pivotal, at least in the minds of officials and report-writers, who chalked up the era's "epidemic strike fever" to "world political unrest" inspired by similar labor action in Europe, and influenced especially by the Bolshevik Revolution, which was thought to have awakened Indian workers "from their 'slumber.' "[56]

Factory managers especially saw extremists and agitators everywhere. Their paranoia may have been unfounded, but workers were certainly vocal and knowledgeable about unfair wages and intrusive disciplinary regimes. This was due to trade union organizing but also to workers' own hostility toward fifteen-hour days, short breaks, and oppressive toilet rules. In Kanpur in 1919 spontaneous strikes by mill workers and others were common.[57] The Mazdur Sabha, the oldest union in Uttar Pradesh, likely grew directly out of the strike committee, which was in turn deeply involved in Congress nationalism for the next two decades. Even as district magistrates worried about the threats to everyday order, they also worried about the perception that police action and excessive arrests would further inflame public sentiment. The extent to which some of them tried to micromanage the strike effect is instructive. District Magistrate Clay wrote a script for how the Kanpur workers should present themselves to him in the interests of ending the strike. It involved "praying for mercy on their misguided brethren," admitting to having been misled by "agitators," and recognizing that any end to the action be represented as "an act of pure grace" on his part. Provincial officials knew they were facing a "crisis of legitimacy."[58] They were, of course, also ready to resort to coercion if need be. Rumors had it that authorities at the Elgin Mill in Kanpur in 1923 used boiling water from cannons against strikers who refused to leave the premises—a rumor so powerful and believable that the "khooni" or bloody cotton mill episode became a metaphor for state violence in the context of other disturbances.[59] Such responses were no guarantee of peace. In 1922, in Hong Kong, when police fired on striking workers organized by the Chinese Seamen's Union, sympathy for the strikers was so widespread that the port was paralyzed and the government and the shipping companies were forced to back down.[60]

It was not unusual for colonial officials to try to dull the strike weapon by intervening at the behest, or in the interests of, managers in factories or in mines. At the Boson mine in Mozambique in 1905, Shaangan workers armed themselves with sticks and gathered outside the mine offices. The compound manager seemed inclined to take them on, revolver in hand, but the native commissioner interposed and the workers were denied their wage claims and driven away from the offices.[61] Class struggle and political turbulence were linked in a wide variety of locations, at times by connections made by workers themselves. The strikes in Sydney and Shanghai between 1920 and 1939 are a case in point. Although "White Australia" was different than "treaty port" China, Hong Kong protesters sought to expel British influence from "slabs of imperial real estate." The Australians, for their part, recognized Chinese labor activists as fellow travelers; one, the YWCA secretary in Shanghai, described "International Action" as the equivalent of "the spider's light filament" even as she predicted that "a weaving has started that cannot easily be stopped."[62] Significantly, witnessing British imperial violence against Chinese workers not only cemented the ties between them, but also sharpened Australians' critique of British imperialism and the nation's place within it. In this case, the spectacle of anticolonial self-determination in Shanghai galvanized unionism in Sydney, highlighting Australians' awareness of potential ruptures in the geopolitical landscape of empire.

Street and strike protest were the twin forms through which labor unrest was manifested across the length and breadth of empire during this tumultuous period. Crowds of 8,000 people and more energized strikers in the South African harbor town of East London in the late 1920s and early 1930s in what was to become the most effective rural and urban poor black political movement in South Africa."[63] The Industrial and Commercial Workers Union had been founded in Cape Town in that "red" year of 1919, drawing on urban workers in East London but also migrants from the Ciskei and Transkei. Despite its internal ideological fissures, its leadership crises, and its uneven alignment with the issues of concern to the laboring poor, the ICU, together with the IICU (the Independent ICU, founded in 1929), helped to orchestrate new forms of racial consciousness in response to state-sponsored segregationist policy. For this they had fertile ground. Wage levels were notoriously low; the fall in the price of wool in the crucible of 1929 exacerbated unemployment and the wage slump; and township health conditions were so atrocious that they drew the attention of the municipal health inspector, chiefly because of fear the health standards of white East London were in danger of being affected. Threats to the security of white middle-class life made their way into IICU speeches: "The European Mrs. will have to do the washing and cooking and all her housework," ICU branch committee leader Alfred Mnika warned, "if she is not prepared to pay the native girl sufficient wages."[64]

Mnika and his comrade Clements Kadalie were bold and ambitious: they readily claimed "agitator" status and addressed the whole spectrum of indigenous work life, from domestic service to railway and harbor employees, in the months leading up to the 1930 strike, which began on January 16 and lasted in its most active phase until the arrest of Kadalie on January 28. Dockworkers took up a sympathetic stoppage and by day three, a general strike was announced. On day four, a crowd of 4,000 was assembled and Kadalie claimed: "It is only a question for me

to light the match and you will see the whole country ablaze."[65]
The next day he and the other IICU leaders were invited to a "private negotiating session" with the district commandant of the South African police, whereupon they were promptly arrested. Although the strike was considered to have been of comparatively short duration, and Kadalie himself ordered the strikers back to work as soon as the end of January, the strikers' impact was in fact far longer. The East London magistrate wrote in his confidential report of 1931 that the strike had "lasted nearly six months and involved some thousands of natives" and saw "a large number of men and women out of work and penniless."[66] The IICU action was a disruption to norms of civil as well as economic order precisely because it brought local community together en masse and in force in ways that compelled the state to respond defensively, rather than with disinterested authority or official indifference.

Kadalie was a major player in these struggles, which leading Pan-Africanist George Padmore aptly called "bitter resistance."[67] A Tonga from Nyasaland, Kadalie founded the ICU and helped it become a major voice for African protest in the region in the early 1920s.[68] Kadalie was connected to international movements like Garveyism, and the overthrow of "white oligarchy" was in his sights.[69] As important as his voice was, it was not the only one, Zabuloni Gwaza of the ICU in Umvoti galvanized fellow Africans in 1927–28 around a combination of wage demands and the return of farms to their rightful owners,which led Jacob Dladla to recall, "What I heard was that when labour tenancy was abolished the country would belong to Africans."[70] In this context, the ICU meant "I SEE YOU"—hailing black workers but also putting white settlers and vigilantes determined to crush black economic power by whatever means necessary on notice.[71] Young African men were critical in this collective fight, but African women were too. So key were they to the mobilization phase of the 1930 strike that strike organizers sought their support before they could even contemplate confronting employers. This was in deference to women's social and cultural authority in the townships but also to their growing power in the labor force: between 1924 and 1932 the female laborers in manufacturing rose from 12 percent to 17 percent.[72] Though the trade union movement as a whole was slow to respond to these shifts, the state responded as early as 1930, when the first legislative attempts to control the flow of African women into urban areas were imposed.[73] In East London, it was women beer brewers who kept the strike going in the spring of 1930, prompting the police and the town council to take stiff action against the possession of liquor and related informal-sector activities.[74] Because these activities were crucial wage supplements, the women were central to the political economy of the strike, in all its dimensions, and served as a critical front line against the state and in their own communities.

By far a more homosocial employment sector, African mining witnessed the same intensification of strike activity in the wake of 1919, shaped by some of the same factors that were impacting workers elsewhere in the empire, primarily postwar inflation and the flu epidemic. One of the most impressive protests was the 1927 Shamva strike, which brought out 3,500 workers and was led by Tom Rikwawa, who, having come from the Rand, knew enough about the discrepancies of wage rates across regions to give the strikers real ammunition. In the context of *chibaro* (forced labor) in the Rhodesian mines, there were "defensive" strikes and "offensive" strikes, the former ones being those that allowed workers to return to the status quo rather than be prosecuted for their resistance. In either case, the ICU encouraged workers to link their industrial experience specifically to the exigencies of colonialism. Were these workers and their leaders fighting imperialism or capital?[75] Kadalie and crew were, above all, nation-builders and that drew them into discussions of dispossession at the hands of whites and, in turn, to anti-imperial critique. East London, for example, was a place with deep imperial histories. As "South Africa's most fiercely contested frontier zone," it was an arena of conflict between British settlers and troops, on the one hand, and Xhosa chiefs on the other, in the 1850s and 1870s—clashes that left an impression on the region's collective memory.

IICU speakers in 1929 told audiences to stop asking God to save King George and pray for their own chiefs instead. Promising to build a "free black nation," the IICU and its representatives frequently invoked "the injustices of the white man's conquest."[76] They looked to links with other blacks struggling against colonial oppression: not just to Garveyites but to American blacks, and colored communities and Indians in South Africa as well. Indeed, the Indian independence movement was such a powerful model that it became an analogy for African struggle.[77] Whether they knew about the actual general strike being waged by gold mine workers in Mysore in 1930—a strike that local Congress party organizations tried to harness for its own purpose—is unknown.[78] And though there is no evidence they referenced the Irish, worker movements in Dublin from at least the 1910s made the same links between economic freedom and the end to interlopers and trespassers and other imperial aliens. The "road to Easter week" (1916) was paved, literally and figuratively, with figures like James Larkin, the union organizer who looked forward to the role of workers in bringing about Irish independence precisely because, in his words, "there are no real Nationalists in Ireland outside of the Irish Labor movement . . . [which] alone rejects [British conquest] in its entirety, and sets itself to the Reconquest of Ireland as its aims."[79] In a variety of imperial contexts, then, labor radicalism was linked to radical nationalist, as well as anti-imperialist, sentiment that expressed itself in the language of local causes and allied with existing nationalist organizations in equally localized ways.

Taken together, these labor struggles and the specific cauldrons from which they emerged give a selective yet consistent impression of the extent to which the representatives of British imperialism on the ground were thrown back on their heels in wartime and throughout the interwar period, decades when Britain was struggling to maintain its global positioning under the weight of war debt and the emergence of the United States as an increasingly ambitious imperial power. Yet while 1919 was clearly a pivotal moment in the history of labor agitation and anti-imperial protest, strikes had followed the empire most of its life, into many if not all of its colonial outposts. Some of these were enmeshed in the creation of formal labor organizations, with short-term implications for both racial and "national" politics. White workers were key to a number of significant strike actions in the later nineteenth century, prime among them the 1875 Black Flag Revolt on the Kimberley Diamond Fields. Here the Combined Diggers Association mustered a paramilitary outfit that contested the growing interest of mining conglomerates, not to mention the disposition of a racialized labor force in which the lines between "master and servant" were blurred and black-owned claims in the mines were also at issue. Indeed, the white diggers' main motivation was "to exclude non-whites from the mining industry in all capacities" and thereby to secure a tightly controlled black labor force. The strike put an end to Sir Richard Southey's government—but not before he had sandbagged the Legislative Council Room, the police barracks, and other symbols of imperial power and authority on the ground.[80] The strikers, among whose leaders was an alleged Fenian, Alfred Aylward, were arrested and acquitted by a jury of their peers.

Nonetheless, London recalled Southey for his failure to manage the situation to their satisfaction.

The shearers' strike in 1891 in Australia offers another example of white laborers' resistance to the changing realities of settler capital, specifically the increasing capitalization of farms and the consequent marginalization of local labor power. In this case the strike was quickly and summarily shut down by colonial officials and dramatized the need for workers to organize, first in Labor Leagues and ultimately into the Australian Labour Party. The shearers' action was prompted by the growing power of big station owners; by the industry thirst for fencing, clearing, dam-building, and other incursions onto land; by pastoralists' aggressive associationalism; and by the advent of mechanized shearing, which required little or no skill and generated a higher percentage of wool per sheep than the skilled shearer alone could.[81] The strike lasted for four months, fueled by "blackleg"/scab labor, open-air meetings, and the presence of the military to maintain order and arrest "rioters." Though very few were killed, both sides were armed to the teeth, and there were rumors that one laborer, John Cassels, had Australia's premier, Sir Samuel Griffith, in his sights. Some Brisbane delegates to the Intercolonial Trades Union Conference in Hobart in 1889 had refused to drink to the Queen and called three cheers for the Australian Federated Republic. [82] The Australian Labour Federation, for its part, called for the nationalization of wealth and a "People's Parliament Platform" as well. Rural violence included the burning of sheds and wool bales. Closer to town, strike camps were set up by the railways lines that brought the blacklegs. Rallies turned quickly into anti-government demonstrations, with 9,000 men thought to be among the strikers at the height of the labor action.

Without conflating white labor action with either indigenous protest or anticolonial dissent per se, it is possible to appreciate strikers like these as troublemakers in the eyes of metropolitan officials and as very real threats to colonial stability on the ground. Significantly, the shearers were charged with sedition, partly on the grounds that they had made derogatory references to the Queen, though these were denied. In an indication of the muted panic these events caused, an official census report claimed that in the western districts the strike "threatened to assume the character of a revolution."[83] Despite the rousing cheer of Henry Lawson's poem—"we must fly a rebel flag / as others did before us"—a letter predicting an Australian revolution cited in the conspiracy charges appeared to be of questionable authenticity.[84] The strikers lost because they could not, in the end, fight a legal system that effectively made it a crime to be a prominent unionist and was prepared to back that equation with military force.[85] Perhaps predictably, the ties between agricultural capital and the colonial government grew tighter in the course of the action and in its aftermath. The landmark compulsory arbitration law that eventuated in 1894 had many origins, the strike certainly among them.

A similar dilemma for labor was in evidence in the context of the 1908 "cribtime" strike in New Zealand, which revolved in part around the refusal of a worker and union leader, Pat Hickey, in the Blackball Mine to limit his lunch ("crib") time to a quarter of an hour. The strike lasted ten weeks and threw a considerable wrench into the compulsory arbitration system that had been established over a decade before. The catalyzing effect of the crib protest aside, Hickey and his fellows were powerful labor critics (they complained "very strongly" to the mine manager about the bad ventilation and violations of the Coal Mines Act); determined strikers ("free socials and football matches" were organized to sustain morale); itinerant labor evangelists (Hickey traveled all over the North Island trumpeting the strike); and revolutionary socialists with a vision (branches of the Socialist Party collected money for strike support, and Hickey and others rallied for the creation of International Workers of the World branches in New Zealand).[86] As in Britain, strike action continued apace in the years leading up to 1914. Contemporary observers may not have had a global-imperial view of labor unrest, but those with an eye for the possibilities of social transformation recognized what they saw: in the words of the reformers Sidney and Beatrice Webb, the country—and by extension, the British imperial world—was gripped "by a spasm of industrial insurrectionism."[87]

While strikes might have "local" origins, they not only reverberated near and far, they also cast wide nets of collective feeling and displayed the capacity of workers to disrupt the often loose-fitting links between economic order and political order in situ. Nor was this only a land-based phenomenon. Seamen across the empire contested their wages, conditions of work, and exclusion from work and other opportunities as non-whites as well. Anti-Chinese agitation was rife across the Australasian maritime world from the 1860s until the end of the century, resulting in the New Zealand 1896 Asiatic Registration Bill and impacting the shape and tenor of the legislative enactments that constituted the White Australia Policy (1901). In New Zealand, the state used race to exercise control over labor and economic relations, though not necessarily successfully in terms of the quelling of labor strife—and not necessarily with metropolitan consent.[88] At the turn of the century, Britain saw punitive colonial responses to anti-Chinese labor agitation as a threat to its larger strategic interests in the region, specifically its attempts to palliate Japan in the decade leading to the Russo-Japanese war. The ship deck was arguably an indigenous space, which made it ripe for conflict cast as "labor agitation" but which is more accurately understood as a struggle over the place of "coloured" seamen in the making of maritime capital that had reverberations for the stability of the empire as a whole well into the twentieth century.[89]

Strike action, then, could signal the potential for larger systemic breakdowns and, in the process, map transcontinental interruptions and nationalist solidarities. This was certainly the case during the Telegraph General Strike in India in 1908.[90] Here, peons and clerks joined signalers to challenge stagnant wages and workplace indignities, but, as significantly, to demand transparency in management plans to institute flexible hiring and firing in order to maximize profit. The clerks were mainly Indians and Christians; the signalers, Europeans and Eurasians. They joined together in Calcutta in a strike action that spread to Bombay, Karachi, and Madras and commandeered the very communications system they worked for. The sheer volume of messages between telegraphers, not to mention the wave of petitions and publicity it generated, shocked and frightened management, reaching the desk of the director of criminal intelligence himself. It was bad enough that hundreds of men were on strike; their actions were like an illuminating dye, revealing the capillaries of mutiny and resistance to technologies that had been established to facilitate information control and profit. The strikers pulled off an amazing feat of coordination, which they telegraphed under the rubric "Diabolic 15" to signal a general strike at a specific time across multiple offices and sites. Alarm and panic were palpable. Local newspapers following the strikers observed the "complete breakdown" with a combination of factuality and muted amazement.[91]

The strike was a success insofar as it dramatized worker power to management and to the virtual relay of strikers themselves, but it did not secure for them the redress they sought. Without a more developed platform, even organization and a sense of solidarity could not sustain a long-term labor movement around the issues that sparked the strike.[92] In the aftermath, community identities were hardened: the signalers were rehired if they agreed to the new working hours, whereas the peons were not taken back. What remains remarkable is these workers' vision. They anticipated the effect on imperial management when its agents experienced a single disruptive action emanating from multiple centers. These workers also anticipated some of the strategies employed in both the Easter Rising of 1916 and the Bolshevik Revolution of 1917, where the seizure of communication networks—the post office and the telegraph—was critical to the uprisings. Marx was prescient about the role of these infrastructural questions for the long-range security of empire, arguing in 1853 that "the political unity of India ... imposed by the British sword, will ... be strengthened and perpetuated by the electric telegraph." Lenin's observation sixty years later, in 1918, that "socialism without the postal service, the telegraph ... [is] nothing but empty words" was a comparatively belated echo of the anarchic work of Indian telegrapher strikers across the subcontinent.[93]

The Diabolic 15 episode is a reminder that despite the spectacular nature of labor protests in 1919 and after, strikes and other forms of industrial or work-related action had long been common occurrences in various quarters of empire. In India, strikes were a regular feature of the industrial landscape well before they intensified in the postwar period. The first mills were established in Calcutta and Bombay in the mid-1850s (cotton and jute, respectively); by 1880 almost 50,000 workers were employed in cotton mills; and by 1889, almost 60,000 in jute mills.[94] As District Magistrate Buchanan observed in the 1930s, "From the beginning there were loosely organized refusals to work," connected mainly with the dismissal or reprimand of a jobber, or recruiter, "whose ill treatment could take out an entire body of workers in sympathy." Testifying for the Royal Commission of Labour in 1892, N. A. Moss, chief inspector of factories for Bombay, estimated two strikes a year per factory, though he emphasized they were short-lived, with no strike "resulting in the absolute stoppage of a mill even for a day." Colonial labor leaders, such as N. M. Lokhanday, were less sanguine, in part because they tended to read short interruptions as strikes rather than hold to the full-scale stoppage as their standard.[95] Imperial officials, for their part, strove to minimize the strike threat, preferring to categorize labor unrest as a question of social rather than political or even economic order—even as workers in some mills in India struck over the fact that employers withheld their pay to keep them at work and (ostensibly, illogically) to stabilize the precarious workforce more generally.[96]

Vernacular newspapers saw things differently, reporting both strike violence and its repression in considerable detail. Where union methods were ascendant, divisions of caste and language might be breached and workers convinced of the possibility of contesting cuts in wages. By the early twentieth century, strikes in Indian mills and on the railway were being organized and coordinated by Congress nationalists. Bipin Chandra Pal, a Congress militant, commenting on the Clive Jute Mills strike of 1906, observed that Indian workers were being transformed "from unthinking brute instruments of European exploitation into men who know that they have . . . rights which by combination they can defend." [97] Not all labor historians have agreed. Labor unrest in Mumbai's cotton mills was considered such a normal and natural part of industrial life that labor protest did not necessarily mean a lack of commitment to work. In fact, willingness to strike might mean just the opposite—an acceptance of the industrial way of life.[98] What is notable is not how well colonial workers adapted but how quickly they learned to exhibit solidarity and became adept at "manipulating the wage economy to their advantage," causing trouble virtually everywhere that it intruded.[99]

The hartal, so famously associated with Jallianwallah Bagh, was a feature of the 1908 textile workers strike in Bombay, where it shut down the city for six days.[100] By then the labor movement in Ceylon was also well underway: the six-day printers' strike in 1893 prompted the formation of a proper union, a move considered "novel, startling and ... daring" to some observers.[101] As in India, militant labor activity took off in 1906 and after, stoked by nationalist leaders and "Buddhist" agitators who were influenced as much by Japan as by India and Britain. The carters' strike of 1906 threatened the carriage of goods that was so critical to Ceylon's growing plantations sector. Though the mayor of Colombo hoped for the collapse of the strike, he gave in after three days and withdrew the offending bylaw, which imposed a fine for road infractions that was equivalent to their monthly wage. A colonial officer observed that the strike was evidence of "the unsettled state of feeling in Ceylon," and Sir Henry Blake, the governor, worried that the fact that "5,000 carters should abandon their work at a word shows a power of combination and organization that cannot be ignored in considering the possibilities of the future."[102]

The carters were led by John Kotewala, known for his physical prowess and his audacious challenges to colonial economic policy and other aggressions of imperial rule. A Buddhist, Kotewala reputedly struck back at violations of his personal space, thrashing a European who had bumped his rickshaw and knocking down "several British planters who had provoked him in the refreshment car of a train."[103] He was legendary in his own time, memorialized in folk ballads. Labor action might, then, reflect a complex of individual grievances, as well as a collective feeling mobilized against the economic face of imperial rule, showing up its vulnerability to disruption and even violence, however short in duration or limited in immediate effect. It could also reveal, in spectacular form, just how precarious the jurisdictional authority of empire was on the ground. The power of labor to mobilize shocked the imperial state into the realization of its limited

capacity, in terms of money and personnel, to halt common protest if not, ultimately, to control the local economy. Though rare,
in such moments, "the 'thin red line' of the British empire" was
exposed for all to see, regardless of which side of that line one
was on.[104] Few of the colonial state's representatives would have
been willing to admit such weakness, especially in the face of
strikers and other challengers to imperial capital. Yet the archive
of imperial defense is full of indications of their tenuous hold.
As J. C. Curry, a senior police officer in Bombay, opined after a
career of such experiences: "The first and last rule of conduct for
all ranks is to go straight for any trouble and deal with it before
it becomes more serious. There can be no excuse for failing to
learn of a small low cloud on the horizon which . . . may quickly
obscure the sky."[105]

Strikes by Any Other Name

The word *strike* has been in use in English at least since the
London and Newcastle Port actions of 1768. It derives in part
from the practice of striking, or "downing," one's tools, or "from
sailors' practice of *striking* (lowering) a ship's sails as a symbol of
refusal to go to sea." As the *Oxford English Dictionary* would have
it, the term had moved from sailors to hatters by 1769 to col-
liers by 1793 to "journeymen biscuit-bakers" by 1801 to London
omnibus men by 1892. Over time, even the mates in Thomas
Hughes's *Tom Brown's Schooldays* (1857) were striking against
their fifth-form betters, and lecturers, in Anthony Trollope's
novels, against their students. The strike can and should be
interpreted beyond the immediate context of industrial action,
as natives and settlers, slave and free, drew on a range of practices shaped by the exigencies of production and exploitation,
as well as of recruitment and work discipline, to protest their

condition as workers in the age of empire. Take the plantation setting for a start. Supervision and management were key to profit, to be sure, but they were also critical to staving off outright rebellion that might imperil those twin forms of authority. Masters clearly understood the "fundamental role of terror in the maintenance of the slave system."[106] Harsh conditions over months or years could provoke an uprising, and it was typically the buildup of exploitation and grievances that produced uprisings large and small. But new arrivals with no investment, literally or figuratively, in the local plantation project might also resist new routines, as was the case near Taylor's Golden Grove plantation in Jamaica in 1765. There the rebels decapitated the overseer in St. Mary's and managed to burn buildings before they were hunted down and killed in the woods. Dramatic and spectacular forms of punishment via public burnings and hangings in gibbets and other ritual forms of counterinsurgency were common. These were designed to instill fear in the slave population the rebels left behind, but they are as indicative of the everyday insecurity of production, profit, and personal safety as of anything else. Masters like Taylor knew that they were as likely as not to have their throats cut, on or off the plantation. In short, targeted retaliations against the combination of imperial, racial, and economic authority most whites, whether men or women, represented was part of the cost of daily business.

If many such acts were episodic and even unreported, others left indelible imprints on the metropolitan imagination and on politics at the highest levels. The Christmas Rebellion, also known as the Great Jamaican Slave Revolt of 1831–32, mobilized thousands of slaves in what was intended to be a peaceful general strike for better wages but evolved into a full-scale uprising. Hopes for emancipation were fully entailed in this action. The rebels were mission-educated, and as such, they were aware of the abolitionist movement in Britain; they looked to Baptist leaders to forward their demands in Britain, a hope that the governor of Jamaica summarily dashed. Their counterparts on the east coast of Demerara a decade earlier had shared this combination of reformism and revolution: they wanted "land and three days in the week" off in addition to Sunday, and there were rumors that the king offered freedom while the plantation owners stood in their way. Those rebels had mustered 12,000 slaves and held their part of the island for a week.[107] As in Demerara, the Christmas Rebellion was brutally, mercilessly suppressed. That suppression was led in this instance by British forces under Sir Willoughby Cotton (later of Afghan war fame), with the considerable help of the plantocracy, who saw property damages upward of £1 million. In Jamaica, the planter's road to ruin came shortly thereafter. Historians have suggested that the spectacle of slave rebellion in December 1831 impacted the tenor of reform in 1832 and immediately after.[108] Ultimately, "King Sugar's fall" came about through the efforts of the champions of antislavery in the halls of a laissez-faire London parliament, whose 1833 Act of Abolition blighted sugar plantations with remarkable thoroughness—which meant that only those who were willing and able to exploit their workers to the fullest were able to survive.[109]

With abolition came apprenticeship, the fate to which former slaves were delivered until "full emancipation" in 1838. Though the law originally slated a two-stage process and an end date of 1840, the sitting governor was forced to confront vociferous protests in Trinidad in 1834 ("Pas six ans!") as he tried to stand behind the six-year waiting period decreed by the act.[110] Meanwhile, plantations across the British empire remained spaces of active labor resistance. As sites of harvest as well as semi-industrial production, they typically had docks and warehouses, and even, in some cases, small-scale mill and refining capacity, from which slaves and then "free" laborers might withdraw their labor or attack imperial interests in direct and subtler ways. Short of carrying out full strikes, workers could interrupt or slow production, frustrating overseers and, indirectly, profits. While this routinely occurred before abolition, it became a topic of shared concern among planters, abolitionists, and the Colonial Office alike after 1838. At Montpelier, a planation in Jamaica that Isaac Jackson had begun managing in 1839, the very survival of the sugar estate was at stake. The labor shortage was chronic, and Montpelier had a variety of neighboring competitors. Former slaves in the area who might be recruited found "the facility of comfortable subsistence" a major disincentive to plantation work; indeed, the range of choices they had, from farming to squatting, together with their ability to negotiate their own terms of work either by themselves or through a headman, only exacerbated Jackson's problems. Those he did manage to engage either struck or simply stopped performing specific tasks. Jackson noted that women in particular refused "to dig a cane hole," while other workers declared the carrying of cane "too hard work." Significantly, those who struck on Montpelier in 1840 did so "to obtain an advance of wages so that they could pay the increased rent and gain time to work on their provision grounds."[111]

Though recovery in Jamaica was slower, by the 1860s, sugar production had surpassed all expectation, and Guyana was second only to Cuba in the region.[112] This was due to Asian-Chinese and Indian indenture in and migration to the sugar colonies and to the brutality, categorical and material, of the indentured system to which they were subject. Physical violence was both random and routine, often a direct response to workers' demands—whether for payment in arrears, disputes over workloads, or the most minor infraction of immigration laws.[113] If beating, and nose breaking, and other forms of assault were common responses to individual insolence or belligerence, strike activity was an equally routine part of plantation life—at the heart, in other words, of this particular "foreman's empire."[114] Given Guyana's contributions to the sugar economy in the post-apprenticeship period, it is not surprising that the history of plantation production there parallels its history of strikes: Devonshire Castle in 1872, Non Pareil in 1896, Friends in 1903, Lusignan in 1912, and Rose Hall in 1913. Strikes in these locations were often the direct result of grievances over the inappropriate behavior of managers and overseers toward Indian women. This was true of events at Non Pareil, for example, where the death of a worker, Jungali, was the result of a triangular struggle between him, his wife Jamni, and the acting manager Gerard van Nooten.[115] That event, in turn, gave some notoriety to Bechu, "a coolie radical" and estate driver whose testimony to the subsequent Norman Commission (1897) and writings in the local press drew unprecedented attention to labor struggles. It also earned him a place in radical black working-class history thanks to the notice taken of him by the prominent Guyanese historian and activist Walter Rodney.

"Strike" in this context covered a range of actions and methods, including minor work stoppages, assaults on plantation officials, and the setting of fields and property ablaze. Collective work stoppages increased markedly during the depression of the 1880s: between 1870 and 1901 there were at least fifty-two strikes, stemming from complaints about wages, forced Sunday labor, and "excessive tasks." Among the best-known of the violent clashes between workers and police in this period is the Muhurram or Hosay riot of 1884 in Trinidad, when Indian workers defied a public ban on processions in order to stage this annual Shiite Muslim festival.[116] Muhurram—what one observer in the *Trinidad Sentinel* in 1857 called "the tumultuous HOSEM"— blurred the lines between labor unrest and related cultural forms of resistance to imperial capital under indenture—that new system of slavery.[117]

On the one hand, the 1884 riot grew directly out of accumulated histories of anti-Indian violence, including the murder several years earlier of the sirdar (foreman) Harricksingh in connection with plantation disturbances in Palmyra. These disturbances fed into the Hosay procession in 1882, resulting in a series of ordinances prohibiting the festival from moving through public roads in Port of Spain or San Fernando. Official anxiety was not simply keyed to public order but to the mingling of Hindus, Muslims, and Afro-Creoles; rather, it was a response to the threat to those straightforward lines between colonizer and colonized, owner and coolie, that the full polycultural mix the plantation system required posed on a daily basis. But historians differ widely on the interpretation of events. Was the purpose of the ban to keep religious racial tensions between the estate worker to a minimum in the city centers? To prevent plantation grudges from spilling out in the street and endangering white property and public space? To suppress the rite because it was a full-throated display of "heathen" practice?

Whatever its meaning, military troops were called in to help the local police enforce the ban and at the end of the day, October 30, 1884, sixteen were dead with over a hundred casualties.[118] News of the riot and of colonial response to it spread through the metropolitan press, stoking the arguments of reformers and other critics of indentured labor migration. For H. W. Norman, who was dispatched from the Colonial Office to investigate the situation, the whole episode was dangerous because it underscored the "rather turbulent character" of the growing sense of "national" consciousness among Indians in Trinidad. "There can be no doubt," he warned in his 1885 *Report on the Coolie Disturbances in Trinidad*, "that the Coolies feel their power, or, I should say, have an exaggerated idea of that power."[119]

Although worker intention is challenging if not impossible to interpret from such a complicated, fraught set of circumstances,

Mohurram does offer an example of "surreptitiously offensive" actions of subjects against the forces, in this case, of imperial capital on the ground."[120] Indeed, practices like desertion—an endemic plantation problem—and sabotage surface, albeit fugitively, in the archive of anticolonial protest, evidence of how ordinary and ostensibly powerless people targeted oppressive economic systems like the plantation. Wherever they worked under coercive systems, they made the owners and other imperial witnesses take notice. Industrial resistance was less common on the sugar estates in Queensland, Australia, than in the Caribbean, though the Pacific Islanders bound to the plantations there in the latter quarter of the nineteenth century did strike against living and working conditions.[121] They also malingered, "back-chatted"—that is, talked back to their supervisors in conjunction with refusing to do allotted tasks—"skulked," "sulked," "shirked," and otherwise slowed down production, "giving a great deal of trouble" and insubordination, according to one official.[122] Given the temporal requirements of colonial plantation work—from contract at the macro level to daily work schedules at the micro level—this stealing back of time is a kind of micro aggression with multiple meanings and effects.[123] Pilfering, arson, crop concealment, verbal abuse, and gestures of contempt were all modes of resistance in post–World War I Burma and India, where cultivators might refuse to work the land, use landlords' fields to "pasture their cattle or plant subsistence crop," or refuse to cooperate with the tax collector—part of a large repertoire of denial, exit, and retribution strategies. In the context of chronic labor shortage, those who intervened in conditions of work in this variety of ways held the long end of the stick; they could wreak manpower havoc not just for European owners but for local elites alike. These strategies were not casual; they required tremendous planning and commitment and, when it came to flight or desertion, a willingness to leave kith and kin behind with no certainty of future reunion let alone health and safety on the run. In the Bengal jute industry, widows were often deserters, pushed by a desire to escape unhappy kinship duties or strictures as much as pulled by the appeal of urban anonymity and wages.[124]

This is not to discount violence inflicted on plantation laborers, whether when new arrivals were being broken in or when those too long under the lash fought back. A plantation worker might bring a successful action of assault and battery against an overseer, as Morlay, an Islander working at Fairymead plantation in Queensland, did in 1884.[125] But this was rare. All the more reason to appreciate the fact that, though desertion may have looked passive, it was a micro strategy of insubordination that marked the itinerant worker's power to push back against incursions of market capital, whether by outright defiance or indifference. Indeed, even the remotest expression of independence of thought or action was so threatening to the plantation complex that it served as the pretext for the violence by planters and colonial administrators alike.[126] In fact, plantation administration and the administration of violence were so closely allied precisely because of the high stakes of minimizing social disruption in the service of maximizing profit, at whatever cost.

On land and on sea, the colonial state was invested in segmenting labor markets, not just by commanding labor itself but by restricting the workers' room to maneuver spatially, and contractually as well. In the South Asian context seamen were converted legally into "docile lascars" (seamen from South Asia) whose "freedom of contract" was sharply limited and whose rebellion against its strictures brought a stream of them up on charges, as when Fazel Ahammed and his fellow seamen went to court in 1921 to protest conditions on the *SS City of Norwich*. In part because of cases like theirs, desertion was such a powerful weapon that it could become an expressly racialized legal category. No white seamen could be incarcerated as punishment for "absence without leave," according to the Indian Merchant Shipping Act of 1923. A clearly defensive response to lascar antagonism and a particularly apt example of "race classification" for indentured labor, this is also a stark example of how labor conflict actively produced racial difference in the course of attempting to manage it.[127] That the cause of Ahammed and his crew was taken up by the United States Circuit Court of Appeals (the ship had docked in New York) and sparked the interest of a US journalist, whom the British Consulate suspected of being both anti-British and pro–Sinn Fein, suggests that even low-level deserters might trouble the certainties of Britain's extraterritorial guardians of empire.[128]

In Asia as in Australia, laborers who interrupted and thwarted work regimes on land or sea may have been drawing on long, precolonial traditions of protest as well as shaping their practice to the particularities of colonial capital. Like North American slaves, they likely had their own alternative plantation landscapes, learning to exploit whatever opportunities, big or small, their environment afforded them.[129] They operated, in other words, with a combination of rational calculation and strategic self-interest in a moral economy in which choice was narrow but agency was still possible. When they did strike outright, they often chose their timing purposefully, to coincide with moments in the harvest or production cycle that would cause the maximum inconvenience and expense. They could be stealthily or directly destructive, of the crop itself or of tools, food, and fodder crops. Sometimes these actions were linked to larger protests, sometimes not. In colonial Malay, passive resistance in the form of not reporting to work and claiming illness was more common than direct action or strike violence, due largely to the powerful influence of Chinese headmen and the vertical pressure they exerted on the workers below them. Thanks to the kangani system, their

Indian counterparts were equally agents of capital in this context, a reminder of how racial hierarchies were not always black and white. Here, as elsewhere, the late 1930s was a convulsive decade, with strikes spreading through the support of the Malay Communist Party.[130]

Motivated by hunger and stringent rationing, plantation workers also stole food, raided chicken coops and gardens, and nicked articles of clothing as well. Mass desertions were rare, but they did occur, specifically among immigrants recruited to Queensland from New Guinea in the mid-1880s. They were the least proletarianized, and, like laborers around the plantation world, many had been recruited under false pretenses.[131] Using a range of strategies from foot-dragging to flight, workers, both coerced and free, practiced many forms of avoidance protest across the empire.[132] In Assam, tea plantation owners tried to retain "the quietest men" in the face of a workforce that was largely "'turbulent, obstinate and rapacious." Attrition was high, in some cases 50 percent, an indication of the struggle managers faced as they tried to secure a stable labor force and balance local with migrant labor. And even those who would work would only do so for a few days at a time, itself form of resistance, perhaps even of indifference as well. In Assam, workers struck on payday and otherwise routinely deserted, much to the chagrin of local Company officials who confessed to be powerless to either trace them or bring them back.[133] Indentured women faced tremendous hardship and violence; in addition to the weight of regular work, they had to navigate the reign of terror condoned by all levels of management, with foremen often the biggest offenders. Women's defiance, which included their refusal to take responsibility for "sex-related problems" on plantations empire-wide, could cost them their lives, but many braved it anyway.[134] For those less self-possessed or subject to brutal work regimes far from home, suicide was also a possibility, the last resort, especially among cultures like those in Melanesia, where it was considered "a rational and honourable escape from unbearable circumstances" for men, and even had its ceremonial dimensions.[135] In parts of rural colonial Africa in the context of changing economic circumstances, women's suicide rates were higher than men, though there is no indication that it was associated with an honorable way out.[136]

Surreptitious "small" acts abounded in contexts of extreme repression and control, where the opportunity or possibility for large-scale opposition was limited. Some of those acts—telltale signs of defiance and dislike—are themselves fugitive, as historian Philippa Levine notes in the case of resistance the Contagious Diseases Acts. The archive registers the fact of colonial prostitutes' opposition to the regulation of venereal disease, but no more.[137] Although the British colonial plantation and the imperial city witnessed full-scale anticolonial rebellions, these do not capture the range of micro aggressions that shaped the terrain of imperial capital in its less crisis-ridden modes.[138] Women who were subject to imperial rule or the forces of market capitalism it sponsored, for example, developed a variety of evasive practices designed to exert their economic independence in the face of shrinking trade. In early twentieth-century Kenya, the combination of indigenous men, both elders and youths, and colonial economic policy shut women out of trade. For some, this provoked outright labor action, as in the case of Nyanjiru; for others, it meant escape to the city in search of new or supplementary sources of income, including prostitution. Such choices, whether affirmative or not, brought indigenous women into conflict with the regulatory power of the colonial state and the moral authority of tribal leaders, for whom chastity and other signs of embodied purity were critical bargaining chips in the context of indirect rule. They could also bring the colonial state to bear directly on women's movement, whether via "emigration" acts or other regulatory forms aimed more directly at sex work. In Nairobi, some prostitutes gained property and the means to subsidize family farms and other holdings, meaning this escape route could be a form of capital accumulation for at least a few. This was by no means true everywhere. Among indentured women in Mauritius, for example, wives and daughters who deserted had left coerced marriage situations; they abandoned their men without necessarily having anywhere to go or anyone else to go to. In Guyana, flight from indenture might mean flight into sex work, coerced or chosen. Meanwhile, contributions to the family economy did not prevent urban prostitutes from being reviled and denigrated by those they supported back home.[139]

These and other "productive relations" were always built into "political relations," which is what made them such a flash-point.[140] This spark often produced what Luise White calls the central contradiction of colonialism: that the state could create a wage force, but, in the face of the migrant repertoire of evasion and resistance, it could not maintain the labor regimes it desired, at least not without interruption.[141] When market integration strategies reshaped conditions of work in a variety of imperial possessions in the twentieth century, and where the shift to a cash economy allowed for some freedoms, conjugal relations were impacted at the most macro level. For women in colonial Asante, divorce represented "a viable strategy for withdrawing labor," albeit one whose price was high in financial and repu-tational terms alike.[142] If for some colonial women, "serving a man … [was] wasted labor," not all who participated in eco-nomic protest were antagonistic to the male interests entangled in their own. Women like Amelia Twayi and Annie Erasmus, who took to the streets in Johannesburg and Bloemfontein in 1913 to protest pass law requirements were workers themselves as well as the wives of skilled laborers. Their calls for "common justice" upended public order in the Orange Free State and raised the distinct possibility of a general strike among black workers."[143] Whether in open-air protests or in the back streets of colonial cities, colonial women's militancy often began in the context of labor.[144]

No account of challenges to the colonial economic order, however selective, would be complete without some attention to the hunger strike, the ultimate form of withholding, evasion, and withdrawal through body politics. The death of Bobby Sands in Maze Prison in 1981 linked the hunger strike in late twentieth-century minds with Irish protest against the last, fierce remnants of British colonial rule in Northern Ireland, and with expressly political struggle as well. Sands was elected to Parliament in the middle of his ordeal. Though it was little commented on at the time, Sands and his fellow strikers were taking up an act of resistance that had a history in anticolonial struggle. Gandhi embarked on a number of fasts "to the death" to protest aspects of British rule and to secure communal cooperation, always in the name of the "downtrodden." Fasts and hunger strikes often began in prisons and were seen as extensions of militant movements even though they were promoted by the deplorable disciplinary conditions imposed on political prisoners jailed for sedition, or suspicion of such.[145] And they were not, of course, limited to the subjects of the British empire. Transnational and "transcolonial," they came through Russian traditions of protest and precolonial practices in the first three decades of the twentieth century.[146] Marion Dunlop, the suffragette who took up a hunger strike during the campaign for women's rights in Britain in 1909, drew on a wide variety of colonial and precolonial traditions from Ireland and India—part of both brehon and Brahmin traditions, as the mid-Victorian work of Sir Henry Maine, jurist and ethnologist, had suggested.

Given the meanings of hunger in Ireland over the three centuries of British rule, it is not perhaps surprising that fasting was mobilized "as a form of compulsion, intended to place a sanction upon another part, to force them to act in accordance with a law or an ethical cause."[147] The protocols were quite particular, suggesting the kind of thoughtful agency that was often at the heart of modes of resistance deemed passive. As a number of Gandhi scholars have suggested, satyagraha, with its signature asceticism and self-denial, grew out of Hindu practices of dharna and *traga* (self-harm) as forms of boycott, typically in the context of debtor relations. The latter was an especially common feature of the spiritual landscape of Kathiawad, Gujerat, where Gandhi had grown up—a weapon considered so powerful, in fact, that the British sought to criminalize it.[148]

Less fully appreciated in this context, perhaps, are Gandhi's struggles in the turn-of-the-century South Africa, where he was at the heart of conflicts over the registration system for Indians. As historian Keith Breckenridge has shown, Gandhi was comparatively slow to recognize how adept the racial state was at co-opting biometric knowledge—in the form of fingerprints—for its own ends in an attempt to control mobility, labor capacity, and segregation. All the same, by the time he wrote *Hind Swaraj*, Gandhi had come to understand through these anti-state struggles how dependent the regime was on the cooperation of citizens—and how vulnerable it was when that cooperation was withheld. It was an insight that shaped his thinking and his practice thenceforth.[149] The complex of methods Gandhi called on Indians to use to withhold the self from the Raj might be called "dialogic," in that they not only drew the imperial state and its representatives into conversation but also compelled it—even though Indians, not imperialists, were the real audience for Gandhi's fasts.[150] This is one indication of why the hunger strike did not occupy some kind of pure, autonomous space outside or beyond politics; to the contrary, it was, and is, a fundamentally communicative device. In the context of empire and its humanitarian narratives, hunger was, quite simply, a political critique, aimed as much at the conditions of political economy as at the machinery of empire. In this sense, Gandhi was out of step with contemporary discourses on hunger and their precedents, for he did not link his fasting to famine. Although he had his critiques of market economy, to be sure, his was a moral attitude that tended as much to Indians' ethical well-being as it did to the ravages of British imperialism, if not more so.[151] And yet, in the end, like the other modes of protest that colonial subjects mobilized across the landscapes of the British empire, the hunger strike was economic warfare by any other name—waged, as the tea and sugar boycotts of the late eighteenth and early nineteenth centuries had been, by making any presumed consensus about the exchange of goods an occasion for battle. Such modes were disruptive and disorienting, symbolically and otherwise, for those who anticipated that empire was—or could be—simply business as usual.

Evasive Histories

If one way of narrating the modern British empire is as a story of the unevenness of global economic integration—of production and consumption and of colonial subjects as well—that "unevenness" is often taken to be a measure of the British empire's territorial vastness, of the way that local difference shaped the terms of economic incorporation. Thus, P. J. Cain and A. G. Hopkins have observed:

> White colonies ... were populated by "ideal pre-fabricated collaborators." In "backward" areas, the Palmerstonian assumption that trade and financial flows would automatically westernize indigenous societies proved illusory. In these

alien environments, economic penetration depended more obviously upon the success of informal political influence. The degree of power exercised by Britain in any particular area was itself a function of her relationship with the other great powers and resilience of the indigenous culture.[152]

"Resilience" may be a euphemism for protest and other forms of pushback. It is also a sign of the work that colonial subjects of all kinds did to prevent the smooth operation of everyday work and consumer life across the extended territorial ambit of British imperialism. What may look like the inevitability of colonial market governance and its socioeconomic entailments must be seen instead as the result of "successive struggles and significant setbacks" across the dispersed and discrepant terrains of aspirant imperial sovereignty and would-be possession—an ineluctable consequence of the political economy of servitude.[153] Though the colonial archive leaves more traces of their actions than of their intentions, those actions alone should prompt us to ask whether people who boycotted, struck, deserted, and otherwise denied colonial capital its due were as sanguine as its investors about the possibility that global integration could actually be realized. Even their largely unsuccessful attempts to resist bear witness to alternative political and economic futures—other than imperial subordination and exploitation—that are worth noting.[154]

Nonetheless, the overall success of capital integration remains one of the master narratives of British imperial history. Some colonial officials attempted to write a script of untrammeled domination or ready hegemony; in other words, there were efforts, in moments of crisis, on the part of empire's masters to control the story of how imperial capital went forth and civilized. Yet the tendency to construct an arc of progressive victory over worker-rebels is far less evident than in military narratives. Taken on its own terms, war might be won. But by its own dynamic logics, capital was, perhaps, never settled, never over and done. Meanwhile, the unpredictability of labor availability and consumer cooperation was reflected in both official and commercial discussions in mining, in jute factories, on plantations, and on the imperial high seas.[155] And then there are the truth sayers, such as the incisive "half-coloured native" in Lower Umkhomazi District (Natal) who told a group of Africans assembled to discuss the coming hut-tax rise in 1860: "Don't you see that the Government are meeting you on your own terms? They never talked of increasing the hut tax until you increased the amount of wages for your labor."[156] Direct evidence of this kind of local skepticism is a rare enough. It survives as a reminder of how boycott, protest, and evasion were at once forms of anticolonial withdrawal and reversal—a turning-the-tables strategy that was readily available and often used to reverse the narrative of capital's certain settlement.

In many respects these two imperial domains—economy and war—cannot be easily segregated, especially since police and military force were often deployed to avert or suppress common protest, and war itself was a pretext for dispossession, resource extraction and white settler capitalism. By isolating collective economic protest in this chapter I have tried to disembed the proactive aggression of empire's producing and consuming subjects. I don't make any claim to see or understand the economic rebel "for herself," or to suggest that those movements that had imperial authority and its representatives as their target are even the most significant for the state of perpetual unrest described here. As historian Ranajit Guha exhaustively documented thirty years ago, in the category of "peasant" insurgency alone there were no fewer than 111 risings in the 117 years between 1783 and 1900 in India—a roster with patterns, to be sure, but patterns in which the alien oppressor is just one of many subjects with whom colonial subjects did battle through collective action.[157] This is to say nothing of the times and places when vernacular capital—shot through everything from mill ownership to maritime investments to public trusts—colluded with imperial authority and its coercive machinery to control colonial labor in its own often ruthlessly defended interests.[158]

Though mainly episodic and uncoordinated across empire, economic protest actions do cluster, the most obvious temporal nexus being the lead-up to 1919 and the subsequently intense strike activity in response to accelerated processes of capital agglomeration, economic depression, and geopolitical crisis in the twenty or so years following the Treaty of Versailles. But there are opportunities to see new narratives and to consider unanticipated transfer points as well. A retrospective look shows what a dense moment 1908 was, from Bombay to Dunedin to East Africa and Dublin. Scholarship on both native tenure and diasporic labor suggests that 1913 was a moment of global ferment, from California's "Pacific Slope" to the shores of colonial Natal. A long tradition of white settler history—from Canada to the trans-Tasman world—has shown that the 1880s and 1890s are notable for the challenges to the emergence of neoliberal colonial/imperial state formations, the United States included.[159] This was also a period of intensified labor militancy in Egypt, mainly on the part of foreign workers in the garment, printing, and metal industries, when Egyptians were sometimes used as strikebreakers.[160] The challenges to urban capital (industrial or finance) and its administrative agents are not adjuncts to the 1919 story any more than economic protest—or insurgency of any kind—is supplemental to the histories of empire writ large. To the contrary, they represent different manifestations of the regular instability that was the lived condition of empire. If, in the context of modern imperialism, historical investigation itself has been the handmaiden to the "colonial task of managing and controlling" the social, economic, and political order on the ground, this is in part because that order was, in Rajnarayan Chandavarkar's inimitable phrase, always "at anarchy's edge."[161]

The kinds of acts, large and small, chronicled here do not, in the main, account for the patterns of decline and fall that tend to undergird narratives of British imperial modernity—whether that downward arc is implicit or explicit in the actual texts of imperial historians. Yet, as Charles Van Onselen wrote of the Chibaro strikes, "indifferent success . . . was not failure."[162] More to the point, what routinely failed, or was regularly imperiled, was the certainty of imperial economic stability, which had ramifications for the modern social, cultural, and global order. Intermittent ruptures in the chain of connection between British ambition and the colonial subjects on whom it relied for its maintenance dramatized for colonizer and colonized alike the limits of colonial power, the possibility that capital might be thwarted, and the likelihood that imperial hegemony was not irreversible or was, at the very least, eminently contestable. Students of imperial history need to begin with a skepticism about empire's infallibility rather than with a conviction about its reach; we must see when and where challenges to it cluster; and we must be alive to those everyday moments when colonizers came so close to outright resistance that they could see the whites of their subjects' eyes. Given the strictures against interracial fraternization, or proximity of any kind, these fractious encounters between colonizers and colonized were arguably some of the most emotionally charged, if not intimate, between rulers and ruled. Those who took responsibility for, and pride in, the daily operation of the British empire lived with a palpable sense of its uncertainty. They well knew that they were, in the end, not emperors of the world but, rather, the unenviable lords of misrule wherever they settled down, arrogated power, or sought profit.

Chapter 3

Subject to Insurgency

Enemies of Empire and the Challenge to Governability

Never in all the revolutions of fate and fortune have you
seen one of those nations of its own motion establish what
we, from a western point of view, call self-government.

ARTHUR JAMES BALFOUR, *1910*

In a revolution, when the ceaseless slow accumulation of centuries
burst into volcanic eruption, the meteoric flares and flights above
are a meaningless chaos and lend themselves to infinite caprice
and romanticism unless the observer sees them always as projec-
tions of the sub-soil from which they come.

C. L R. JAMES, *preface to The Black Jacobins, 1938*

If manifestations of economic unrest in the modern British
empire had their common dynamics and rhythms, they were
always specific to local histories and patterns of imperial settlement, capital and migration. Connections between economic
protest and organized political resistance, whether short- or
long-term, were thus by no means predictable. When such connections did emerge, they might be tenuous at best. What is evident is the recurrent challenge to imperial political order that
imperial officials faced whenever they sat down at their desks.

Like economic order, political order was not simply imposed. It had to be struggled for on a continual basis by those who ran the empire. Moments of crisis offer opportunities to examine a number of patterns, including recurrent recognition on the part of nationalists and radical movements that imperial jurisdiction could and should be breached—that is, that political legitimacy was eminently vulnerable to challenge by the colonized. From time to time there was a knock-on effect, but nationalist groups did not, in the main, actively share agendas or coordinate their movements, even though they may have known of common critiques and circulated in similar circles, physically and imaginatively.[1] Yet if challenges were not routinely pan-imperial, they were nonetheless what cell biologists call *pluripotent*: full of developmental possibility and capable of differentiating into many types—making empire, in turn, susceptible to manifold insurgencies that could provoke and disable, if not dismantle or overturn.

The focus here is on the variety of insurgent individuals and movements that emerged in the wake of the most chronicled act of colonial rebellion in the history of the British empire, the Indian Mutiny. To begin with the aftermath of 1857 is to acknowledge its centrality to cyclical narratives of empire and then to decenter it—to right-size its claim to be the signal moment of modern anticolonial insurgency by re-situating it in wider contests over imperial power and in the variety of challenges to that power made by the enemies of empire in the 1850s and after.[2] Victorians who lived through the events of 1857—whether as combatants or as metropolitan observers of the spectacle of colonial resistance and British savagery that was available in newspapers and eyewitness accounts—may well have been reassured by the Proclamation of 1858, which reset the terms of imperial sovereignty in India. Queen Victoria pledged that the Crown would be "bound to the natives of our Indian territories by the same obligations of duty which bind us to all our other subjects."[3] But as the subsequent decades made clear, Pax Britannica was no simple task, and India was not the only terrain on which challenges to imperial authority and stability were made. Political order and imperial security were routinely subject to challenges emanating from economic-cum-political crises rooted in both regional conditions and global developments. Planters and other capital interests required political stability in order to function, thrive, and profit, as both government and the investors it aimed to protect understood. That link was equally well understood by colonized subjects: those subordinated by a combination of planter rule or settler sovereignty, on the one hand, and imperial political authority, on the other. In the 1850s and after, colonial subjects in a variety of discrete places took to the streets and the fields in outrage over a variety of grievances, transforming their initial protests into radical, if short-lived, anti-state challenges that aimed to break the link between economic exploitation and political hegemony. In the process, they threw the very presumption of empire's political legitimacy into doubt, revealing the defensive positions imperial policy makers were forced to adopt as they sought to routinize imperial political order on the ground and to carry on with government as usual.

Aftermaths of Revolt, 1858–1880

In March of 1860, John Peter Grant, recently appointed the lieutenant governor of Bengal, returned to Calcutta following an extended tour of neighboring Bihar, which had been a site of intense indigo cultivation by British planter interests since the early nineteenth century. To his dismay, he "found his desk piled high with accumulated reports from his district officers telling of the indigo disturbances which had erupted in Nadia District during his absence."[4] Grant immediately sent military police to Nadia "to forestall a possible outbreak of widespread violence by the ryots," cultivators who were subject to economically punishing contracts. Though the indigo contract was technically entered into freely, effectively, it was compulsory. The ryot was compelled first to sign the contract—here, a blank, stamped piece of paper—then to take an advance, from which the value of the indigo would be deducted when the crop was delivered. The costs of seed, rent, and portage were still owed (often to the head ryots as well as to the factory), meaning that it was nearly impossible for the ryot to get out of debt, let alone prosper on his own terms. While indigo was grown elsewhere in India with little or no problem, in north Bihar it was not integrated in broader cropping patterns. This, in combination with the ryot system, made it both popular and unstable. Though historians rightly acknowledge the hyperbole of one observer's claim that "not a chest of indigo reached England without being stained by human blood," such sentiments were promoted by the exploitation that the "Indigo Mutiny" made visible during Grant's short tenure in Bengal.[5]

Collective resistance to this system took the form of "manifestations." In Krishnagar, Jessore, and other districts, ryots assembled to contest the indigo system and its abuses.[6] Resistance also involved a variety of forms of noncooperation with planters, accompanied by declarations of refusal that were notable indictments of a corrupt and abusive economic system. Nafar Das of Lokenathpur, for example, stated that "he had been deprived of profit by 'coercion and fraudulent commutation' of his produce." Haji Molla of Nischindar, for his part, claimed "he would 'rather beg than sow indigo.'" Ryots took up nonviolent forms of resistance by withdrawing essential services and recruiting Indian plantation servants in their work stoppages. Well before the age of Captain Boycott, villagers were boycotting indigo plantation complexes, "often cutting off supplies of essential bazaar goods and excommunicating them."[7]

Resistance was not only passive, nor was it disconnected from local nationalist impulses. In a letter to the *Indian Field* in February 1860 one German missionary, the Reverend C. Bomwetsch, described how the peasants organized into "companies" to resist the *lathials* (stick fighters) one planter had sent to enforce the new contracts; they used slings and brickbats, and women turned pots and pans into weapons to fight the planters' forces. In Jessore district, Bishnucharan Biswas and Digambar Biswas, a moneyed landlord and a moneylender, respectively, organized a number of peasants against the landlord William White. They were not the only men to try to capitalize on peasant unrest through armed struggle. Such disturbances incensed the planters, who understood as well as their enemies that if the colonial plantation was not synonymous with the imperial state, their interests were so closely tied as to make them practically coterminous. Planter ire helped to generate Act XI of 1860, which called for the temporary enforcement of the contract system and a commission of inquiry into its workings. [8]

The Act was a defensive response to ryot unrest and local reaction and, like the commission that ensued, it signals the pressure Grant was under not simply to control the immediate unrest but to develop long-range solutions to the problem of political order posed by economic crisis. Already more sympathetic to ryot grievances than his predecessor, Grant understood the urgency of palliating colonial opinion in particular, in part because of long-simmering tensions around "race, commerce and politics" in connection with the indigo question. In 1857, Britons and Indians had gathered at the Calcutta Town Hall in significant numbers and unruly gatherings to debate the indigo system. One "sober young classicist," Rajendralal Mitter, made the global stakes of Indian opposition to the system perfectly clear in a public speech that ranged empire-wide:

> Devoid of the merits which characterise a true Englishman, and possessing all the defects of the Anglo-Saxon race, these adventurers from England have carried ruin and devastation to wherever they have gone. Ask the red Indian in the prairies of South America and he will say that the antagonism of the Anglo-Saxon adventurers has within a hundred years reduced their number from half a million to forty thousand. What is it, but the antagonism of the sweepings of England and Holland that has driven the Bosjeman and the Caffre to the inhospitable sands of Central Africa? In Australia and New Zealand the battle is still being fought, and ere long the natives of these places will be numbered with the things that were. . . . [The English] talk of their energy, education, and high civilization. They boast of the capital that they bring to India, and the vast number of men who find employment from their wealth. . . . The country could not have a greater curse than the Anglo-Saxon planters, who have been by their own missionaries denounced as the greatest tyrants to have ever been permitted to fatten on the ruination of the inoffensive and helpless peasants, men whose like can be had only in the slave owners of Virginia.[9]

Possibly with such subversive rhetoric in mind, vernacular newspapers and religious men alike weighed in on the unjustness of the indigo system in 1860. English missionary James Long wrote anonymously to the *Bengal Hurkaru*, describing what he called "a reign of terror" in some districts, where "certain planters can make use of Black Holes as Saraja Dowla did, while the violation of their daughters will teach ryots how they complain of the Indigo sahib." This reference to the Black Hole of Calcutta, where the Nawab of Bengal held British prisoners of war in the 1750s, suggests how readily the planters were vilified in terms that imperial officials would understand—and that conjured the specter of sexual violence against white women as well. As for the commission, he claimed that "well applied bribes and the black hole will make the ryot testify to anything the planter wishes."[10]

Missionaries had their own agenda in the disturbances: some (though not all) believed the unrest interfered with their evangelical work and tried to exert influence on the commission. Long himself was tried and sentenced for libel in connection with his role in disseminating the play *Nil Darpan*, written by Dinabandhu Mitra and translated as *The Indigo Planting Mirror: A Drama. Nil Darpan* enacted the coercion and violence at the heart of the indigo system and gave credence to images of a blood-soaked commodity chain of indigo production. The two main planter characters, J. J. Wood and P. P. Rogue, "commit every conceivable outrage ever attributed to the planters of Lower Bengal," including no compensation for planting, physical violence and intimidation against the ryots and "outrages" on village women.[11] Such reports awaken the rural *bhadralok* (middling classes), represented by the Basu family, whose son is killed after striking down a planter. Though the focus on the controversy was Long's translation, the real focus—and the main legal proceeding—was against the story itself, which was performed in Dhaka and Calcutta "amid much fanfare."[12]

For metropolitan observers with vivid memories of the recent sepoy mutiny, such specters were alarming. The viceroy himself was disturbed by the prospect of agitation: the indigo strikes had caused him "more anxiety than I have had since the days of Delhi." He worried that "a shot fired in anger or fear by one foolish planter might put every factory in Lower Bengal in flames."[13] Speculation abounded in the early 1860s about the links between the indigo unrest and anti-British political movements.

A translation of Long's play by the poet Michael Madhusudan Dutt ensured its reproduction and circulation throughout Bengal Presidency, while local officials treated it as seditious material, and the Landholders and Commercial Association denounced it as "foul and malicious libel."[14] Though there was no collective nationalist organization on the subcontinent in this period, the *bhadralok* and the colonial intelligentsia took up the ryots' cause, in part because it was more anti-planter than anti-British, which suited the liberal, civil-order orientation of the Bengali middling classes. The "blue [indigo] mutiny" and especially the prosecution of Long left a deep and enduring impression on many Bengali nationalists, who saw strains of later anti-British movements in these disturbances.[15]

News of the Indian Mutiny had coursed through the "thinly stretched network of bureaucrats" and governors general across the British empire, touching off a panic from Mauritius to Australia that centered on the potential of a local emergency to ignite imperial-global unrest wherever colonials might take up arms.[16] Grant's troubles in Bengal may not have had the same reverberations, but they were part of a dense moment of localized imperial uprisings that foretold a troubled period for imperial stability in the mid- to late-Victorian period. Just as the indigo riots were being quelled, a more severe test of imperial legitimacy was afoot thousands of miles away. On October 11, 1865, Paul Bogle, a black Jamaican Baptist who had recently been made a deacon, led a contingent of several hundred black men and women to the court house in Morant Bay, on the southeastern side of the island. They brandished sticks, cutlasses, and, according to one witness, arms they had taken from a police station on their way into town. They carried a red flag and were heard swearing that they would kill "every white and Mulatto man in the Bay," and then head for the estates.[17]

The crowd may have seemed to those occupying the courthouse like a mob, but observers would later report that they marched in rows. They were "'packed together close behind," accompanied by a fife and drum, and they came into town "with some intention."[18] This was the second time in less than a week that a crowd associated with Paul Bogle had menaced the courthouse. On October 7, over one hundred men had come to protest a proceeding involving a young boy being tried for assault. A scuffle ensued, and the police and rioters went at it. But the main event on the seventh was a case of trespass on land bordering Paul Bogle's village, Stony Gut. Some tenants who owed rent to a planter got into a disagreement with the planter's representative, claiming they had been to the Record Office and discovered that the land had in fact been "given to them, free, some years ago," and demanding a rent reduction. Among these was Bogle's cousin: his horse had strayed onto the planter's land, and he faced a fine that Bogle encouraged him to contest. While the case was being heard, the crowd who had come into town with Bogle and had scuffled with the police filled the courthouse in support of the plaintiff, kicking up enough noise and general disorder that the justices were too intimidated to arrest them that day.[19]

Three days later, police were dispatched to Bogle's village to execute warrants for his arrest. At this point several hundred people came to Bogle's aid; the police were entrapped and forced to take oaths swearing their allegiance to blacks and ceasing to "cleave" to whites. Bogle drew up a petition to the governor seeking protection from the courts and the police; by the next day, he was leading his supporters to town. Defended only by a volunteer militia that was totally unprepared for a crowd of people of color chanting "war, war!," the courthouse was quickly under assault. By the end of the day seven black protesters and eighteen whites were dead; the unrest continued for several days, during the course of which two white planters were killed as well. Retribution was swift and merciless. Eyre wasted no time in declaring martial law, fearing an islandwide rebellion that he was convinced would pit "the coloured against the white man."[20] As he put it, time was of the essence because a failure to respond "might have lit the torch which would have blazed in rebellion from one end of the island to the other."[21] Soldiers, some of whom were 1857 veterans or were otherwise experienced in colonial warfare—Abercrombie and Nelson had been in Afghanistan—hunted blacks and killed them indiscriminately, whether they had participated in the uprising or not. Trials occurred at lightning speed, and many of those accused and convicted were unaware of the charges against them. Bogle was hanged by October 25, as were his brother and a dozen others who were with them that day. Lashing was random, fierce, and utterly routine; no one was spared, not even pregnant women. In the words of one deputy adjutant general, "civil law can do nothing . . . do punish the blackguards well."[22]

As in India less than a decade before, counterinsurgency and its reign of terror were indices of the rebellion's power, both symbolic and real, to shake the foundations of civic and political order. In this sense, "terror" here, as elsewhere in empire, was revolution by any other name.[23] Despite the arms that Bogle and his supporters managed to rustle up, the threat of total rebellion in Jamaica was scarcely real—even allowing for Bogle's attempts to round up maroons.[24] Eyre, for his part, was deeply paranoid. A month after order had been restored he was convinced that Jamaica was "still on the brink of a volcano,"[25] perhaps because Eyre knew that the political stakes of the rebellion were exceedingly high. And he knew from his recent past history with a variety of local black men how contested imperial jurisdiction was in everyday island politics. Among these men was George William Gordon, a Jamaican businessman and politician, the son of a Scottish planter and a mixed-race slave. A member of the Jamaican Assembly, he saw himself as an advocate for the ex-slave population. An early critic of Eyre's, he was demoted from his position as magistrate, although, with Paul Bogle's help, he was returned to the assembly. Between 1862 and 1864 he was in and out of office three times, subject to the machinations of the local clergy. Though there is no indication that Gordon was in any way involved, one of the magistrates, Baron von Ketelholdt, was brutally beaten and murdered on October 11, in the midst of the rebellion, and Eyre was determined to hold Gordon accountable, if not for that specific incident, then for his role in the uprising, for which there was very little evidence.

With Bogle having acted as his political agent, and with both of them having pressed the interests of settlers, Gordon was easily folded into the category of rebel before the events of October 1865. His willingness to challenge local authority and to take on Eyre's legitimacy in the process— Eyre called him an "evil-doer" in court and "a plague-spot on Jamaica" in writing—practically sealed his fate. Well before rebellion broke out he was heard to say in public that Eyre was an oppressor of blacks and that, under such tyranny, "you must do what Hayiti does."[26] In the wake of the uprising, he was remanded from Kingston to Morant Bay, where he was summarily tried without due process and executed along with Bogle, despite the fact that Eyre was aware that all resistance had ended well before the period when Gordon was accused of fomenting rebellion. In the midst of all the hysteria and paranoia, Eyre's call for Gordon's execution was nonetheless adjudged "a cool, deliberate, well pondered deed."[27]

The Haiti link was no mere metaphor. It was evidence of the way that "racial fear was vividly in play from the beginnings of the press coverage."[28] London papers that reported the rebellion viewed Morant Bay as part of an international postemancipation black conspiracy, a theme also taken up by several New York papers, which ran headlines such as "Sketches of the Leading

Assassins."[29] Although his remarks about Haiti had been published in the local press at the time, Gordon denied them at his trial; the mere possibility that he might have invoked the 1791 revolution was considered so inflammatory that even his allies at the time distanced themselves from him.[30]

Debates about Jamaica in Britain and beyond had been lively in the months and years leading up to Morant Bay and, more broadly, in the wake of the abolition of slavery in 1833. There was no dearth of opinion about the cause of Jamaica's distress leading up to the march on the Morant Bay courthouse: local Baptists, white and black, had been involved in heated discussion of the impact of the depressed sugar economy on the black workers and the government's failure to acknowledge, let alone intervene in, the crisis.[31] A memorial to the Queen was also introduced.

The presence of Gordon and other men of color in the assembly brought race politics and economic protest together. Given Gordon's own struggles over his elected seats, when an armed group of blacks marched on the courthouse, they were coming to protest their exclusion from both the estates and political power, whether he had sanctioned this personally or not. They sought redress and representation both discursively and in real terms. The question of dispossession and reclamation was also on their minds: George Craddock, one of the rebel leaders, "believed that the people would now take charge of the island." According to a witness, he was heard to say, "This country would belong to them, and they were about getting it, to take possession . . . it had long been theirs and they must keep it wholly in possession."[32] Other rebel sympathizers bemoaned the death of Gordon, "the poor man's friend," and expressed their intention to "kill you and kill ourselves if you don't bring back every black man you take away from Kingston . . . we will bring judgment to Jamaica, at once, at once."[33]

Like the Blue Mutiny a few years earlier, the Morant Bay rebellion was rooted in plantation system abuses. It started in peaceful discussions and a petition, it grew into an armed rebellion, and it had anti-state as well as anti-planter dimensions. John Peter Grant, who followed Eyre as governor of Jamaica, figured in both events since he, like other colonial administrators, typically moved from post to post (Eyre had been lieutenant governor in New Zealand before coming to Jamaica). Even if neither his superiors in London nor the rebels on the ground made the connection between India and the Caribbean, Grant most certainly did. He wrote of Morant Bay that "no one will ever believe the things that were done here in that mad, bad time."[34] In Jamaica, as in Bihar, there was a post-event commission—called because of Governor Eyre's brutal response to the event—which "revealed a highly politicized society, with a vocal dissident group developing in opposition to the government."[35] The commission detailed why the rebels had taken up arms against colonial representatives in Jamaica and how their economic protests were linked to larger questions of political order. It also underscores the role of religion, and of missionaries, in stoking or at the very least shaping the circumstances under which political authority was challenged. In Bihar, it was the Calcutta Missionary Society that petitioned the government about the indigo system, while in Jamaica the Underhill report, chaired by the secretary of the Baptist Missionary Society of Great Britain, was crucial to the pre-1865 tensions. Confessional strife arguably undergirded Gordon's animosity toward Eyre, who was a pronounced Anglican and hence suspicious of Baptist influence, no less than of Baptist converts like Bogle and Gordon. At stake for missionaries was "the moral and social improvement of the people."[36] At risk for the government was the security of the very machinery of imperial government and of the economic interests it was drafted to safeguard.

Nowhere was the link between religion and rebellion as long-standing as in Ireland. Antagonism between a Protestant state and its Catholic subjects made Ireland a model of recurrent anarchy. In party political terms, the lines were well drawn by the 1870s: Catholic Emancipation had anticipated the liberal reform measures of the first decade of Victoria's reign, and Gladstone's long-standing investments in an Irish solution tied the Liberal Party to Home Rule in ways that were to prove costly for him and for his party well into the twentieth century. In nineteenth-century terms, Gladstone's quest for Irish self-government was quite radical: even as late as the 1880s, the notion of Irish Catholic fitness for self-rule was considered dubious and dangerous, on racial and confessional grounds alone. Yet it was well within the patterns of incorporation into the body politic that had been unfolding as part of both Whig and Tory calculations about how democracy might both flourish and be preserved in its English constitutional forms. The reform acts of 1832 and 1867 were said to have staved off class warfare and unrest in part by enfranchising larger segments of able-bodied white men. Nineteenth-century Irish politicians, from Daniel O'Connell to Isaac Butt, participated in this broad consensus about the prudent, assimilationist character of Victorian democracy; and again, though their rhetoric and their tactics might provoke hostility or scorn, they nonetheless played inside the lines, seeking an extension of rights and recognition within the system rather than aiming to upend its basic structure. The challenge to that consensus came not in the form of a politician but in the body of a mass movement: the Irish Land League (ILL).

The League was founded in 1879 in the spirit of the slogan "The Land of Ireland for the people of Ireland," a phrase coined by Michael Davitt, a Fenian, labor agitator, and League founder. The ILL grew out of decades of Catholic peasant tradition that "saw landlords in general as ruthless predators, against whom the tenant farers were engaged in a chronic war for survival; and this shaped his view of the land system as a monstrous and alien 'feudalism.' "[37] In this tradition, the Union was the guarantor of alien possession, and possession was an act of tyranny linked to conquest and British imperial dominion. As James Fenton Laylor, a member of the Young Ireland faction, put it, the goal was "not to repeal the union, but to repeal the conquest . . . to found a new nation, and raise up a free people . . . based on a peasantry rooted like rocks in the soil."[38] A radical notion, its basic premise—that the Union was an act of conquest and that its undoing was the task of agricultural laborers determined to expel the aliens and establish a new nation—was nonetheless taken up by moderate nationalists in the 1850s and 1860s, among them Charles Gavan Duffy, John Blake Dillon, and Sir John Gray.[39] By the late 1870s, the issue was not just the inalienability of the land but the question of landlordism itself: that illegitimate claim to proprietorship exercised by imperial overlords, which, in the view of Irish nationalist leaders and labor organizers, required nothing less than direct challenge and, ultimately, overthrow. To this end, one of the first principles of the ILL was "to facilitate the obtaining of the ownership of the soil by the occupiers."[40]

If not all Irish saw the English as colonial masters, the most radical among them most certainly did. The ILL mounted its challenge to imperial occupation in a variety of ways. "Monster" processions and meetings dramatized the sheer demographic power of anti-landordlism, and the fiery speeches that typically accompanied them demonstrated to both officials and the British public alike, not just the injustices of the landlord system, but as well the determination of Irish nationalists to seek redress within the law, but "from an Irish point of view."[41] Branches quickly sprung up all over Ireland and Scotland, even as ILL spokesmen traveled to the United States to raise funds in support of the campaign. Rent strikes and boycotts were rampant. Women participated in

League activities in a variety ways, not least because as wives of tenant farmers and as tenants themselves, they were as invested in protecting the family's economic interests as anyone else. And they did more than simply call for the harvest to be held: they took repossession of their land in the face of eviction and courted prison for their actions, like anyone else.[42]

Not unlike Bogle in Jamaica, the League (with 200,000 members at its height) denounced violence and illegal tactics, but it did not necessarily control the activities of the militants associated with it. Killing and intimidation were part of the civil unrest that erupted, after a long history of resentment, conquest, and confiscation, in response to the kinds of sectarian justice that agrarian secret societies had long viewed as utterly characteristic of British response to perceptions of Irish racial and civilizational difference—especially, when such difference threatened imperial economic interests.[43] Such tensions were exacerbated by the convergence of a populist movement and a parliamentarian, Charles Stuart Parnell. By the middle of 1880, Ireland was in the grip of an all-out revolution against landlordism as Irish nationalists wed economic protest with a direct challenge to imperial politics as usual.[44]

Parnell had a fine line to walk. Himself a Protestant gentryman, a landlord, and the leader of the Irish Parliamentary party, he saw an opening for Irish Home Rule in allying with the tenancy movement in 1877–78; by 1879 he was drawing expressly on the rhetoric of dispossession in his developing anti-landlord platform. As in the case of Bengal and Jamaica, a commission was seated. This resulted in the Land Act of 1881, which offered some security against unfair rents and evictions but made no guarantees of what the League was really after: proprietorship. Parnell and others were jailed for sabotaging the Act, considered by many to be inadequate for addressing the tenants' conditions, which had been exacerbated by the bad harvests and economic downturn of the late 1870s. The land wars raged on, entangling the machinery of government at Westminster in the morass of nationalist politics, from which neither Parnell nor Gladstone would emerge unscathed. Amid his determination to pass Home Rule, Parnell was brought down by a divorce scandal, while Gladstone's attachment to Irish self-government cost the Liberal Party: they lost in 1886 specifically because of a Home Rule bill and remained out of power for all but three of the following almost twenty years.

What did the Irish Land League accomplish? Beyond the immediate and considerable havoc it wreaked on an already fragile parliamentary consensus about the possibilities of Home Rule, it had long-range consequences. If it could not ultimately break the link between landlordism and British rule in its heyday, it helped to weaken landlordism as an economic force. The Wyndham Land Purchase Act of 1903, one important legal outcome of this long struggle, eventually made it possible for tenants to buy out their landlords, a provision that helped to transfer nine million acres to owner-occupiers by 1914. It also arguably laid the basis for the future Irish state, linking the nineteenth-century principles of proprietorship directly with twentieth-century nationalist outcomes. More immediately, the League compelled the liberal Gladstonian state to respond illiberally via coercion acts, the suspension of habeas corpus, and other forms of legal repression. Both legally and psychologically, then, one consequence of state terror was to cement the connections among Irish nationalism, Home Rule, and the disintegration of empire in unprecedented and long-lasting ways. As J. O'Connor Power wrote in the *Nineteenth Century* in December 1879,

Never since O'Connell summoned the mighty multitudes to his standard in the struggle for Repeal, has Ireland be en so deeply moved or so thoroughly roused to public action, as it has been by the cry for land reform which has rung so loudly throughout he country during the last autumn.... Those who look upon agitation generally as a mischievous cannot find terms sufficiently odious and condemnatory in which to describe an agitation which has thrown all former agitations for the last thirty-five years entirely into the shade. Persons of this class tell us that the agitation is a crusade against property, 'an audacious incitement to violence and murder,' or, in the language of the Irish Chief Secretary, a movement of 'undiluted communism,' or one which, in the words of the Secretary for Foreign Affairs, has promulgated 'doctrines which have never before been seriously raised in any civilised State.'[45]

If this was class war, it was a decidedly anti-imperial class war that appeared to throw the confidence of English claims to both sovereignty and civilization into serious doubt. It also brought terrorism to the very threshold of the Victorian imperial state, whose leaders struggled to develop a counterinsurgency policy and methods in ways that protected imperial interests and "generally met the test of liberal acceptability in Britain."[46]

The Struggle for Africa: Rethinking the Scramble, 1880–1929

If the story of the ILL—or more broadly, the accumulation of uprising and disturbance across the 1860s and 1870s—looks like a local challenge to imperial legitimacy, manifested in sporadic if targeted attacks on a colonial state that was rather more or less in control of its own destiny, depending on the time and place, we might be justified in dismissing it as insignificant to the history of political order in the empire. Yet while discrete and highly contingent on the particular conditions under which formal and informal rule operated, these eruptions add up to something approaching both revolution and state failure. The notion of "chaotic pluralism"—a term that John Darwin has used to characterize the haphazard practices of territorial acquisition in the mid-Victorian empire—might be germane here to register the ongoing processes of doing and undoing, becoming and unbecoming, that the quest for imperial legitimacy actually entailed.[47] One way to appreciate these unstable processes is to take the view from Whitehall or the Colonial Office. Looking at Gladstone's foreign policy beyond Ireland, especially during his second ministry (1880–1885), reveals the extent to which empire was perpetually on the ropes during the so-called high noon of British imperialism, facing challenges of management and administration from different quarters and struggling to keep up with the changing conditions, splintering factions, and burbling opposition and unrest on the ground. Reckoning with how and why anticolonial nationalisms posed a complex of problems not readily resolved by occupation, let alone by state-sponsored rhetorics of the evangelical civilizing mission or its demographic correlative, white settlement must be done in the context of that persistent narrative marker of imperial hegemony, the "Scramble for Africa."

Egypt is a fitting location for examining resistance to British interests, since the urgency of controlling resources there involved Great Britain in the Sudan, Uganda, and East Africa from 1882 to 1954. Imperial debt and anticolonial revolution thrust Egypt into the global headlines in the late 1870s, though even observers skeptical about Britain's capacity to manage the complex interimperial web of money and geopolitical investment there were likely unprepared for the events to come. A vassal state of the Ottoman empire to which it paid tribute, Egypt had a governor, known as the Khedive, who was a puppet in thrall to French and British banks, partly as a result of the Suez Canal. The singularity of the claim "Egypt for the Egyptians" made it appealing as a nationalist slogan. Unwittingly or not, it also referenced the multiplicity of competing interests—European, Ottoman, Turkish—that stood in the way of even an elite Egyptian monopoly of state power, broadly conceived. The prelude to revolution was politically long and socially deep. With origins in cultural salons, guild organizations, and even the armed forces, the unrest that erupted in the summer of 1882 may have looked terribly eventful, which is to say, provoked by immediate street fighting and popular unruliness. But it was the product of a growing multiclass antipathy to European territorial encroachments, bureaucratic and otherwise.[48] Though not typically labeled a mutiny, it was nonetheless led by an army general of peasant origins, Ahmed Urabi. His rebellion failed but his defiance helped to launch the political career of Egyptian nationalism.

Urabi challenged the khedival state by founding the Egyptian nationalist party, which sought to eliminate the privileges accorded Europeans and Ottoman Egyptians.[49] He may have been just one player in the contest for Egypt, but he articulated the problem for Gladstone and his government in no uncertain terms. On the eve of the British bombardment of Alexandria he told Gladstone, "Egypt is ready still, nay desirous, to come to terms with England, to be fast friends with her, to protect her interests and keep her road to India ... But she must keep within the limits of her jurisdiction."[50] If Urabi's revolutionary bid did not succeed, it signaled the very real possibility that there were jurisdictional limits to British imperial power in Egypt, and that those under its thumb, even those who might be inclined to be collaborators or allies, saw them and seized the right to denominate them as such. The specter of that kind of boldness,

and the recognition of the thin jurisdictional line it revealed
between anticolonial movement and full-fledged nationalism,
threw Evelyn Baring, later Lord Cromer and the consul-general
of Egypt, into a quiet frenzy.[51] Recalling in his memoirs Urabi's
rank insubordination with palpable astonishment at the thought
of the ramifications of Urabi's revolt, Baring asked "at what point
the sacred right of revolution begins or ends, . . . at what stage a
disturber of the peace passes from a common rioter . . . to the
rank of a leader of a political movement?"[52]

Proconsular anxiety about the potential repercussions of
local imperial crises must have been absorbed Gladstone as he
turned, almost within the year, from the occupation of Egypt
to the Sudan crisis of 1884. The two were hardly unrelated: the
Khedive whom the British had intervened to safeguard was the
ruler of Egypt *and* the Sudan, which his great-grandfather had
conquered and which the British treated as an imperial possession. Charles George Gordon was a British army officer whose
experience in dealing with internal security issues, from the
Sudan to the threshold of Uganda in the 1870s, must have made
him seem the logical man-on-the-spot when rebellion broke out
in the Sudan in 1884. As the governor general of the Sudan he
had managed an almost constant series of outbreaks in Darfur,
as well as along the Abyssinian frontier. Like John Grant in
Jamaica, he did not simply sit behind a desk. He spent more
than half his time in the Sudan outside of Khartoum, patrolling
the edges of Egypt's empire and logging over 14,000 kilometers.
The security problems he faced—including violent rebellions by
slave traders—were chronic and threatened the very stability
of the khedival regime, indirectly impacting British interests as
well.[53] These details serve as reminders of frontier instability in
all quarters of the empire, even at the height of its territorial
ambition and even at moments of apparently successful pacification and occupation.

Major-General Gordon was nothing less than the bane of Gladstone's foreign policy existence. Gordon was called in to quell a major uprising by the Mahdi, Muhammad Ahmad bin Abd Allah, an Islamic cleric and messianic leader who saw himself as the "rightly-guided one" who Islamic doctrine prophesied would come at the end of time. The Mahdi drummed up an impressive army of followers who gained control of northern and central Sudan and put Khartoum on the defensive.[54] Gordon not only failed, but also resisted Gladstone's efforts to rein him in. He died a popular hero in the process, memorialized as "the Martyr-Hero of Khartoum," a one-man army, and "apostle of duty," who embodied the Christian idea of the "Ever Victorious Army" of Christ for empire. Indeed, his martyrdom and the cult it inspired became a central preoccupation of British colonial rule in the Sudan.[55] As General Kitchener prepared to retake the Sudan ten years later, "the humiliation and anger which had been aroused at the news of Gordon's death were still rancorous" among Britons at home. And as the post-1898 Sudanese administrator Wingate observed, "That a new and better Sudan will be raised up over the ashes of Gordon . . . is the fervent hope of every well-wisher for the prosperity of Egypt."[56] Kitchener, for his part, was known to his troops as "Gordon's Avenger."[57]

The disaster at Khartoum was catastrophic in both public relations and geopolitical terms.[58] The Mahdi had proclaimed his antiestablishment movement in 1881, on the eve of unrest in Egypt proper. That establishment was known as the Turkiyya, a Sudanese term for the Egyptian-Ottoman regime onto which the British sought to superimpose themselves, first through the Suez Canal in 1869, and then through occupation in 1882.[59] Claiming to be a descendant of the prophet, the Mahdi joined his revivalist movement to the Sufi tradition; the Egyptian authorities responded by threatening to arrest him. He, in turn, declared jihad, reasserted his claim to being the Mahdi, and marched with his *ansari* (supporters) to Khartoum. Though he had dogmatic and other conflicts with regional ulema, he and his followers utterly overwhelmed the Egyptian forces and laid siege to al-Ubayd in the year before Gordon's debacle at Khartoum. The Egyptian army, led by General William Hicks, was futile against the Mahdi and his now 40,000-strong army. Gordon was killed defending the city, and when his head was given to the Mahdi he ordered it to be displayed in a tree, "where all who passed threw stones at it" and "the hawks of the desert swept and circled about it."[60] Afterward Queen Victoria herself lamented, "Our power in the East will be *ruined* . . . we shall never be able to hold our heads up again." Meanwhile, the Mahdi declared triumphantly that "the affair of the Sudan is finished."[61]

The presentation of Gordon's head as tribute to the Mahdi was an omen of things to come. The Mahdi's army clocked victory after victory, sequestering Anglo-Egyptian control to the limited spheres of Suakin and Wadi Halfa, for whose defense the British, after invading and occupying Egypt, depended on an Egyptian army they could scarcely afford to equip.[62] Though the Mahdi died of typhus shortly after Gordon's death, his movement lasted ten years, serving as a hostile regime at the fringes of the eastern African region that was embroiled in the imperial ambitions of Ethiopia as well as Italy and France. The Mahdi's successor regime turned in short order from "a tribal confederacy in the service of Allah . . . [in]to a paranoid autocracy.[63] There is no question that this experiment in jihadi nationalism ended in defeat and imperial pacification; the reconquest was accomplished in part with Egyptian troops and in part with serious machinery: six new British Maxim guns to every one old enemy rifle. Even Churchill thought Kitchener too ruthless in his pursuit of the wounded. As for Sudanese accounts, they measure the battlefield defeats in seconds rather than minutes or hours.[64]

Despite this, Kitchener was not satisfied: he ordered the Mahdi's tomb razed, a move that caused outrage in Britain and provoked a minor insurrection in the Sudan as well.[65] The condominium period that ensued was restive. Though the Mahdists had been severely weakened by their military defeat, a "dedicated minority" remained "Mahdist at heart" and continued to plot the demise of an 'infidel" government."[66] There were two major rebellions in the period between the end of the war and Egyptian quasi-independence in 1922, in addition to many smaller ones, and the condominium government struggled to maintain law and order in the face of ongoing Mahdist agitation. The British brutally suppressed these uprisings, hanging the leader of one such incident, Wad Habuba, without trial in 1908.[67]

Wingate used the specter of security risk to seek funds from Whitehall to extend the railway beyond Khartoum—a ploy that the War Office rejected, in part because it lacked the money and in part because it viewed the railway as one more government installation to be protected. That is to say, metropolitan officials viewed the expansion of transportation networks—those global markers of British technological superiority and economic capacity and modernizing spirit—as a dubious prospect, since the extension of an imperial power and legitimacy that would require more military protection than the government could afford, in symbolic as well as real terms, would further expose forces on the ground.[68] Mahdist anticolonial agitation continued through World War I and beyond, making law and order perpetually vulnerable in principle and in practice. Nor was opposition limited to religious men: Sudanese bureaucrats joined in the 1924 uprising, whose tenor was presaged by public festivals where *effendiyya* (middling classes) sang odes whose anticolonial rhetoric British officials failed to decipher.[69] Meanwhile, the Mahdist state was quite elaborate and highly functional, with its own judiciary, coinage, and military—a rare enough accomplishment for any millenarian movement in the context of European empire.[70]

The 1898 battle of Omdurman, on the outskirts of Khartoum—where Kitchener crushed the army of the Mahdi's successor—fits neatly into the classic narrative of the Scramble for Africa. One way to tell that story is as a process whereby "suddenly, in half a generation, the Scramble gave Europe virtually the whole continent . . . Africa was sliced up like a cake, the pieces swallowed by five rival nations—Germany, Italy, Portugal, France and Britain" with Belgium's King Leopold standing by "controlling the heart of the continent" in the Congo.[71] Britain certainly had its eye on the ambitions of rival European powers to carve up the continent into spheres of influence subject to their own hegemony and profit. Gordon himself had been approached by King Leopold II to help administer the Congo Free State, a reminder of the pure pragmatism at the heart of nationalist projects of empire-building and imperial capital accumulation. Yet the Scramble was not simply a competition among European powers; as profoundly, it was a struggle with and against indigenous forces to get and hold those territories that western leaders assumed to be rightly theirs. Indeed, Britain's attempts to secure its tenuous continental holdings were particularly intense in the 1870s and 1880s. The year 1879 alone saw the battle for Natal, Urabi's opening gambit in Egypt, and stirrings in the Sudan (as well as the onset of the second Anglo-Afghan war). In this unstable context, the proposition that the Congress of Berlin, where Africa was so famously carved up into spheres of European influence, was a defensive response to a deepening crisis rather than the offensive strike leading to decades of conquest, is worth considering.

Admittedly, the General Act of the Congress—which focuses chiefly on the Congo—presumes European dominion and registers no possibility of a trace of indigenous presence, let alone indigenous rights or resistance. Yet the most irritating, if not the most significant, indigenous challenges to British imperialism in African persisted well after the 1885 declaration of sovereignty—beginning with Islamist defiance of Britain's imperial power, whether real or by Egyptian proxy, as embodied by the Mahdiyya's rival regime in Cairo's backyard. For the next two decades, the British fended off a variety of colonial challenges to its claims to political legitimacy, scrambling to devise a successful response to the question of what imperial jurisdiction meant on a continent that was apparently legitimately open to divide and rule by European kingmakers who, however, faced a host of equally determined indigenous kingdoms on the ground.[72]

The kingdom of Buganda is an instructive counterpoint to claims of ready-made conquest and hegemony. Lord Lugard's methods in Buganda were notoriously high-handed. In 1890 he forced a treaty on the *kabaka* (king) of Buganda, Danieri Basammula-Ekkere Mwanga II. The latter signed under protest and after much foot-dragging—to such a degree that Lugard admitted that he subjected his Maxim gun to particularly close inspection in order to reassure himself that the outcome would be favorable.[73] Having capitulated to the Imperial British East Africa Company (IBEAC), Mwanga carried on what might be called the war of the flags: Mwanga refused to allow the standard of the IBEAC to fly, which Lugard saw as trifling but which Mwanga clearly viewed as a statement about the limits of the company's jurisdiction. Lugard, for his part, saw the flag as a symbol of a treaty that would enable him "to do the rest quietly."[74]

Mwanga's tenacity in the face of imperial capital's would-be sovereignty was not suggestive of any organized opposition. In fact, the kingdom of Buganda was internally divided among Protestants, Catholics, and Muslims in ways that made his authority tenuous; his relationship with the neighboring kingdom of Bunyoro was also fractious. Yet Lugard was seriously rattled by the possibility of war, even if he did not attribute sufficient agency to the Buganda to read them as indicative of Mwanga's determination to hold on to some kind of strategic autonomy. In the face of these lingering challenges, challenges shaped by the conflict between the Catholic and Protestant missionary factions and exacerbated by Muslim raids on the north border in collusion with Kabarega, their Bunyoro ally, it was clear that Buganda was far from secure for the IBEAC. When Lugard returned from an expedition to try to prevent such raids, he discovered that Mgwana "was flying an enormous flag on a very high flagstaff (cutting out in height and dimension that British flag)." He pronounced this "not good," noting that it "proclaimed to the whole country that the King was not with us, but apart altogether."[75] Lugard was convinced that he had to wage a war of definitive conquest, which he conducted and won with the help of Sudanese troops and the Maxim gun. Shortly after the provisional treaty ending the war was signed in 1893, the Union Jack was once again flying.

As in the indigo and Morant Bay revolts, missionaries were critical to how these battles unfolded; Catholic officials were Mwanga supporters and the white fathers played a significant role in his later "royal" rebellion.[76] Yet the 1893 Buganda treaty was by no means the end of the story. First of all, the Banyoro (Bunyoro people) were an important second front in Lugard's war on behalf of IBEAC supremacy, and his battle against them lasted four years. The Bunyoro leader conducted a fierce guerilla war, to which Lugard responded with an equally brutal scorched-earth policy. As one historian of that war has written, "Despite its ultimate failure, the almost decade-long Banyoro resistance nevertheless slowed down the rate of occupation since the British involuntarily had to work out each advance with regard to the scale of opposition likely to be encountered and to be overcome."[77] Just as the Bunyoro resistance ended, Mwanga returned in full-fledged rebellion mode, provoked by significant incursions into traditional monarchical realms such as the household. The revolt that broke out in 1897 was a "royal rebellion," in which Mwanga allied with his Bunyoro counterpart Kabarega and even with chiefs who had previously been hostile. There is also evidence that it was not entirely spontaneous: missionaries were aware weeks and even months in advance that "something [was] growing under the surface."[78]

The insurrection took two years to subdue, and, in the end, though it did represent the culmination of nearly a decade of resistance to colonial takeover, its leaders were not able to scale it up and make it a full-fledged war of independence. As with the Bunyoro movement on whose heels it came, Mwanga's second rebellion not only slowed down the course of occupation, but also shaped the very character of protectorate rule going forward. Buganda was "not to be so easily sidelined" as Lugard had imagined.[79] Even historians not given to skepticism about the imperial hegemony in this region concede that the pushback of powerful leaders like Mwanga and Kabarega conditioned the terms of engagement and chastened colonial administrators into greater appreciation for the resistance of local leaders to the extension of imperial jurisdiction, in this case via the extension of instruments of capital exploitation and extraction. In the case of the IBEAC, "pacification" was not either an end in itself or an end to the story. It represented the beginning of an ongoing, fitful process of subordination "in the teeth of a populace that was not uniformly content with its new circumstances."[80] One need not make a protonationalist argument to concede that the kind of qualified imperial governmentality at the heart of the Bugandan version of Lugard's infamous formula for indirect rule was predicated on the forms of resistance and strategic autonomy that Buganda-Bunyoro leaders had exhibited in the decade before the matter of the protectorate was finally, if not fully, settled.[81]

If Africans proved resistant to the Scramble, it was not necessarily in patterned or predictable ways. Buganda was not, for example, Matabeleland. There the Ndebele had had an ethnically diverse nation with a capital city, Bulawayo, organized by Mzilikazi Khumalo. The discovery of gold made kingship challenging for his son, Lobengula, who received concessions in exchange for allowing the British South Africa Company (BSAC) a foothold—only to see it turned into a royal charter in 1889 and a takeover by Cecil Rhodes and a group of white settlers by the early 1890s. Much as Lugard had done in Buganda, this was accomplished by fiat; Matabeleland and Mashonaland were declared protectorates, though, again, not without a fight. The first Matebele war was a disaster for Lobengula; he was reputed to have 80,000 troops but they were no match for the voracious Maxim gun. Yet, in a scene reminiscent of Britain's failures on the northwest frontier and at Ulundi, Leander Starr Jameson—soon of Jameson raid fame—was not able to catch Lobengula, who left Bulawayo burning in his wake.[82] This led to the debacle of Shangani Patrol, where the Matabele routed all but a few British officers. As in Buganda, resistance here was a two-stage process: a second war was fought in 1896 in support of the Ndebele revolt against the BSAC. This rebellion was led by Mlimo, a spiritual leader who convinced the Ndebele that white settlers had brought the ecological crises—drought, locusts, and rinderpest—that threatened cattle and crops upon indigenous economies. By then substantially weakened by the failed Jameson raid, the BSAC was ill-equipped to defend its territories, and the war raged on for nearly a year. Known as the First Chimurenga—in Shona, "revolutionary struggle"—it ended somewhat improbably by Cecil Rhodes asking the *impis* (local regiments) to drop their arms. It remains a touchstone in Zimbabwe as the first war of independence, evidence that Africans were in no way predisposed to cede ground in the face of European geopolitical aspiration, technological assault, and rapacious company settlerdom.[83]

What do these outcomes indicate? In the case of the Matabele, colonial administrators were preoccupied by the unrest that the power vacuum left in the wake of the 1896 war—a preoccupation that continued well into the 1920s with attempts to reinstate Lobengula's grandsons. In the interim, efforts by royal allies to seek tribute from commoners and build a political base left British officials perpetually fearful of insurrection.[84] Seen in this light, the most important thing may be simply to acknowledge uprisings like the Ndebele's in all their halting eventfulness, since the story of the Scramble for Africa is and remains a winner-took-all narrative, burying the heat and light of the actual struggle for Africa under the smug certainties of empire-builders like Lugard and Rhodes. Indeed, anti-British rebellions like those mounted by the Buganda or the Ndebele attest to what we might call ungovernability with agency—that is to say, disorder that is neither purely circumstantial nor fully coordinated, but which poses a distinctive threat to jurisdictional claims, whether in the form of the planting of the flag or the settling of uitlanders (migrant workers) or the unleashing of Maxim-assisted carnage. The wars fought in the 1890s by Lugard and Rhodes both ended in protectorates, but rather than easy conquests or untrammeled impositions of benevolent order, those regimes were the product of a disordered and halting set of victories for the conqueror. They did not necessarily or self-evidently lead to anticolonial nationalism, but they do represent a notable form of collective counteraggression that took on the legitimacy of jurisdictional protest by creating a state of perpetual insecurity through war and its challenges to political takeover, even after treaties had been signed and the Union Jack firmly planted.

Though it has made little impression in grand narratives of the Scramble for Africa, this insecurity was not abstract. Fear

of colonial uprising and overrun was endemic to settler societies across the British empire, regardless of their longevity. To
be sure, administrators might be caught up short by the eruption of anti-white violence, as the "gentle and idealistic" Lord
Grey undoubtedly was when he heard about the first stirrings of
rebellious activity in Matabeleland shortly after his arrival there
in 1896.[85] But settlers, who lived atop the impossibly unstable
demographic volcano that white settlement tried to manage,
were typically less sanguine; like the British state itself they lived
"nervously" in the shadow of native communities whose sovereignty might be more or less consolidated but whose potential
to become a formal enemy was part and parcel of daily life.[86] As
Shula Marks has written of the Bambatha rebellion in Natal in
1906, "The fact that many locations were 'natural strongholds'
from which it was believed that Zulu armies 'could sweep the
country in a single night and return with their plunder' was as
much a source of anxiety and suspicion in 1900 as in the 1850s."[87]
Settler insecurity here, as elsewhere, was highly gendered and
rooted in anxieties about the sexual safety of white women and
the specter of miscegenation. "Outrages" against settler women,
both imagined and real, were a constant feature of colonial rumor
and drove fears about the security of settlement, not just in the
context of war but as part of everyday lived experience as well.

Given the calculus of settler sovereignty in Natal in particular, fears about Zulu takeover were a characteristic feature of settler life. In a context where whites' relentless land hunger had
pushed Africans into squatting or reserves, where poll taxes were
oppressive and increasingly nonviolently resisted, and where
martial law was easily resorted to, fear of an African uprising was
"strong, enduring and at times almost pathological" especially in
the wake of the end of the Boer war. In this particular setting,
"rumors that the Africans were about to rise and unite against
white rule were rife all over South Africa"—so much so that

some magistrates dismissively called it the "annual hysteria."[88] Such hysteria was both general and highly localized. Such was the case in East Griqualand in the 1890s, when indigenous anger over land questions was palpable, fears of the theft of stock, and other expressions of disaffection, combined with knowledge of local and regional rebellion in previous years, produced anxieties about imminent revolt, though no shots were ever fired.[89]

Elsewhere in nineteenth-century southern Africa, this state of affairs had resulted in settlers and their guardians vowing to inflict "a proper degree of terror" and to "shed Kaffir blood" wherever necessary in the process.[90] The Bambatha rebellion—a Zulu revolt against British taxation in 1906 in which Gandhi famously commanded a corps of Indian stretcher bearers to tend to wounded British soldiers—was ultimately suppressed, at the cost of many thousands of Zulu lives. Bambatha's attempts to secure his own chiefly power in the face of British fiscal incursions were more easily and quickly suppressed than in Buganda and Matabeleland. But the fact of its eruption is no less significant: the necessity of martial law was an embarrassment to the Liberal government in Britain and a sign that white settlement was under threat.[91] As historian Shula Marks observes, "There was a strong undercurrent of fear in the race attitudes of white Natal: fear of the savage and unpredictable tribesman, fear of the newly emerging educated African, fear of the Zulu who had only been brought under Natal control in 1897."[92] Even if we concede that imperial officials and their agents had the capacity to suppress dissent and bring agitators to heel, white fears persisted nonetheless. Rebellion was not, in other words, a one-off; it was only the most spectacular manifestation of the insecurity that underwrote empire on the ground every day, waiting to erupt in acts of defiance large and small no matter how formal or "informal" colonial control might be.

As with the scripting of formal battle "victories," so, too, with the writing of imperial narratives about the conquest of

Africa. The so-called women's war of 1929, which was provoked by census-taking as a prelude to taxation and began as an attack on a British-appointed warrant chief, Okugo, is a powerful example not just of the way that gender contributed to unstable conditions on the ground, but of how imperial history has periodized the phenomenon of the Scramble itself. Begun in Oloko (Owerri province, Nigeria), the protests spread and turned violent as police shot on and otherwise harassed women who were not only assembling but also raiding banks and court buildings, looting, and burning government establishments. Though they were brutally repressed, the Igbo women kept up their protest actions in the 1930s and 1940s, in which context the memory of 1929 was an important touchstone.[93] Yet the women's uprisings of 1929 are not typically understood as an extension of the post-Berlin settlement. Indeed, their contributions to the long-term crises of British colonial Africa are typically forgotten in imperial histories of rise and fall because they appear to fall between stools: they are neither war nor rebellion in the conventional sense, in part, of course, because of the gendered forms of expressions through which they were mobilized. Through targeted campaigns, riots, and ritual performances like dancing and sweeping, African women embodied forms of contest and claim-making that addressed intrusions of colonial market governance and other manifestations of the collaborative patriarchy of indirect rule.[94] Ordinary African men and women did the same wherever Europeans sought to colonize and settle. Perhaps 1900 is too soon, then, to declare the Scramble for Africa over and done. Though the Africans were undoubtedly defeated in the ways that tend to count in imperial history, they themselves remained the drivers of imperial insecurity well beyond the decisions taken in Berlin, doing their undisciplined work to shape the parlous conditions of colonial ambition.

Chasing the Enemies of Empire at Home and Abroad, 1850–1930

If Britons were privy to the perpetual challenges to imperial power and legitimacy through newspaper accounts, *Boys' Own* and *Girls' Own* adventure tales and the heroic empire landscape of novelists like G. A. Henty—who chronicled everything from the Afghan disaster to "the march to Coomasie" in vivid fictional accounts—they did not, for the most part, experience the disruptions at home. The costs of imperial expansion, while real, were far removed from the daily lives of the average inhabitant of the metropole, whether she lived in London or Suffolk, Limerick or Glasgow, Bishops Stortford or Hay-on-Wye. To be sure, relatives of emigrant women, soldier boys, and military men might come closer to appreciating what empire was on the ground, though this would not have brought them into direct contact with colonized people except perhaps as ugly abstractions: wogs, mutineers, fuzzy wuzzies, to name just a few in the distorted catalogue of terms available to "native" Britons at home who cared to take note. Increasingly, of course, colonial peoples themselves came to the metropole in search of education or work. While there had long been a population of Africans and Asians in Britain, since the Elizabethan era in fact, these numbers accelerated in the early twentieth century, bringing native Britons into contact with a variety of the Queen's subjects on the streets, at the docks, in shops, and, when interracial friendships or marriages occurred, at the dinner table too.

Yet if empire remained mostly remote, a matter of parliamentary debate rather than daily life, there were a number of turbulent events that brought its direct costs and domestic dangers starkly home. In 1865, the same year as the Morant Bay rebellion in Jamaica, the Irish Republican Brotherhood (the IRB; also known as the Fenians) planned an uprising in Britain that aimed at establishing an Irish republic and, through it, a revolutionary challenge to British rule in Ireland. The IRB had emerged in the wake of the failed rebellion in Dublin in 1848. Its founder and chief strategist, James Stephens, created an oath-bound secret society with multiple cells and a transatlantic development machine that capitalized, literally and figuratively, on the huge sympathy for Irish independence among Irish Americans.[95] Founded in 1858, the IRB grew fitfully in its first few years, as Stephens sought to recruit members from the older 1848 cadres; resolve tensions between different strands of radical traditions in Ireland; deal with clerical opposition, mainly from Archbishop Paul Cullen; establish a newspaper, the *Irish People*; and coordinate the streams of money and men coming from the United States. This was an underground mass movement designed to overthrow British imperial rule and to undo the hold of the Church on the Catholic middle class in the process. Among the Fenians' supporters in Ireland were artisans and school teachers, laborers and small shopkeepers—tailors, ironworkers messengers, clerks, bricklayers, weavers, dyers and porters, a considerable and representative slice, in other words, of the Irish working class. By autumn of 1864 they were said to number 54,000—a figure Stephens thought was extremely conservative—and to have 8,000 recruits in the British army in Ireland and abroad.[96]

Despite their size and years of planning, including the steady shipment of American arms, the much-anticipated 1865 rebellion did not occur. The British government carried out preemptive raids, including on the offices of the *Irish People*, and Stephens himself was taken into custody. Lord Wodehouse, the viceroy, declared his arrest "the heaviest blow we have struck yet against the seditious faction."[97] He could not perhaps have foreseen that this was the beginning of decades of giving chase to Irish revolutionaries determined to throw off what they viewed as illegitimate British rule in Ireland and to use physical force throughout the United Kingdom to do so. The Fenians broke Stephens out of Richmond jail and got him into hiding—an act of daring that sent the British authorities scrambling in anticipation of an uprising that they believed could erupt anywhere in Britain. Fearing the symbolism of St. Patrick's Day 1866, the British purged the army of suspected Fenians via 150 court-martials, suspended habeas corpus, and undertook a massive dragnet, detaining over seven hundred people without trial.

Though these tactics created serious challenges for the IRB, 1866 was nonetheless a year of tremendous upheaval in Britain proper, and Stephens was determined to cultivate allies through sub rosa connections and in legitimate political circles. The Reform League, which sought to extend the franchise to the working classes, held demonstrations in Hyde Park in July that had the police on the defensive and, in the words of one observer, had the makings of "desperate deeds and revolution."[98] Stephens made overtures to British radicals even as he continued to cultivate transatlantic alliances, including with the agent of the International Working Men's Association in New York. Meanwhile, the Provisional Government of the Irish Republic was established in secrecy off the Tottenham Court Road (London), and it issued its proclamation in February of 1867. With its direct address to "the Irish People of the World" and its unflinching claim on Irish territorial sovereignty ("the soil of Ireland, at present in the possession of an oligarchy, belongs to us, the Irish people, and to us it must be restored"), the proclamation was a call to arms as well as an announcement of republican intention.[99] It was also a declaration of political war on the British empire at home.

The Fenian rising, called for March 5, was a notorious failure. Despite minor, short-lived successes in Kerry and Dublin, plans for an all-out rebellion fell disastrously short. In Britain, an attempt to storm the castle at Chester also failed. Britons following the drama would have been most riveted by the so-called Manchester martyrs—William Philip Allen, Michael Larkin, and Michael O'Brien—whose attempts to free IRB prisoners resulted in the killing of a policeman and their swift arrest. The Manchester Irish were terrorized when the police raided their quarters in an attempt to hunt them out; following their conviction they were hanged in short order outside of New Bailey prison in Salford in November of 1867. The British press sent up a chorus calling for "retribution swift and stern." Fenian panic was general all over Britain."[100]

But it would be a mistake to read the IRB's challenge to empire only through the lens of this singular event or to dismiss it because it ended in failure. The Fenian threat and its associated manifestations remained an irritant, and a menacing one, in one form or another until the Easter Rising of 1916 and the formation of the Irish Free State in 1922. This was in part because Irish republicanism was an international movement; and because the Irish were a global diaspora, Fenianism was the nursery of a worldwide conspiracy against empire as well.[101] It was also a potent reminder to the liberal establishment in Britain that that state monopolies on violence should not be overestimated, and that institutional force was not necessarily an indelible marker of state power.[102] In the nineteenth century, fomenting "terror" at the very heart of the empire was a pluripotent IRB method. Though broken by the execution of its leaders, Irish radicals continued to target British interests on British soil: that is, to bring its claims about the illegitimacy of British rule directly to the sightline of Britons at home. Following shortly on the heels of events in Manchester, the Clerkenwell bombing of 1867 was the first of these. Richard O'Sullivan-Burke, a Fenian arms agent, was taken prisoner and put in Clerkenwell jail. An attempt was made to free him via explosives, which took out a wall and, unintentionally, a block of houses. Twelve people in all were killed and Karl

Marx, for one, feared it would permanently alienate the English working classes: "one cannot expect the London Proletariat to allow themselves to be blown up in honor of the Fenian emissaries."[103] Popular opinion did rally to the government, but the nation—and as importantly, the Home Office—was gripped by fear of what was to come. Rumors abounded of Fenian conspiracies to kidnap Queen Victoria, who expressed disappointment that more men were not punished for this incident. She recommended that Irish suspects should be held without trial and "'lynch-lawed' on the spot."[104]

This was just the beginning of the "dynamite war" that Fenians waged in late Victorian Britain. That campaign was every bit as psychological as it was physical. Here, gender had its impact: in addition to the role Irish women played in Fenian disruptions, the image of "Bridget and the bomb"—that is, the specter of domestic servants bank-rolling Fenian activity—compounded fears that Irish terrorists were a threat to the well-being of women and children and hence were outside any legitimate political imaginary.[105] They continued to cultivate American financial and political support, which enabled them to continue to press Irish demands at the heart of the empire by whatever means available. As historian K. R. M. Short has noted,

Between 1880 and 1887 three of Britain's major cities came under attack from teams of bombers whose leadership, finance, and most of whose personnel came from two Irish-American organisations based in the United States of America, Jeremiah O'Donovan Rossa's Skirmishers and Clan na Gael. Although Liverpool and Glasgow were to suffer in the initial phases of this struggle against English "imperialism," it was London which for almost 5 years daily faced the threat of gunpowder and dynamite explosions occurring the City of London, the streets of Westminster, the Tower of London, the House of Commons, under London Bridge, in its railway stations' left luggage rooms, and the tunnels of the underground. The goal of the dynamiters was to force Westminster to withdraw from Ireland and allow the development of a free and independent nation. London was to be held ransom.[106]

Terror was a political strategy, albeit it a slow and steady one. The ultimate goal was revolution, but in the wake of the failed Fenian uprising, incremental attacks, like the skirmish, were employed. A commentator in the *Irish World* in December 1875 remarked, "The Irish cause requires Skirmishers. It requires a little band of heroes who will initiate and keep up without intermission a guerilla warfare."[107] Though skirmishing has been attributed to O'Donovan Rossa, the exiled Fenian who coordinated the bombing campaigns in the United Kingdom from the United States, it was in fact the brainchild of the Ford brothers of Brooklyn, whose so-called Skirmishing Fund was enormously popular and linked readers of the US-based *Irish World* newspaper with antiestablishment struggles in Europe and across the empire. Beyond the United States and Canada, Fenians were linked mainly imaginatively to other anticolonial struggles, though the coincidence of the most intense years of the dynamite wars with British imperial campaigns in Africa is suggestive of links historians have yet to fully explore. As a symptom of the state in crisis, Fenianism must be understood as "a political movement in a violent age rather than a violent movement in an age of peaceful politics."[108]

Meanwhile, serious damage was undeniably done in Glasgow and in central London. The 1883 bombing of the District Line by Clan na Gael wrecked a train, shattered coaches and sent seventy-two injured passengers from the third-class carriages to St. Mary's Hospital.[109] Though "native" Britons may not have experienced the generalized anxiety of white Natal settlers, urban dwellers and those responsible for the security of the imperial nation-state were undoubtedly rattled. Fears were afoot about the safety of Queen Victoria's rail travel, fueled by the knowledge that Irish partisans were everywhere. Poison-pen missives were sent to British consuls in America, including the one in Washington, DC, as follows: "Sir a friendly note to the English govt, tell them to kiss our arse we want war with them you will be poisoned or shot and your place blown up your fate will strike terror in Europe." There was a regular relay of anxiety and reassurance between American and British officials about this "open traffic in crime directed against the subjects of a friendly state" and the safety of well-heeled Britons traveling in the United States was much worried over as well. [110] Much of the apparatus of the Metropolitan Police and Scotland Yard was established or fine-tuned during the 1880s to combat the kind of guerilla warfare the Fenians and their allies were determined to wage in order challenge the permanency as well as the legitimacy of British rule. Though it's obvious to many in our own time how and why state complexes of intelligence and policing arise or intensify in response to threats at home, it's worth recalling that "states did not think strategically about how to contain their political opponents; their actions were reactions to the crises and challenges that first arose in the late nineteenth century."[111] It was terror in the imperial metropole that was responsible for the modern domestic security state in Britain. This includes the Met's Special Branch, a direct result of Fenian anarchy at home and one of the origins of the vigilant state.[112]

The Fenians' work in the two decades between the 1860s and the 1880s enabled them to produce more generalized *strurm und drang* than specific results toward their ultimate goal of an end to British hegemony in Ireland. Yet what they accomplished was more than simply anticolonial activity. They modeled a deterritorialized strategy of political sovereignty that was to become the characteristic form of anti-imperial politics in the first three decades of the twentieth century. The Fenian uprising of 1865, which failed in Britain, extended into Canada, coordinated by Stephens's counterparts in New York and Ottawa, among others. From 1866 through 1871 they attempted raids and "invasions" that were rebuffed by Britain's proxy army, the US military. The London *Times* covered the events extensively and with increasingly seriousness, as it became clear to metropolitan observers that the demographics of the Irish diaspora meant that Fenian rebellions were potentially everywhere, from Tipperary to Sydney—where a Fenian sympathizer made an attempt on the life of the Duke of Edinburgh, the son of the Queen, in 1868. This reading of a deterritorialized revolutionary ambition is not hindsight; the very language of its global imaginary was endemic to the time. The assassin's purpose, according to the *Times*, was "to show that the murderous society was world-wide in its organization, and could strike down a victim even on the other side of the globe."[113]

The same might be said of Indian nationalism in the following century. Indeed, the connections between the two movements originated in the nineteenth century and traveled along many vectors.[114] Like Irish radicals, some Indians were ready, willing, and able to imagine an extraterritorial form of anti-imperial sovereignty, one that viewed as its destination the end of empire through a transnational, even global set of alliances woven via print culture, mobile agents, and a canniness about how to elude the growing surveillance state that empire had to become in order to track, let alone manage, the insurgencies directed at it. Though he abjured the violence associated with conventional notions of insurgency—and, indeed, had serious moral, political, and tactical disagreements with the Indian nationalists, who espoused terror as a means of achieving the end of the Raj—Gandhi was considered both a dangerous radical and a revolutionary anticolonial subject by defenders of the Raj in the first three decades of the twentieth century. His calls to swadeshi, his mobilization of the salt marches and other forms of mass mobilization, and the Quit India movement of 1942 that he inspired each articulated the conviction that British rule had no long-term future in India. And the quiet ferocity of satyagraha—manifested in peaceful public demonstrations that massed thousands of Indians in protest against the legitimacy of British rule—arguably reterritorialized the very notion of sovereignty. Gandhi's nonviolent resistance methods made Swaraj (self-rule) the watchword for a new form of authority, one that operated through the interiority of the individual psyche as well as via collectivity of an aspirant postcolonial nation-state.

Notwithstanding Gandhi's impact on the imperial and the global imagination, his were by no means the only forms of insurgency that Indians seeking an end to British rule mobilized. Like the Irish, Indians within and without India mounted a frontal assault on the territorial integrity of the imperial nation-state, throwing the very notion of a nation-bounded nationalism into question. Three decades after the Fenians disrupted British soil with their "dynamite war," an Indian radical named Mohan Lal Dhingra, a mechanical engineering student at University College London, attended a reception held by the National Indian Association at the Imperial Institute where he pulled a pistol and killed Sir William Curzon Wyllie, aide to the secretary of state for India. A Parsi doctor, Cawas Lalcaca, who tried to intervene, was also fatally wounded. Ostensibly motivated by the racism he had experienced in London, Dhingra was said to have been plotting the bombing of a P&O liner as well as the House of Commons in order "to create the greatest amount of sensation" among a domestic British public whom he believed held Indians in contempt. Dhingra was convicted, sentenced to death, and executed in Pentonville in the summer of 1909, becoming a martyr just weeks after the assassination.[115]

As a tactic, the threat of assassination was not an uncommon feature of the global imperial security landscape. Anyone following the metropolitan news in the 1880s would have known the impact of the Phoenix Park murders—where two high ranking officials, Lord Frederick Cavendish and Thomas Henry Burke, were slain on their way to the Viceregal Lodge in Dublin. And governors-general were well aware of the danger to lesser representatives of Her Majesty's empire on the ground via targeted killings that were political assassinations and alarmed consul and commoner alike. Dhingra, for his part, belonged to a large and growing Indian student population in London associated with India House, or Bharat Bhavan, in Highgate. Founded in 1905 as a hostel for Indian students by Shyamaji Krishnavarma, a Balliol College graduate and an admirer of Herbert Spencer, it quickly became a nursery for Indian radicals, some of whom were inspired by or connected with terror movements in Bengal. Though Indian students in Britain had been under surveillance for quite some time because of the suspected revolutionary ideas and activities of Krishnavarma and his colleague, the poet and playwright Vinayak Damodar Savarkar, Dhingra's actions drew renewed attention to the community of diasporic Indians in Britain with varying degrees of sympathy for pre-war Indian nationalism.[116]

India House—home not only to a community of radicals but also the site of short-lived but politically and intellectually influential circulars like the *Indian Sociologist*—was shuttered, and those associated with its publications were arrested and imprisoned. Among these was Savarkar who, like Dhingra, was radicalized by his time in Britain. Savarkar was the author of *The Indian War of Independence*, a revisionist account of 1857 that argued for the collective, nationalist impulses of the uprising in direct response to the fiftieth anniversary "commemorations" of it staged by empire chauvinists. Viewed as seditious by colonial officials, especially in the already inflamed context of terrorism in Bengal and elsewhere in the empire, it was banned until the end of the Raj, though it made its way surreptitiously into India inside book jackets that purported to cover copies of Dickens's *The Pickwick Papers*.[117] David Garnett, an early twentieth-century scholar of Hinduism and supporter of the Indian revolutionaries, vividly recalled Savarkar reading aloud from his "extremely propagandist history of the Indian Mutiny" at India House, after which students and others listened to "Vande Mataram" on the gramophone."[118]

In a move that signals the jurisdictional morass that anti-colonial politics threw into bold relief, the authorities invoked the 1881 Fugitive Offenders Act of the Indian Penal code and extradited Savarkar to India, where he would receive a harsher sentence than had he been tried in Britain. He remained in jail until 1921 and upon his release continued to be an avid critic of both imperial rule and Congress nationalism, advocating for a Hindu Rashtra as an alternative political form. What was at stake in Savarkar's 1910 arrest was the operation of the kind of legal exception that that the colonial state arrogated to itself when it came to violence—an exception that underwrote the long life of British power in India. Men like Krishnawarma and Savarkar were not just alive to this exceptionalism but in avid intellectual and practical dialogue at India House about the provocation to revolution it posed. Their work, both literary and political, represents a rejection of the possibility of accommodating Indian nationalist desire through conciliatory measures ranging from constitutional nationalism to Gandhian passive resistance.[119]

While Dhingra and his fellows undertook sedition in the metropole, terrorists were getting up to all kinds of trouble in

Bengal, including bomb throwing and assassination attempts against officials at all levels, and with mechanisms that carried plenty of meaning as well as firepower. In 1907, Hem Chandra Das cut an oblong hole in Herbert Broom's 1,000-plus page treatise *A Commentary on the Common Law Designed as an Introductory to Its Study*. The target of this "biblio-bomb" was the local presidency magistrate.[120] The first decade of the twentieth century was critical to the character and trajectory of terrorism there, both in terms of actual violence and in terms of intellectual/ political rationales for armed struggle against the Raj. Terrorist and terrorism, though arguably loaded terms because they were mobilized by the imperial state to cover a wide range of subversive practices, are contemporary to and commonly used by defenders and enemies of the Raj alike.[121] Indian women figured crucially in terrorist activities, sometimes as assassins: Bina Das shot at the governor of Bengal in 1932. They might be members of the Indian Republican Army: Kalyani Das and Priti Lata Waddedar helped storm the Chittagong Armoury in 1930. Or they were activists in organizations like Bhaghat Singh's Lahore Students Union, preparing for events like the Kakori Train Robbery in 1925. Waddedar was unapologetic—she had been training for her mission all her life—proclaiming that "armed women of India will demolish a thousand hurdles, disregard a thousand dangers and join the rebellion.[122] Others, like Suhasini Ganguli, faced torture and jail for their role in such plots and were revered for their courage and self-sacrifice.[123] Not all nationalist women in the empire took up armed struggle, of course. Cumann na mBan, the Irish feminist organization, did not endorse physical force for Irish women, preferring "practical assistance" instead. This did not stop them from gun-running, participating in the Citizen Army, or carrying their own weapons. There were, in short, a number of ways for women to be "loaded with sedition."[124]

"Freedom fighters" empire-wide might have been united by their revolutionary commitments, but they often took a variety of approaches to ending imperial rule. A figure like the poet-nationalist Aurobindo Ghose may be representative of Indian revolutionary thinking, but his retrospective comment in 1938 that he favored "an open armed revolution in the whole of India" as opposed to individual acts of terrorism suggests the range of views among the enemies of the Raj in this period.[125] Valentine Chirol, the *Times* journalist who had connections with a number of powerful imperial men, viewed all such lawless actions as derivative of "the Irish Fenian and the Russian anarchist"—a patronizing remark that reveals much about the global drumbeat of sedition that pricked the consciousness of the defenders of empire in the first decades of the twentieth century.[126] *Bande Mataram* agreed, proclaiming in 1909 that Dhingra's shot had been heard "by the Irish coterie in his forlorn hut, by the Egyptian fellah in the field, by the Zulu laborer in the dark mine."[127] By 1930, that shot was echoing from Dublin to India as the Indian Republican Army planned their amoury raid to commemorate the 1916 Easter Rising.[128]

Meanwhile, radical activity flourished outside the borders of empire as well, specifically in the United States, though by no means only there. On the frontiers of British Canada, unrest had been brewing at least since the 1830s; among the most notable insurgents was Louis Riel, the metis leader of two uprisings (1869–70 and 1885) who was thought to have Fenian connections if not transnational networks. His trial and execution in 1885 was a global media sensation and earned him the contemporary moniker "the Catholic Mahdi of the Northwest"—which indicates how rebel iconography might travel and captures the violence at the heart of postcolonial state formation in all its varied forms. It is also in danger, perhaps, of obscuring other axes of connection and disconnection, and in Riel's case, of disappearing how disengaged indigenous peoples in the Northwest were from the events of 1885, at least, and by extension, of flattening the unevenness of the terrain on which local eruptions occurred across different spaces of once and former empire.[129]

Though the historical reasons were different, Indians, like the Irish, created enduring networks of sedition and insurgency from bases in the United States, from which they imagined and attempted to execute a variety of plots aimed at bringing down the British empire. Thanks to the work of a variety of exiles and diasporans—from the Punjabi laborers who worked on the Western Pacific railway lines to the political radicals who generated pamphlet material and raised money for sorties in the heart of the Raj—some of the most significant forms of radical thinking and action occurred outside India proper.[130] Some of this activity began at the turn of the century, aided by the prodigious political energy of such exiles as Lala Lajpat Rai and Taraknath Das—perennial seditionists who fled India for America, where they saw, at least initially, the possibility of freedom and equality.[131] The foundation of the Ghadar Party in California in 1913 was a major milestone in the development of a dispersed, extraterritorial, anticolonial, radical movement that unequivocally aimed at bringing down the Raj.

Derived from an Arabic word meaning revolt, *ghadar* is an Urdu/Punjabi term; it speaks to the movement's origins among Punjabi workers and its broader appeal to Punjabis as well. *Ghadar* was, significantly, the name of both a party and a newspaper. In both forms, it sponsored tentacled networks of radical agents and ideas who carried revolutionary principles through global matrices that relied on colonial circuits even as they worked to elude imperial surveillance machinery thrown on the defensive in a prolonged "cat and mouse" game from the first years of the twentieth century through the granting of formal independence in 1947. Indeed, the influence of the Ghadar movement is evident from official reports of where *Ghadar* (the newspaper) was intercepted: Trinidad, Sudan, Aden, Morocco, Manila, Siam, Java, Madagascar Reunion, Nairobi, Fiji.[132] Though it was banned in India, *Ghadar* circulated all over the world well into 1920, carrying headlines like "Ghadar and Guns" and "Philosophy of the Bomb" and serving as the calling card for the movements that were evolving anticolonial, anti-racist strategies.[133] The party also ran the Ghadar Press, which printed pamphlets and other ephemera in both the vernacular and English, written by party leaders and, in some instances, by the laborers who made up its ranks.[134] Poetry was common in Ghadar Press publications and spoke of everything from reconciliation to guerilla warfare, from soldier allies to the need for science colleges, from secret societies to the Delhi Mutiny. Though the term *organic intellectual* postdates their activities, Ghadar was the nursery for a heady ferment of ideas dedicated to the revolutionary end of empire.

The onset of World War I opened up all manner of opportunities for the enemies of the Raj, including liaisons with the Germans, who were as eager to break the British empire from within as from without. German agents in the United States leant support to the Ghadarites, who, in turn, encouraged Indians to support Germany in headlines as bold as "O Hindus, Help the Germans" and equally incendiary copy: "Germany is going to defeat England. German [*sic*] have taken the whole of France: and Russia too has been dismantled." By December of 1915, *Ghadar* was calling for Indians to rise up, "for the day will come when your flag will be respected throughout the world . . . Soon, with the aid of the Germans and Turkey, your enemies will be slain. This is the opportune time."[135] There can be little doubt about the party's political intentions. When the new party headquarters were opened, the revolutionary Har Dayal wrote, "This is not an ashram but a fort from which a cannonade on the English raj will be started." And when war was declared, he exhorted, "Your duty is clear. Go to India and stir up rebellion in every corner of the country."[136] Lest the seriousness of this intention be doubted, *Ghadar*'s editor endorsed an open letter to Bhagwan Singh, a luminary of the revolution, urging him to start a press in Siam and Batavia, thus signaling the broad geographical ambit of the party's political ambition.[137]

Revolutionary movements across the empire were interconnected through the circulation of print culture, including revolutionary materials that British officials were at pains to track. But the British knew how inspirational the Irish were, especially for the Bengali radicals—and they used counterinsurgency tactics borrowed from the Irish Civil War to respond to Indian dissent.[138] Ghadar's internationalism is historically significant; it was a mobile corps of empire's enemies who saw opportunities with other anti-imperial sympathizers and did not hesitate to identify with them.[139] Its perpetual motion, together with the ability of its agents to elude surveillance during the planning stages, meant that it strove to stage pan-imperial protests as opposed to strictly localized ones. The 1915 conspiracy plot is a major case in point. Conceived as an army-wide revolt, the plan was to coordinate Indian nationalists in India and diaspora with help from the German Foreign Office and even some Irish republicans. Hundreds, if not thousands, of foot soldiers and sympathizers were drafted in the process. Capitalizing on already established revolutionary cells in India that had been holding public meetings and stirring up minor disturbances since 1907, and comprising just one strand of a global network of communications that arguably had its origins a decade before Singapore, Ghadar commandeered ammunition as well as recruits in preparation for a February 1915 uprising.[140] As they had done in the Fenian case, British authorities penetrated the cadres and forestalled a multi-sited rebellion. The sepoys in Singapore did, however, mutiny, thanks in large part to the planning work of an enterprising Ghadar agent, Mansur Singh. Though the British at the time characterized the mutiny as a strictly local affair, the regiments who rose up were politicized through multinational channels from Canada to Hong Kong. The "British" response was also multinational, growing out of and tied to both European and East Asian metropoles, not to mention Canadian and US ones.[141] Rebels who were caught were tried under the Defense of India Act in 1915, and forty-two were sentenced to death. If the 1915 plot failed, it did so in part because of traitors like Sagar Chand, who passed information to British intelligence and helped subvert the rebel cause. If Ghadar was ultimately unable to bring the empire down, it continued to favor revolutionary tactics over legal ones and, in so doing, to reject the approaches used by many moderate Indian nationalists before 1919.[142]

In the midst of the war, then, the British were fighting anticolonial nationalisms of varying types on multiple fronts, politically and geographically. That the seriality of the 1916 Easter Rising—a failed revolutionary attempt rooted in notions of blood sacrifice—and the more successful 1917 Bolshevik Revolution—unnerved the British imperial nation-state, there can be little doubt. "The Communist menace" consumed British politicians at home, in part because of the fear that, in the words of a Special Branch officer, conditions among the working class in Britain were as close, if not closer, "to those laid down by Communist philosophers as being necessary before a Proletarian Dictatorship could be imposed."[143] Even as failures, the Easter Rising and its martyrs had given powerful voice to the view that "the government of Ireland by England rests on restraint and not on law"—a slogan that may not have inspired Constance Markievicz's "buy a revolver speech" to the Irish Women's Franchise League, but that helped to galvanize Cumann na mBan, the revolutionary women's group, nonetheless. In 1917, the *Irish World* confidently proclaimed "All Hail Russia!" and predicted that "the Irish [will] become fit partners of the Russians in the regeneration of the world."[144] Even King George V recognized that "everything which touches Ireland finds an echo in the remotest parts of the Empire."[145]

Meanwhile, the War Office and related agencies in Britain had kept close watch on the Irish and the Indians, whom they monitored for evidence of Soviet plots and attacks; concerns about the "Muslim Bolshevik fanatic" were as acute as fears of Jewish radicals, a paranoia that beset the Calcutta police with particular sharpness, despite the "tiny communist nucleus" there.[146] The Indian Political Intelligence (IPI) archives offer evidence of how the British imperial state tracked Irish-Indian radical connections especially. Surveillance ranged from the close scrutinizing of the newspaper coverage of radical activity or communist sympathies to the tracking of individuals such as Shapuri Saklatvala, who had been under surveillance since 1910, was elected as an Member of Parliament in 1922, was known to be a great friend to Irish nationalism, and was a regular visitor to Ireland in the early 1930s.[147] By 1934, the links between the Indian Independence League and the Irish Republican Congress were intensifying, severed partly by Saklatvala's untimely death in 1936.

Anti-imperial movements did not simply find common cause and pose daily challenges to British intelligence operations. They proactively threw the imperial nation-state on the defensive and compelled a host of repressive responses, from the suspension of habeas corpus to the promulgation of legislation like the Rowlatt Acts (technically, The Revolutionary and Anarchical Crimes Act, though referred to rarely enough as such). In some cases, alliance-makers were bold about their solidarities, as when V. J. Patel, the ex-president of the Indian Legislative Assembly, visited Dublin in 1932. His first stop was St. Stephen's Green, where Éamon De Valera was unveiling a memorial to the revolutionary Countess Markievic.[148] This kind of traffic was arguably more

common by the 1930s. In any case, the British were plagued by
the fear that colonial radicals might reach out to other disaf-
fected rebels across the disintegrating landscape of the pre- and
post-Versailles world, making alliances that crossed imperial
boundaries in their quest for a globally reconstituted geopolitical
landscape. Ghadar's pre-war history is instructive here. During
the war, its Berlin committee hosted Persians and Turks; it culti-
vated an Istanbul community; and it sponsored Calcutta-Batavia
and Siam-Burma schemes. In many ways it fulfilled the promise of earlier, Victorian radical fantasies about the possibility of
global solidarity among the enemies of empire and anticipated
later transnational manifestations of such sympathies as well.
While these schemes did not succeed in the conventional
sense of the word, the British were not fully prepared for the new
multi-axial and semi-coordinated forms of resistance that anti-
colonialists were increasingly resorting to in the years before and
after World War I. Indeed, they were holding onto older models of nationalism and of state-building as well. Nowhere is this
clearer than in postwar Iraq, where the British were busy setting
up the new government on what officials called an Indian model,
a kind of protectorate that was bound to fail. If this was not true
at the start, then it was certainly the case by the late 1920s,
when the Britain realized that "it could not afford to devote the
time and money needed to build an efficient, sustainable, liberal democratic state in Iraq" and settled for a quasi-state from
which it hoped to disengage easily. For all that the Versailles
settlement heralded a new Anglo-centric global order, Britain
was underequipped to handle emergent international norms of
self-determination of the extraterritorial, insurgent kind that
both preceded it and followed in its wake. [149]

Even as those responsible for imperial security relied on a certain kind of intra-imperial network, as in the Singapore Mutiny,
they often failed to recognize, or to stay ahead of, developments

in anticolonial resistance that had been going on since the nineteenth century Fenian operation—a mobile movement that they were arguably preoccupied with, but over which they exerted limited control. Indeed, even the IPI was not foolproof: Indians routinely evaded its surveillance apparatus, remaining "off the map" and out of reach for years at a time, during which revolutionaries learned how to use disguises, make bombs, and elude the net of the imperial security complex.[150] In the context of this defensiveness and disarray, the historical significance of the global "Hindu conspiracy" against the Raj cannot be underestimated. The subterranean work of Ghadar and its sympathizers sought to join other sworn enemies of the imperial nation-state in a shared project whose ends were clear: to foment worldwide revolution through a pluripotent set of threats in which physical violence was paramount. It threatened the security of empire, shaped the emergence of the twentieth-century surveillance complex, and served as a highly visible index of how anticolonial nationalism might hobble the ability of an imperial regime to remain offensive in a changing global landscape. If the transnationality of anticolonial activity can be said merely to have mirrored the kind of extra-imperial sovereignty the British empire and its agents aspired to, it is not clear who preceded whom. The vigilant state and its tentacled apparatus look very much like a defensive response to the challenges of managing a multisited empire and its pluripotent crises.

Waging Resistance: End-to-Empire Visionaries

As historian Maia Ramnath has detailed, despite the massive crackdown on it, the Ghadar Party shifted its weight toward the Third International, establishing bases in Turkey, Persia, and

Egypt after the war. By the late 1930s, Ghadarites were in direct contact with Moscow, sending students to its "university" and setting its sights on China and Afghanistan as potential allies.[151] This kind of transnationalism was by no means unique to the Ghadarites. The League Against Imperialism, founded in Brussels in 1927, was both a defensive response to the liberal imperial internationalism that emerged from Versailles and a proactive form of international anticolonial solidarity. Patronized by Albert Einstein and funded by the Comintern (the Communist International), the league's 1927 meeting brought delegates from China, Palestine, Syria, Egypt, North Africa, Peru, the mainland United States, and Puerto Rico together in to develop strategies that would bring about an end to empire. Nehru remembered the meeting many years later as a crucial experience in his political development, a moment when he began to understand "the problems of colonial and dependent countries" in the same frame of analysis.[152] Although Africans did not have a major voice at Brussels, the pan-African movement was its own force to be reckoned with. The African Association founded in 1897 by Henry Sylvester-Williams, a Trinidadian lawyer, had support in his endeavors from Irish and Indian nationalist leaders. By 1900, London itself was the site of the first Pan-African Congress, an event that drew people of African descent and a variety of imperial critics and served as the occasion for W. E. B. Du Bois's prophetic speech in which he named the color-line as *the* defining problem of the twentieth century.[153]

Some British observers of the conference cautioned against political alarmism, approving the tone of the speeches and professing hopefulness about the possibility "genuine wisdom" to be found there.[154] Yet, as historian C. L. R. James showed with remarkable clarity from the vantage point of 1938, a global consciousness of shared struggle was the very condition of pan-African revolt from Haiti through Garvey, from Turner's revolt to Harry

Thuku, and beyond. Actual linkages between the movements are as yet undocumented. What twentieth-century pan-Africanism had in common with the Ghadar movement was a recognition of the strategic advantage of operating not just transnationally but geopolitically as well. They appreciated the advantage, in other words, of prioritizing thinking and working outside the spatial parameters of the nation and/or empire and beyond their temporal limits to imagine and work for a world in which racialized imperial state power was no more.[155] This was true even as black radicals struggled to compel the proponents of working-class and communist internationalism to appreciate the global-scale revolutionary potential of black people.[156] Characteristic of the end-to-empire posture that interwar radicals shared was a modus operandi predicated on networks—intraregional or cross-border networks that might run at odds with or parallel to imperial ones and that might be animated by a charismatic figure capable of generating counter-publics either in his own time or beyond it. Whether or not they were motivated by theological doctrine, and whether they were tight or loose, many such networks—like the Fenians—were chiefly, if not exclusively fraternal. Women revolutionaries and terrorists did exist, participating in both spectacular acts and more mundane activities to promote the cause. These networks were also often religious, whether via their forms of associationism or their cultural origins. In such cases, imperial loyalty might be tested and found wanting, as the case of the Khilafat movement (1919–1924) illustrates.

For Muslims under British rule, the prospect of a global caliphate was a source of inspiration that created tensions between imperial authority and political fealty. When Sultan Abdul Hamid II ascended the Ottoman throne in 1876, under an Ottoman constitution that nominated the Sultan as the Khalifa, the modern Khalifate movement was born.[157] As Indian Muslims began to look toward Constantinople—an orientation enabled by the transnational circulation of a rich and textured Islamic print culture in the late nineteenth century—British policy in the East became of increasing concern. One school of thinking traces the rise of pan-Islamism in India to the Russo-Turkish war of 1876–78; even the London *Times* spoke anxiously of Muslim "restiveness" over Britain's Ottoman policies. By 1906, a pan-Islamic society had been established in London by Abdullah Suhrawardy, an Islamic scholar who would later be elected to the Indian Legislative Assembly. Indian Muslims were roused by Britain's ultimatum to Turkey that same year—and by the Anglo-Russian convention in 1907, which appeared to ally Britain with Turkey's archenemy. According to one Muslim journal in Calcutta, "The Musalmans will look upon the fame of England's influence in the East with distrust and abhorrence . . . [they] will lose their faith and friendship in the English and thus create for her a great difficulty in the future."[158] The Balkan wars further alienated Bengali Muslims, as did British neutrality in the face of Italy's incursions into Libya.

As an official anti-imperial protest campaign, the Khilafat movement emerged in full force in 1919, gaining ground following the Treaty of Versailles, when the Ottoman empire was on the block, and especially after 1920, when the treaty of Sevres partitioned its remains and the new geographies of the "modern Middle East" were created, literally, by mandate. Prior to this, at an All India Muslim League meeting in Delhi in December 1918, leaders expressed grave concerns about the future of Turkey, especially its role in the "guardianship of the Holy places in Islam." By 1919, an all-India Khilafat Committee had been set up in Bombay; among its first resolutions was the observance of Khilafat Day by all communities in the subcontinent. By November of the year, its first open session had been called and Gandhi was elected to the chair. Khilafat committees were established all over India; boycotts were put into motion, and it was not long before "Khilafat" and "Swaraj" were intertwined through a joint commitment to noncooperation.[159] As historian Abu Yusuf Alam puts it, "the formula 'no cooperation til Swaraj and Khilafat' was repeated everywhere like a hypnotic chant" and "even the rural areas [of India] were afire with enthusiasm and full of a strange excitement."[160] Volunteers were organized at the district level, conferences were held, and in November of 1921 the Bengal Congress and the Khilafat Committees called for a hartal to protest the Prince of Wales' visit to Calcutta. In a sign of official recognition of the threat to public order, Congress and Khilafat offices were rifled, papers seized, and workers arrested. This dealt a blow to the movement, but not before the Bengal government had pronounced the political situation "volcanic." Meanwhile, as late as 1925, Sir Malcolm Hailey, the governor of the Punjab, continued to rank the "shock" of the Khilafat movement with that of Gandhi's noncooperation campaigns.[161]

British officials charged the leaders with conspiracy but were eager to avoid popular agitation over the arrests from turning them into martyrs.[162] The Khilafat movement was eclipsed in 1922 by events at Chauri Chaura, where Gandhi followers were shot at during an antigovernment protest. Such aggression promoted some protesters to storm and set fire to a police station, which resulted in the death of twenty-two policemen, massive arrests, and the escalation of both Gandhi's ahimsa campaign and more revolutionary mass movement tactics. With the victory of Ataturk in 1924 the Khilafat movement was effectively over: the new Turkish leader summarily abolished the Caliph role and that link with India, at any rate, was severed. In terms of the internal history of Indian nationalism, the Khilafat movement proved the occasion for division, as some Muslim leaders (Dr. M. A. Ansari and Maulana Abu Kalam Azad) supported Gandhi while the Ali brothers threw their energies into working for the Muslim League. But the pan-Islamic impulses that had emerged in the immediate postwar crisis were not confined to Khilafat. Despite the fact that revolutionary terrorism in Bengal had a Hindu bias—the Dacca Anushilan Samiti expressly forbade Muslim participation, while in other groups Hinduism was presumed if not policed—pan-Islamic secret societies sprang up in Calcutta during the Balkan war of 1912-13.

Men like Azad, who had himself taken a tour of the Middle East and Turkey in 1908, knew firsthand about the revolutionary ferment taking root outside India among fellow Muslims, and he carried news of it home via the newspaper *Al-Hilal*. While Azad's "apocalyptic millenarian" vision alarmed the British (he appears in their intelligence records), he viewed the front against the British as "a long-term policy, to be pursued even at the cost of immediate Muslim interests." Such a conviction hardly dulled his anti-imperial fervor. In 1916 Azad wrote, "For jihad it is not always obligatory that there should be a battlefield, a sword or a military operation. But . . . it is obligatory to inflict injury by any means which may cause to the enemy loss in life, property, land, nationality, commerce and morals"—the whole register of British justification for imperial legitimacy, in short.[163] Significantly, Azad traveled in international radical circles, one conduit for pan-Islamism to and from India. Indian newspapers closely followed the creation of British mandate Palestine, which Gandhi openly condemned as "an act of treachery toward Indian Musalmans and of pillage against the world's Musalmans." Less well known, perhaps, is that a Palestine Arab delegation visited India in 1923–24, partly to disseminate pan-Islamic materials. Though these attempts to forge and sustain links between co-religionists were sporadic and even ineffective in terms of generating real cooperation, they had the effect of keeping possibilities alive and realizing some tangible impact, however singular. The successful staging of a Palestine Day in May of 1930 was the event with the greatest support in Bombay.[164]

Both Constantinople- and India-based leaders, Muslim or not, used the Khilafat idea to their political advantage—and to their geopolitical advantage, to boot. Palestine was equally instrumental to Indian nationalist agendas: "it could be used as a revamped Khilafat grievance which would foster Hindu-Muslim unity and in doing so, strike British rule at its very bedrock."[165] This may explain why Congress was resolutely anti-Zionist. Yet by no means all Muslims were enamored of the possibilities for transnational connection that the Khilafat movement and its predecessors held out. In a remarkably postmodern turn of phrase, the influential Muslim jurist Syed Ahmad Khan deplored the "extraterritorial romance" of pan-Islamism, not least because it threw the security of the British empire into potentially perpetual question.[166] For Muslims under British rule, the question of loyalty had long been an issue—not because of any confessional predisposition toward jihad but for economic and political reasons derived from the combination of economic exploitation that Muslim subjects experienced and the challenge to sovereignty an alien Christian conqueror posed. Despite the fact that some Muslims profited from their collaboration with the state, British rule in South Asia brought impoverishment and immiseration for the many Muslim communities, which made them susceptible to recruitment in 1857. Their availability was provoked by a variety of changes introduced by the Company state in the years leading up to 1847. These included the Bentinck law of 1832 protecting the rights of Indian converts and the steady erosion of Mughal influence and power in the judicial and administrative systems of British India.[167] Though the British were the conquering power, Sir William Muir saw Islam as "a subtle usurper" and the Raj's "mortal foe," a paranoia echoed by perpetual fear of a popular uprising.[168]

In January 1857, Ahmadullah declared a jihad against the British. Credited with the infamous chapati scheme, he fought and was jailed by the British, though he met his death at the hands of an enemy raja.[169] Jihad has a long and nuanced history in British India as an intellectual concept, a spiritual idea, and a political practice. In the case of Sayyid Ahmad, jihad was against Sikhs, though his martyrdom was to have lasting consequences and even recruitment possibilities well into the nineteenth century Maulana Sayyid Nazir Husain Dehlavi insisted a jihad was only legitimate "if initiated by an imam with the Prophet's family" and if there were arms enough to fight the enemy. He preferred a *jihad-ilafzi* (verbal struggle), though the rebels persuaded him to issue a fatwa for jihad nonetheless. Prophecies associated with jihadi power stoked fears and roused rebel passions, though neither the ruling houses of Persia nor Afghanistan joined in to ratify the local pan-Islamic promise of the mutiny, despite hopes to the contrary. In fact, many Muslims were loyal during the mutiny, none more famously than Sayyad Ahmed Khan, who spent much of his intellectual energy denying that the rebellion of 1857 fell into the category of jihad and, beyond that, to insisting on Muslim loyalty to the Raj.

Debate on that question was enlivened by W. W. Hunter, whose 1871 book, *The Indian Musalmans*, responded directly to the question posed by Lord Minto: "Are the Indian Musalmans bound by their religion to rebel against the Queen?" Answering in the affirmative, Hunter organized his book around chapters titled "The Standing Rebel Camp on Our Frontier" and "The Chronic Conspiracy within Our Territory." Here India was perforce a "rebel colony" beset by a "fanatic host."[170] Hunter's particular target was the Wahhabis, a Sunni sect that adheres to a strict interpretation of the Koran and to whom anticolonial sentiment, conspiracy and rebellion were often attributed. Hunter did not deny that there were loyal Muslims; rather, he concluded that "we may enforce submission, but we can no longer claim obedience."[171] Even the most minor grievances had the capacity, in his view, to jeopardize the political authority of the Raj. In this sense, the balance was tenuous and precarious, for even a small infraction might at any time "free them from their duty as subjects, and bind them over to treason and Holy War." If Hunter's book was nothing more than a compilation of European stereotypes about Islam, it also packaged up the most noxious of those stereotypes as imperial intelligence: jihad was, potentially, always only just around the corner.[172]

Those preoccupied with security in Ireland had similar concerns: Thomas Carlyle worried in 1868 about the way the Irish land system bred disaffection, painting Dublin Castle as a defensive barracks and Irish Catholics as rightly antagonistic in the face of "unjust government."[173] But Victorian paranoia about fealty was reserved for Muslim subjects of the Raj. Whether or not such paranoia was warranted, it was a leitmotif for those in charge of the security of the Raj—not least because jihadis were charismatic figures with the power to inspire potential rebels and served as scapegoats for imperial anxieties in need of images around which to coalesce—because, of course, one man's dangerous radical was another's revivalist or reformer (recall the Mad Fakir of Swat from chapter 1). Perhaps no figure was more vexing to British authorities in this regard than Jamal ad-Din al-Afghani. His career is worth detailing in its particulars because though in many ways he was sui generis, he anticipated the transnationalism of later anticolonial men, stirring up trouble as he wandered through a variety of imperial terrains. His particular form of anticolonial movement (in terms of ideas as well as mobility) highlights the tense and tender relationship between nationalism and insurgency and of the possibilities not only of resistance but also of principled non-alignment—an aspect of anticolonial radicalism that British imperial histories have tended to occlude.

Though his origins have been shrouded in mystery, Afghani was born *c.*1838–39, just as the First Anglo-Afghan War was erupting. Most likely born and raised in Shi'a Iran, he traveled to India for the first time in his teens, right before the 1857 Mutiny, an experience that equipped him with what was to become his fierce, unerring critique of British rule. A peripatetic anticolonialist, he was in Afghanistan again in 1866, where, according to British state documents, he encouraged the new emir to align with the Russians. That recommendation encouraged many to suspect him of being a Russian agent, including the emir, who had him escorted out of the country in 1868. From there he went to Istanbul, where he gave speeches on education connected to Ministry of Education. When his arguments drew fire he was expelled and went to Cairo, where he is said to have favored the assassination of the Khedive and to have given fiery anti-British speeches in the tense years leading up to the British occupation, but he does not appear to have been aligned with Urabi.[174] The Khedive expelled him 1879; it was the first time he came to the attention of the British in Egypt, which suggests that intelligence sharing with India was not what it should have been.[175] From there Afghani went to India, where he turned against the followers of Sayyid Ahmad Khan, who he believed, with some reason, to be westernizers.

After 1881, Al Afghani became a defender of Islam, a representative of "Muslim defensive solidarity," and of a pan-Islamism that was taking shape as a genuine intellectual and organizational threat to British political order. In 1882 he in was Paris; he claimed to be the European agent of the Mahdi to Wilfred Scawen Blunt, an Egyptian sympathizer. Somewhat incredibly, Blunt brought Afghani to Britain, to discuss the Sudanese Mahdi situation with Churchill and Leonard Woolf. Afghani was then in touch with Sultan Abul Hamd, though he did not go to Istanbul to meet him until 1892, despite his previous attempts to ingratiate himself—perhaps because the Sultan perceived him as a potential rival for the leadership of the global Muslim community.[176] The 1880s saw Afghani in Tehran and in Russia, where his anti-British opinions brought him the attention of government officials. In 1889 he was invited by the Shah to Iran, but he quickly earned Shah's wrath by critiquing his concessions to foreigners and was summarily driven out. Back in London, he continued his anti-Iran propaganda. After the Sultan invited him to Istanbul, he worked to advance the Sultan's pan-Islamic claims, yet still dallied with his Egyptian friends. The Sultan feared the Khedive would be the focus of a pan-Islamic movement.[177] In 1896 Nasir Ad-din, then shah, was assassinated at what was believed by many to be Afghani's encouragement, if not behest.[178] The Iranians wanted him extradited, though the Sultan refused, likely to protect his own intrigues, about which Afghani knew, perhaps, a considerable amount. In the aftermath of this contretemps Afghani's influence waned, and he died of cancer in 1897—poisoned, some thought, possibly by the next shah himself.

Distinctive for the murky, subterranean trail of intrigue and sedition he left behind, Afghani was one of a number of "fugitive mullahs" and "outlawed fanatics" through whom we can take a measure of English paranoia and insecurity in the Raj. They were "'little men' between big empires"—British, Ottoman, and Dutch—who moved along transnational networks. Their circuits sponsored a kind of "international relations of ordinary individuals" linked to Muslim politics rooted mainly in India though extending well beyond its official borders.[179] Muslim women traveled too, developing their own extensive patronage networks and, in the interwar period, making connections with the international women's suffrage movement, as when they gathered at the Eastern Women's Congresses at Baku in the 1930s. The imperial government was suspicious of the latter, mainly because of their links to their respective nationalist movements, from whom they faced more hostility and even violent opposition on issues of suffrage and divorce.[180] In some instances, Muslim women were linked to conspiracy through male relatives, as Shah Jehan Begum was with Wahhabism through her husband Siddiq Hasan, and as her daughter Sultan Jahan Begum was through her son Hamidullah in connection with the "Muhammadan Conspiracy" at Aligarh. Though they are less well known in histories of pan-Islamism, they caught the eye of the CID (Criminal Investigation Department, India) and even the *Times*.[181] Legitimately or not, the imperial state was on the whole more apprehensive about unaligned Muslim men like Afghani who had mixed origins and motives: they might be reformist ulemas (legal scholars of sharia) or mere opportunists, but they had all left or been forced out of India."[182] Many shared a conviction about the umma, the community of Muslim believers around the world, not just as an ideal, but as the basis of a working alternative to British political legitimacy. In this sense they modeled the deterritorialized sovereignty that Ghadar later publicized but which had deep historical roots across the British empire in South Asia.

They may also have shared a skepticism about the very territorial certainties that undergirded the post–Berlin Conference world. In a 1892 letter to Abdulhamid, al-Afghani observed that among western powers,

> all have only one desire, that of making our land disappear up to our last trace. And in this sense there is no distinction to make between Russia, England, Germany or France, especially if they perceive our weakness and our impotence to resist their designs. If, on the contrary, we are united, if the Muslims are a single man, we can then be of harm and of use and our voice will be heard.[183]

Afghani posed a threat to imperial security because his believed that the West was a common enemy for those who wanted no part of European empires. His ideas impacted not only Mohammed Iqbal and Azad but the All-India Khilafat Conference, whose call in 1922 for an Asiatic Federation was a concept he had promoted.[184]

Interwar Insurgencies Rampant

This book opened with the argument that World War I made the limits of European technological superiority globally apparent. So, too, the 1930s dramatized a disruptive set of challenges to British imperialism for all the world to see. Newspaper coverage of Gandhi's salt march and of the wide variety of nonviolent resistance activities across the subcontinent helped to guarantee this, as did the acceleration of terror activities in India and left-leaning anti-imperial activism in the metropole. Whether they were critics in Britain or from within the Congress Party itself, contemporaries clearly understood that Gandhi had the capacity to create anarchy for empire through nonviolent resistance and its consequences.[185] That anarchy operated both above and below the radar screen. Imperial officials attempting to keep track of the movements of individual revolutionaries had long felt their own inefficacy. Well-known revolutionaries, such as M. N. Roy and Virendranath Chattopadhaya, traveled the radical circuits from India to Berlin and beyond, routinely evading the surveillance of the British Foreign Office. They donned all kinds of disguise and even survived assassination plots, as did Chatto in 1921. Some women revolutionaries, such as Bhicoo Batlivala, also gave the British pause, in her case because of her openly "anti-British propaganda."[186] The poet Sarojini Naidu, seemed at once more and less formidable. According to one agent, "She belongs to the school of the troubadour, the rover, the duel by candlelight!"[187]

Meanwhile, in this same turbulent period, rebellions across colonial central Africa shook the foundations of the colonial regime to its core. Imperial agents nonetheless failed to take initial indications of unrest seriously and were therefore caught perilously off guard. In the case of the Watchtower movement, a millenarian revivalist sect, activists sought to cleanse the people, combining "moral regeneration and political revolution" through a different vernacular than satyagraha, perhaps, but in ways that echoed the purified self/purified nation dyad of swaraj and swadeshi. As with the Indian boycotts, political economy was at the heart of the matter, as Africans were compelled to work for cash; tax was used as a tool of labor recruitment and they sought redress in spiritual idioms. Watchtower adherents in Malawi and Zambia targeted customary rulers by burning villages and attacking ancestor shrines. Those headmen, the custodians and beneficiaries of the British system of indirect rule, were not above using violence against "witches" and other enemies of their interests, as was the case with the Zambian Lala chief Shaiwila from the mid-1920s onward. The administrative response to this trouble on the ground was a campaign of containment, via arrests that focused on the technicalities of vagrancy and tax evasion but largely left the inflammatory subject of religion untouched. As a mode of anticolonial politics, Watchtower remained a major anxiety for the administrator and white settler alike, both of whom were susceptible to rumors of bloodbaths and feared being murdered in their beds. Beyond the crises of the 1930s, such colonial histories remind us that the British were in full possession of political power, either at the inaugural moment of indirect rule or throughout its quotidian, troubled life.[188]

Conditions under the Palestinian Mandate were equally turbulent. The British garrison had been reduced to 5,000 troops as part of postwar economies that included cuts to intelligence service, despite the outbreak of rioting in Jerusalem and Jaffa in 1920 and 1921. Palestine's already thin line of internal security was, for all intents and purposes, erased.[189] The 1920s were "oases of peace" punctuated by riots that included Arab boycotts of Jewish establishments and goods, especially in the context of the riots of 1929, which ostensibly broke out over conflict around Arab and Jewish rights to the Western Wall but which were in fact the consequence of British failure to mediate communal relations. Martial law was declared after rioting in Jerusalem and massacres in Hebron and Safad. The police there were overwhelmed and reinforcements had to be brought in from Egypt and Malta."[190] Tensions between Jews and Arabs, unresolved by a weak and weakening Mandate, came to a head again in the 1936 Arab revolt in ways that further exposed Britain's inability to manage challenges to political order on the ground.

The facts are well known: the immediate spark of the revolt was the murder of two Jews on the road from Nablus to Tulkarm. Though the Jewish press attributed the murders to Arab banditry, rumors abounded that the attack was retribution for the death of Shaykh Izz al-Din al-Qassam, a popular Arab preacher who had railed against both British rule and Zionism ("Obey God and the Prophet but not the British high commissioner").[191] His capacity to rally both urban and rural sentiment—and supporters willing to fight—made him a security threat, and he was killed in a battle with the British mandate forces in 1935. His name and his reputation as the "detonator" of anticolonial insurgency lived on as late as the TWA bombing of 1986, where it was invoked with passion and pride as an antecedent to late twentieth-century anti-imperial causes.[192] A cycle of funerals and assaults was begun in the wake of the travelers' murders, culminating in an Arab general strike and revolt in the fall of 1936. The British response was a series of Orders in Council, emergency measures that were effectively martial law though officials fell short of using the term itself.[193] Thence ensued "the most significant anticolonial insurgency in the Arab East in the interwar period."[194]

That insurgency began in the cities but moved swiftly to the countryside in the aftermath of Britain's call for royal support from Iran, Transjordan, and Saudi Arabia for a Royal Commission of Inquiry; the commission recommended partition into an Arab state and a Jewish state. A call to arms was matched by various forms of assistance on the part of villagers, whose kinship connections linked them to regional rebel commanders and disposed them to help erect barricades and to hide guerillas in their homes. There was considerable complexity and organization to this movement, including rebel courts and a taxation system developed to keep the rebels funded and fed. Some urban Arab women turned their associations into auxiliaries for the cause, and rural women also actively participated in the struggle. The death of Qassam radicalized many in both city and country, but peasant women threw themselves into the fray. They had a keen sense of the local economy and topography; they could destroy provisions to keep them from falling into the hands of the British during raids (in one case by pouring oil over lentils); and they proved themselves capable and willing when it came to smuggling weapons as well.[195]

Imperial histories that underplay the racialized law-and-order concerns colonial rule strove to manage run the risk of obscuring the personal relationships many rural Arabs, especially, had with Jewish neighbors and of painting the Arab revolt as anti-Semitic when it was not uniformly so. Such narratives are also often deeply buried evidence of horrific British counterinsurgency, acts of repression that typically occurred off the beaten path, in these same rural areas, which historians are just beginning to unearth in all their violent detail. Such outrages, termed euphemistically by one contemporary observer "punitive measures," included summary executions of suspected Arab rebels in the streets and in homes, the detonation of mines under a bus full of Arabs, and public beatings and torture "without pity." The archives pertaining to the Arab Revolt and the counterinsurgency that followed are full of cryptic references to deeds so dark on the part of British soldiers against Arabs that witnesses, including at least one clergyman, were loathe to commit them to paper.[196] What references remain suggest village burning and destruction that is more than a faint echo of what Churchill had recorded in the Malakand campaign thirty years earlier. Whether the atrocities committed in Palestinian communities such as Halhul and el-Bassa in 1938–39 were more atrocious or whether interwar officers and soldiers were more vulnerable or sensitive to world opinion is an open question. That a significant segment of the Palestinian Police Force was recruited from the Royal Irish Constabulary and the Black and Tans[197] into the 1950s points to an intracolonial network of training in riot-control tactics that drew on decades of imperial experience (though perhaps not wisdom) in global imperial security management. It is a sign, too, of how mobile counterinsurgent personnel were and had to be as an end to official empire appeared to be nearing.

These events have a familiar ring: dramatic eruptions of rebel action growing from years of low-level unrest and contest; the commission of inquiry; the short- or longer-lived rebellion; the brutal repression. Indeed, the regularity of the crisis-induced commission across the period under consideration is one index of the continuous trouble empire made. Imperial officials were force to take notice in procedural ways which, in turn, created archives of dissent and disruption that—however incomplete—are not available anywhere else. Meanwhile, the Arab Revolt provoked denials about the level of reprisal that are arguably unmatched in other accounts of imperial insurgency before Mau Mau: deniability surely rooted in both shame about and resistance to the idea that these enemies of empire were worthy combatants, whose strength and tenacity were so powerful that they required "disproportionate" force to quell. In that sense, insurgency and counterinsurgency carried out in the 1936 Arab Revolt are part of a long history of resistance and failure in the British empire since the First Opium War (at least). This accumulation of examples means that 1857 simply cannot stand as the avatar of resistance to British imperialism, any more than Gandhian or Nehruvian anticolonialism efforts can. To understand the "ruins of empire" and where they come from requires an emphasis on the multiple, pluripotent forms of dissent and disruption that bedeviled imperial state power wherever it sought to compel authority and create legitimacy, by force of arms or, indeed, by force of the tax man, whether British or native. Such a range of actions did more than throw empire on the defensive. They arose precisely because empire was undefended, or underdefended, against the sheer possibility of them, on a variety of fronts and well beyond the eruption of a "major" event like the Mutiny, however large it continues to loom in the postcolonial imagination.[198]

This blindness can, of course, be attributed to orientalism or racism or whatever sets of belief that account for the incapacity of will or self-governing deficits empire builders only too willingly attributed to those they attempted to colonize. It is an attitude encapsulated by prime minister Arthur Balfour's conviction that "never in all the revolutions of fate and fortune have you seen one of those nations of its own motion establish what we, from a western point of view, call self-government."[199] Somewhat paradoxically, those in charge were unprepared for the trouble they encountered, even as they often believed that the threat of physical struggle was around every corner. They thought the worst of those they governed, believed them capable of betrayal and insurrection, yet they backed into security provisions, formal and informal, that were called into existence by the prospect of threats, some imagined and some very real.[200] Imperial officials may have aspired to a monopoly on violence, but they did not exert total control over subject populations (let alone "domestic" ones). As a result, political order was, both routinely and at spectacular moments, provisional at best. Though many Britons may have imagined it could be so, the prospect of a safe England in a dangerous world was, in fact, wishful thinking -- precisely because there was always trouble with empire.[201]

It seems appropriate, then, to think of, and to narrate, the British empire not through an arc that neatly rises and falls but as a chaotic and pluripotent "terrorist assemblage."[202] Though women were involved, it was a notably fraternal assemblage, predicated on mobility, autonomy, and a sense of transnational brotherhood that was more or less realized depending on time and place. An assemblage is a kind of grid, such as that which personally connected Irish and Indian radicals. It is also a kind of mesh, throwing into bold relief the variety of webs and networks that crisscrossed the worlds encompassed by imperial power. The narrative possibility that the assemblage as method enables us to appreciate is the field of empire as a reticulate form, where reticulation is not merely ornamental or filigreed but vascular and resilient, like the veins of a leaf. As nearly all the examples of insurgency routinely show, agents can act by chance or by design—they may even be thwarted or interrupted—but they always leave a trace in the dense, coagulate field of history, not just in the life of the individual or the movement. Histories built on the trouble with empire cannot simply add insurgencies to our narratives. What we need is a methodological frame that can acknowledge and account for insurgents, insurgency, and the trouble they caused as the legitimate grounds, the veritable starting point, of any British empire history worthy of the name.

Epilogue

Toward a Minority History of British Imperialism

The summer of 2010 saw the publication of the Saville Report, which declared the "Bloody Sunday" killings unjustified. Bloody Sunday refers to the day in January 1972 when Britain's Parachute Regiment killed fourteen unarmed Irish civilians in Derry's Bogside, shooting some of them in the back as they ran for cover. The London papers trumpeted headlines about Lord Saville's findings and about the speech by the new Tory prime minister David Cameron, in which he endorsed the report and apologized for what his country's soldiers had done that day. Simon Winchester, the *Guardian* reporter who had been in Derry when the massacre occurred, declared it "a full stop to Britain's colonial experience" and "a colophon to Britain's unlovely and untidy colonial experience in Ireland." Winchester, who also recounted his own testimony before the Saville commission, called Cameron's speech "one of the most hauntingly memorable of all Britain's post-imperial moments."[1]

Winchester tells the story of Derry from an ostensibly anti-imperial viewpoint: he thinks of Bloody Sunday as the fillip to IRA nationalism and connects it to two earlier anti-colonial events that led, in his view, to the fall of empire. For Winchester, the Good Friday agreement (the peace agreement between Britain and Ireland in April 1998) was a consequence of Derry the way that Amritsar in 1919 (where a British brigadier fired on innocents in the Punjab) led to Indian independence and the bombing of the King David Hotel in 1946 (a deadly attack on the British mandate authorities) "paved the pathway to Israeli sovereignty." This particular postcolonial narrative brings a variety of "nationalists" into the same anticolonial story, while leaving others out; and it gives a redemptive cast to a diverse, chaotic set of violent and convulsive "ends." Winchester manages to give the impression that Britons somehow cheered all this on, watching India, Palestine, and then Ireland fall like dominos in a ratification of the imperial decline saga that looks natural and outright necessary for the collective identity of twenty-first century Britain. "This day," Winchester concludes, "has been a true imperial moment, part of a colonial end-game, in its own way as symbolically important as all those lowering-of-flag ceremonies and the doffings of goose-feather helmets in tropical climes."[2]

A very particular species of imperial time shapes Winchester's account of Derry at the end of the first decade of the twenty-first century. The Saville Report is at once "a true imperial moment" and "part of a colonial-end game": two processes—the end of empire and its continual ending—that are coincident, though apparently unremarkably so. There is no trace in Winchester's account of contemporary wars in Iraq and Afghanistan, to which the late Labour government was so fatally pledged and which remain its legacy. Yet in long and short historical terms, those military commitments are very much an Anglo-American enterprise, part of a "special relationship" that is by no means transhistorical, that has been tested by war and the battle for oil in several gulfs at once, but which remains entangled in the racial and civilizational grids of long-standing global imperial aspiration. Such grids can, apparently, assimilate the Derry Irish (former "terrorists" in the minds of many of Winchester's readers, very possibly) but cannot acknowledge, even glancingly, the

place of 7/7—"Britain's 9/11"—and its contemporary reverberations in the United Kingdom's ongoing postcolonial history.[3]

What's remarkable about Winchester and those who
embrace the Saville report as some kind of endpaper of empire
is the belief they cherish that empires are ever over, or that
their histories can be written as self-contained, rise-and-fall
narratives, however delayed and disjointed. This cyclical
trope—to which even Winchester's "anti-colonial" account can
be assimilated—remains a touchstone for arguments about
contemporary anglophone imperial power and its roadmaps for
success and long life. It may also represent the long postcolonial afterlife of the political unconscious of imperial history—a
halting, stumbling afterlife aided, perhaps, by the anachronism
of a postcolonial theory that remains trapped by forces beyond
its control. Presumptions about the rise and fall of the British
empire persist in contemporary writing about modern imperialism and especially in popular renditions of imperial history.
Even when angst and ambivalence are refracted through such
premises, stories about "the end of empire," and of the Raj in
particular, are still headline grabbers.[4] Histories of resistance
whose endpoint is not the "giving over" of independence or the
inevitable (if vexed) afterlife of empire "at home" have failed to
filter into public perceptions of British imperial power on either
side of the Atlantic. Narratives about empire as a cyclical phenomenon have practically "monopolized the entire system of
representation" available to us, if not across the whole historiography of the British empire, then at least in the still powerful,
if not still dominant, public Anglo-sphere. The prose of empire
is a seductive, distorting mirror and even when we want to, it's
hard to give it the slip.[5]

This is not to say that empire can't be dated, or that it didn't
end formally and officially. But Britain decolonized in much the
same way it colonized—fitfully, haltingly, bloodily—by managing

serial and/or simultaneous crises that verged on states of emergency and produced a variety of "ambiguous victories."[6] During the so-called "endgame of empire"—which in historiographical terms, tends to occur from the Attlee years forward—British imperial power looked insecure and intermittent, evidence of an abrupt decline that must nonetheless have been experienced as ruthlessly slow as well as violent to colonials who were subject to the various "dirty wars" that brought imperialism officially to a close in the postwar/Cold War era.[7] That intermittent hegemony and its correlative misgovernment was characteristic of the modern British imperial project and not simply of its postcolonial denouement. Following the combination of imperial mismanagement and colonial protest that dogged British imperialism between the first Afghan War and the globally apparent imperial crisis signaled by trans-imperial interwar insurgencies, it's hard *not* to see that the history of the British empire is not rise and fall but skirmish, scramble, stumble, recover; not up and down but perpetual crash and burn; not success and failure but fail, fail, fail and make the most of it—with an eye on your backyard and your hand on your Martini rifle. It requires a persistent and willful disavowal of these patterns *not* to see why its mutineers and guerilla fighters and deserters and protesters and insurgents—its enemies, in short—made empire rather than the other way around, or that the dream of imperial hegemony that shapes the arcs of rise-and-fall accounts, even and especially in the shadow of steep downward slope, was just that.

Even so, despite the anarchic work that colonial subjects performed across the globe to contest their imperial fates, histories of dissent, especially those beyond the famous or the spectacular, remain largely elusive in British imperial histories. Though they tend to drive many (though by no means all) narratives that take South Asian, African or Australasian indigenes as their point of departure, they are not, apparently by definition, characteristic of imperial history as such. Through the narratives undertaken here I have tried to bear witness to some instances of a more fugitive empire history. As for the rebels and deserters and anti-imperial martyrs, although the trouble they made for empire's guardians was consequential to how imperial power fared on the ground, it's the unstable terrain they helped to produce and to keep dynamic and unpredictable that is historically significant—signaling the fundamentally insecure conditions to which imperial aspirations were subject, and the setbacks, interruptions and insurgencies that thwarted the fullest realization of those aspirations at nearly every turn. It's the friction they generated, the ragged edges on the colophon, which make them the dissenting ground of empire and its histories.

The Trouble with Empire suggests how attention to turbulence recalibrates the periodization of the modern British imperial timeline. The Mutiny of 1857 is not a one-off example in terms of rebellion and insurgency; 1919 remains pivotal for its global repercussions but it is more characteristic than not in terms of threats to capital that were ongoing across time and space. And far from exceptional, the Victorian wars in Afghanistan deserve a central place in narratives of empire in trouble. On all these fronts dissent and disruption drove imperial experience on the ground and shaped how policy was made on the spot and in London. At the same time, arcs of rise and fall are not destined to disappear. They exert too powerful a hold on the historical imagination. They are vehicles of mourning and loss in many traditions. In the long and short histories of empire, they are also prototypically liberal plot closure devices, and they will likely play a role in the making of big narrative history for some time to come.[8] Perhaps "fatal florescence," a term that has been used to describe the history of American empire in particular, is the best, most accurate way to represent the operations of modern imperial power.[9]

Yet even under that rubric there is no guarantee that such histories will center on the trouble of dissent and disruption. By definition, the histories of collision of events and people that made such trouble for empire are, perforce, minority histories, and they are indispensable as such. To assimilate them to mainstream narratives would be to lose sight of the levers of dissent they render visible and to occlude the provocations and impediments their makers created under particular historical circumstances. The minor yet incisive angle of vision that such troubled histories provide fixes our sights on the vast, kinetic terrain of subject histories that remain: that long line of dissident empire histories yet to be written.

NOTES

Introduction

1. Alan Lloyd, *Drums of Kumasi: The Story of the Ashanti Wars* (London: Longman's, 1964), 13.

2. See Dane Kennedy, "The Great Arch," in Martin Hewitt, ed., *The Victorian World* (New York: Routledge, 2012), 57–58; 62.

3. Frederick Cooper and Ann Stoler, eds., *Tensions of Empire: Colonial Cultures in a Bourgeois World* (Berkeley: University of California Press 1997).

4. I think here of the work of John Newsinger, such as *The Blood Never Dried: A People's History of the British Empire* (London: Bookmarks Publications, Ltd., 2006).

5. Quote is from Joseph Schumpeter, "The Sociology of Imperialism" (1918) in *The Modern History Sourcebook*: http://www.fordham.edu/halsall/mod/1918schumpeter1.html. Accessed April 5, 2014.

6. That is, when they focus on empire at all. See Kumari Jayawardena, *Perpetual Ferment: Popular Revolts in Sri Lanka in the 18th and 19th Centuries* (Colombo: Social Scientists' Association, 2010). Thanks to Jean Allman for encouraging me to emphasize the latter point.

7. Ranajit Guha, *Elementary Aspects of Peasant Insurgency in Colonial India* (New Delhi: Oxford University Press, 1983). See Pierre Bourdieu and Loci Wanant, "The Cunning of Imperialist Reason," *Theory, Culture, and Society* 16, 1 (1999): 41–58.

8. Often, though not always, in the interests of historicizing the pathway between "coercion and the creation of consent." See Dagmar Engels

and Shula Marks, eds., *Contesting Colonial Hegemony: State and Society in Africa and India* (London: I. B. Tauris, 1994).

9. "Macaulay's narrative is of a prosperous, progressive nation, committed to liberty and civilisation, and a love of that vision of nation is at its heart. . . . Empire is one of the fundamental but unstated assumptions, a natural part of England's greatness, scarcely mentioned in the thousands of pages that make up the five volumes." Catherine Hall, *Macaulay and Son: Architects of Imperial Britain* (New Haven, CT: Yale University Press, 2012), xvi; Theodore Koditschek, *Liberalism, Imperialism, and the Historical Imagination: Nineteenth Century Visions of a Greater Britain* (Cambridge: Cambridge University Press, 2011), 2–6, 107, 136, 149.

10. John Comaroff, "Colonialism, Culture and the Law: A Foreword," *Law and Social Inquiry* 26, 2 (2001): 311.

11. Philippa Levine, *Prostitution, Race and Politics: Policing Venereal Disease in the British Empire* (London: Routledge, 2003). See also Elizabeth Kolsky, *Colonial Justice in British India* (Cambridge: Cambridge University Press, 2010); and James Epstein, *Scandal of Colonial Rule: Power and Subversion in the British Atlantic during the Age of Revolution* (Cambridge: Cambidge University Press, 2012).

12. Ashwini Tambe's *Codes of Misconduct: Regulating Prostitution in Late Colonial Bombay* (Minneapolis: University of Minnesota Press, 2009) uses the sex trade and its recurrent regulation by the colonial state as evidence not of a Victorian "restrictive" ethos at work but of the failure of the imperial administrative apparatus to accomplish its disciplinary ambition.

13. I draw here from Doreen Massey's *For Space* (London: Sage Publications, 2005) and from the work in Tony Ballantyne and Antoinette Burton, eds., *Moving Subjects: Gender, Mobility and Intimacy in an Age of Global Empire* (Champaign, IL: University of Illinois Press, 2008).

14. Clare Hemmings, *Why Stories Matter: The Political Grammar of Feminist Theory* (Durham, NC: Duke University Press, 2011), 2, 61.

15. Newsinger, *Blood Never Dried.* "Blood makes noise" is from Suzanna Vega's song of the same name (1992). https://www.youtube.com/watch?v=v6qvIhygLTs Accessed May 12, 2015.

16. See, for example, Anand Yang, *The Limited Raj: Agrarian Relations in Colonial India, Saran District, 1793-1920* (Berkeley: University of

California Press, 1989) and Jonathan Saha, *Law, Disorder and the Colonial State: Corruption in Burma c.1900* (London: Palgrave Macmillan, 2013), esp. chap. 2.

17. John Darwin, "Imperialism and the Victorians: The Dynamics of Territorial Expansion," *English Historical Review* 112, 447 (1997): 641; John Galbraith, "The 'Turbulent Frontier' as a Factor in British Expansion," *Comparative Studies in Society and History* 2, 2 (1960): 150–68.

18. See, for example, John Gallagher's oft-overlooked essay, "The Decline, Revival and Fall of the British Empire," in John Gallagher, *The Decline, Revival and Fall of the British Empire: The Ford Lectures and other Essays*. Edited by Anil Seal. (Cambridge: Cambridge University Press, 1982), 73–153; esp. 73.

19. For the important distinction between anxiety and fear, see Ranajit Guha, "Not at Home in Empire," in Guha, ed., *The Small Voice of History: Collected Essays* (Delhi: Permanent Black, 2009), esp. 445–54.

20. I draw here from the use of assertion by David Hardiman in his book, *The Coming of the Devi: Adivasi Assertion in Western India* (Oxford: Oxford University Press 1987).

21. These kinds of frictions are apparent whether you assume a core-periphery model or a cross-colonial one: in fact, they are evident throughout extant secondary work from the last quarter century at least, and it is largely that body of scholarship from which I selectively draw. For my abrasive approach to connectivity and power, I rely on Anna Lowenhaupt Tsing's *Friction: an Ethnography of Global Connection* (Princeton, NJ: Princeton University Press, 2004).

22. See Tony Ballantyne, "War, Knowledge and the Crisis of Empire," in *Webs of Empire: Locating New Zealand's Past* (Wellington: Bridget Williams Books, 2012), 159–76.

23. See Antoinette Burton, *Burdens of History: British Feminists, Indian Women and Imperial Culture, 1865-1915* (Chapel Hill: University of North Carolina Press, 1994).

24. See Rehana Ahmed and Sumita Mukherjee, eds., *South Asian Resistances in Britain, 1858-1947* (London: Continuum, 2012).

25. See Meenakshi Mukherjee, *The Perishable Empire: Essays on Indian Writing in English* (Oxford, 2000). "Precarious vulnerabilities" is

Ann Stoler's term; see her *Race and the Education of Desire: Foucault's History of Sexuality and the Colonial Order of Things* (Durham, NC: Duke University Press, 1995), 97; see also George Steinmetz, *The Devil's Handwriting: Precoloniality and the German Colonial State in Qingdao, Samoa and Southwest Africa* (Chicago: University of Chicago Press, 2007).

26. Here the most notable recent case in point may be John Darwin's *The Empire Project: The Rise and Fall of the British World System, 1830–1970* (Cambridge: Cambridge University Press, 2009).

27. Elizabeth Elbourne, "Broken Alliance: Debating Six Nations Land Claims in 1822," *Cultural and Social History* 9, 4 (2012): 521.

28. Nicholas B. Dirks, "History as the Sign of the Modern," *Public Culture* 2, 2 (1990): 25–32.

29. I refer to E. Valentine Daniel's *Fluid Signs: Being a Person in the Tamil Way* (Berkeley: University of California Press, 1987).

30. Thanks to Zach Sell for this reference. See http://www.nathan-ielturner.com/whitemastersoftheworld.htm. Accessed February, 15, 2015.

31. Here one can cite Gallagher, *Decline, Revival and Fall*, and Darwin, *The Empire Project*, where the role of enemies of empire in its historic "end" scarcely feature at all.

32. David Graeber, "On Cosmopolitanism and (Vernacular) Democratic Creativity: Or, There Never was a West," in Pnina Werbner, ed., *Anthropology and the New Cosmopolitanism* (New York: Berg, 2008), 290.

33. Ned Blackhawk, *Violence Over the Land: Indians and Empires in the Early American West* (Cambridge, MA: Harvard University Press, 2006), 6.

34. Robert Warrior, "Native Critics in the World: Edward Said and Nationalism," in Craig Womack, Jace Weaver, and Robert Warrior, eds., *American Indian Literary Nationalism* (Albuquerque: University of New Mexico Press, 2006), 197.

35. Damon Salesa observes that for Samoans, "genealogy was a conditioner of living, not simply a pedigree or a line of descent. More than this, genealogy was politics: better thought of as a network of relations than as a personal history." See his "Samoa's Half-Castes and Some Frontiers of Comparison," in Ann L. Stoler, ed., *Haunted by Empire: Geographies of Intimacy in North American History* (Durham, NC: Duke University Press, 2006), 83.

36. Chela Sandoval, *Methodology of the Oppressed* (Minnesota, 2000) and Linda Tuhiwai Smith, *Decolonizing Methodologies: Research and Indigenous Peoples* (London: Zed Books, 1999).

37. George Boyce, *Decolonisation and the British Empire, 1775-1997* (New York: St. Martins Press, 1999).

38. Ritu Birla, *Stages of Capital: Law, Culture, and Market Governance in Late Colonial India* (Durham, NC: Duke University Press, 2009).

39. Brian Farwell, *Queen Victoria's Little Wars* (New York: Norton, 1985).

40. Darwin, "Imperialism and the Victorians," 614–42.

41. See Rudyard Kipling, "The White Man's Burden," *McClure's Magazine* 12, 4 (February 1899): 4.

42. For one example with failure in its sights, see Donald Denoon, *A Grand Illusion: The Failure of Imperial Policy in the Transvaal Colony during the Period of Reconstruction, 1900-1905* (London: Longman, 1973).

43. That is, a global arena where economic supremacy is undergirded by "clear military superiority and ideological hegemony as well." See Thomas J. McCormick, *America's Half-Century: US Foreign Policy in the Cold War and After* (Baltimore: Johns Hopkins University Press, 1989), 5. Thanks to Dave Roediger for this reference.

44. Quote is by Edward Said, cited in Neil Lazarus, *The Postcolonial Unconscious* (Cambridge: Cambridge University Press, 2011), 13. For a different iteration of this claim, and one that I have benefited from, see Inderpal Grewal and Caren Caplan, eds., *Scattered Hegemonies: Postmodernity and Transnational Feminist Practices* (Minneapolis: University of Minnesota Press, 1994).

45. For an energetic start to the former see Dane Kennedy, *The Last Blank Spaces; Exploring Africa and Australia* (Cambridge, MA: Harvard University Press, 2013). Antagonism is a posture Bruce Robbins ascribes specifically to Edward Said. See Robbins, *Perpetual War: Cosmopolitanism from the Viewpoint of Violence* (Durham, NC: Duke University Press, 2012), 12.

46. The quote is from the Newcastle positivist and empire critic Malcolm Quin, cited in Gregory Claeys, *Imperial Sceptics: British Critics of Empire, 1850-1920* (Cambridge: Cambridge University Press, 2010), 94.

Chapter 1

1. Robert Mandel, "Defining Postwar Victory," in Jan Angstrom and Isabelle Duyvesteyn, eds., *Understanding Victory and Defeat in Contemporary War* (New York: Routledge, 2007), 30–35.

2. Paul Fussell, *The Great War and Modern Memory* (Oxford: Oxford University Press, 1975). 8.

3. Fussell, *Great War*, 13.

4. Quoted in Michael Adas, "Contested Hegemony: The Great War and the Afro-Asian Assault on the Civilizing Mission Ideology," *Journal of World History* 15, 1 (2004): 31–63.

5. Quoted in Adas, "Contested Hegemony." For two readable accounts of this and related questions, see George C. Robb, *British Culture and the First World War* (New York: Palgrave, 2002); and Gregory Mann, *Native Sons: West African Veterans and France in the Twentieth Century* (Durham, NC: Duke University Press, 2006).

6. Recent work on the Russo-Japanese War of 1904–1905 has challenged the centrality of the Great War to the perception by colonial peoples that Europeans might not be invincible. See Cemil Aydin, "The Global Moment of the Russo-Japanese War" in his *The Politics of Anti-Westernism in Asia: Visions of World Order in Pan-Islamic and Pan-Asian Thought* (New York: Columbia University Press, 2007). Marilyn Lake's work on Charles Pearson shows that fears of an Asian and African demographic "take-over" were ascendant by the 1890s. See her "'The Day will Come': Charles H. Pearson's *National Life and Character: A Forecast*" in Antoinette Burton and Isabel Hofmeyr, eds., *Ten Books That Shaped the British Empire: Creating an Imperial Commons* (Durham, NC: Duke University Press, 2015), 95.

7. Quoted on the title page of Winston Churchill, *The Story of the Malakand Field Force* (London: Leo Cooper, 1989). Subsequent footnotes refer to this edition.

8. Churchill, *Malakand*, 217.

9. Churchill, *Malakand,* xiv–xv.

10. Churchill, *Malakand,* xiv–xv.

11. Here I use "Pathan" to mean "Pashtun", as in Pashtun speakers who might or might not be Afghans per se.

12. Churchill, *Malakand*, 242.

13. Churchill, *Malakand*, 13.

14. D. S. Richards, *The Savage Frontier: A History of the Anglo-Afghan Wars* (London: Macmillan, 1990), 130.

15. "Military Department, General Order, Simla, the 31st of May, 1895," *London Gazette*, July 16, 1895, p. 4017. http://www.london-gazette. co.uk/issues/26644/pages/4017. Accessed February 15, 2015.

16. Churchill, *Malakand*, 8. For an excellent discussion of how Churchill used the miraculous powers of Saidullah as a pretext for pathologizing him and justifying British intervention, see David B. Edwardes, "Mad Mullahs and Englishmen: Discourse in the Colonial Encounter" in Fernando Coronil and Julie Skurksi, eds., *States of Violence* (Ann Arbor: University of Michigan Press, 2006), 153–78.

17. A. H. McMahon and A. D. G. Ramsay, *Report on the Tribes of Dir, Swat and Bajour Together with the Utman-Khel and Sam Ranizai* (Peshawar: Saeed Book Bank, 1981), 27–28. Originally published in 1901.

18. Ayesha Jalal, *Partisans of Allah: Jihad in South Asia* (Cambridge, MA: Harvard University Press, 2008), 176.

19. Percy C. Elliott-Lockhart, and Edward M. Dunmore, Earl of Alexander, *A Frontier Campaign: A Narrative of the Operations of the Malakand and Buner Field Forces, 1897-1898* (London: Methuen, 1898).

20. Churchill, *Malakand*, 29.

21. Churchill, *Malakand*, 29. Churchill later opined that despite Deane's competency, military men of all ranks tended to see political agents as "marplots" or busybodies in cahoots with "all these savage chiefs [who] were his old friends and almost his blood relations. Nothing disturbed their friendship." Winston Churchill, *My Early Life, 1874-1904* (1930; New York: Charles Scribners; repr. by Touchstone, 1996). 132.

22. Churchill, *Malakand*, 34, 35, 39–40.

23. Churchill, *Malakand*, 40–41, 42–43, 46, 45.

24. Churchill, *Malakand*, 46, 48–49.

25. Churchill, *Malakand*, 49–50.

26. Churchill, *My Early Life,* 129.

27. Churchill, *Malakand*, 63, 64, 65.

28. Churchill, *Malakand*, 3.

29. Churchill, *Malakand*, 3. For a discussion of Victorian martial race discourse, see Heather Streets, *Martial Races: The Military,*

Race and Masculinity in British Imperial Culture, 1857-1914 (Manchester: Manchester University Press, 2004).

30. Churchill, *Malakand*, 3.

31. Churchill, *Malakand*, 120–22.

32. Churchill, *My Early Life*, 146.

33. Churchill, *Malakand*, 139.

34. Churchill, *Malakand*, 69.

35. Churchill, *Malakand*, 69.

36. Churchill, *Malakand*, 78. This is a rare moment not because Churchill acknowledges a native soldier but because he names one—Singh is one of the few native soldiers in the whole narrative with a name, in fact. As Churchill noted, Major-General Blood also acknowledged Singh's bravery, along with that of Lance-Nail Vir Singh, in a dispatch (p. 255).

37. Churchill, *Malakand*, 71, 72, 80.

38. Churchill, *Malakand*, 69–70.

39. Churchill, *Malakand*, 71, 72, 62.

40. Churchill, *Malakand*, 62.

41. A. P. Thornton, *The Imperial Idea and Its Enemies: A Study in British Power* (New York: Doubleday, 1957), 108.

42. Churchill, *Malakand*, 62, 161.

43. Churchill, *Malakand*, 124, 132.

44. Churchill, *Malakand*, 127–28.

45. Churchill, *Malakand*, 141, 143.

46. "The Swat Valley," *Pall Mall Gazette*, Wednesday July 28, 1897, 1; "The New Trouble in Chitral," *Aberdeen Weekly Journal*, July 29, 1897, 5.

47. *Hansards*, House of Lords Deb. 30 July 1897, vol. 51 cc 1588–9.

48. Churchill, *Malakand*, 142; "The Chitral Disaster," *Freeman's Journal and Commercial Advertiser* (Dublin), July 31, 1897; "British Camp Attacked," *Hampshire Telegraph and Sussex Chronicle*, July 31, 1897; "The Fighting on the Indian Frontier," *Lloyd's Weekly Newspaper*, August 1, 1897; "The Indian Frontier Troubles," *The Graphic*, September 18, 1897; "The Tory War in India," *Reynold's Newspaper*, September 19, 1897.

49. Churchill, *Malakand*, 146, 147.

50. David Held, *Global Transformations: Politics, Economics and Culture* (Redwood City, CA: Stanford University Press, 1999), 93.

51. Churchill, *Malakand*, 150.

52. For a different take on the Amir, see Robert C. Low, "The Risings on the Indian Frontier," *National Review* 30, 176 (1897): 192–206.

53. Churchill, *Malakand*, 150.

54. See Paul Robinson, *Military Honour and the Conduct of War: From Ancient Greece to Iraq* (New York: Routledge, 2006), 141–46.

55. Edgar Sanderson, *The British Empire in the Nineteenth Century: Its Progress and Expansion at Home and Abroad; comprising a description and history of the British colonies and dependencies* v. 4 (London: Blackie and Son, 1897), 201.

56. Churchill, *Malakand*, 163.

57. Churchill, *Malakand*, 164.

58. Churchill, *Malakand*, 167.

59. Churchill, *Malakand*, 163, 164.

60. Churchill, *Malakand*, 164, 165, 167.

61. Churchill, *Malakand,* 167.

62. *Frontier and Overseas Expeditions from India*, vol. 2, supplement A (Calcutta: Government of India, 1908), p 1. For an image of Willcocks's attempt to impose terms, see Michael Barthorp, *The Northwest-Frontier: British India and Afghanistan, A Pictorial History 1839-1947* (Dorset: Blandford Press, 1982), 144.

63. Churchill, *Malakand*, 75.

64. Churchill, *Malakand*, 41

65. Sniping, sabotage and theft of arms under cover of night were all tactics they used in the Malakand. Churchill, *Malakand*, 118.

66. John A. Lynn, *Battle: A History of Combat and Culture* (Westview, 2003), 145–46. Lynn quotes Arthur Wellesley, the Duke of Wellington, describing the battle of Assaye, where he defeated a Maratha army of 60,000 (1803), as "the bloodiest [battle] for the numbers I ever saw" (163).

67. Lawrence Stone, *An Imperial State at War: Britain From 1689-1815* (London: Routledge, 1993), 20–21.

68. Martin Ewans, *Conflict in Afghanistan: Studies in Asymmetric Warfare* (New York: Routledge, 2005), 21.

69. See, for example, Patrick Macrory, *Signal Catastrophe: The Story of a Disastrous Retreat from Kabul, 1842* (London: Hodder and Stoughton, 1966) 19. When respect was not grudging, it was because indigenous fighters, like the Pathans and Gurkhas, were fighting with and not against the British forces. See Streets, *Martial Races*, 100–101.

70. In what follows I draw from the introduction to my edited collection of primary sources, *The First Anglo-Afghan Wars: A Reader* (Durham, NC: Duke University Press, 2014).

71. Victoria Schofield, *Afghan Frontier: Feuding and Fighting in Central Asia* (New York: I. B. Tauris, 2003), 65.

72. Arley Loewen and Josette McMichael, eds., *Images of Afghanistan: Exploring Afghan Culture through Art and Literature* (Oxford University Press, 2010), 19. For a fuller account, see Antoinette Burton, "On the First Anglo-Afghan War: Spectacle of Disaster," http://www.branchcollective.org/?ps_articles=antoinette-burton-on-the-first-anglo-afghan-war-1839-42-spectacle-of-disaster, accessed February 15, 2015; Burton, *First Anglo-Afghan Wars*.

73. As Fakir Azizuddin reassured Lord Auckland in 1838, when he was about to meet Ranjit Singh, "The lustre of one sun (Ranjit) has long shone with splendor over our horizon; but when two suns come together, the refulgence will be overpowering." Khushwant Singh, *Ranjit Singh* (London: Penguin Books, 2009), 247.

74. See Hari Ram Gupta, *Panjab, Central Asia and the First Afghan War* (Chandigarh: Panjab University, 1940), 160–62.

75. Schofield, *Afghan Frontier*, 72.

76. J. A. Norris, *The First Afghan War, 1838-1842* (Cambridge: Cambridge University Press, 1967), 379.

77. Archibald Forbes, *The Afghan Wars: 1839-1842 and 1878-80* (London: Seeley and Co., 1896), 135; Frank A. Clements, *Conflict in Afghanistan: A Historical Encyclopedia* (Santa Barbara: ABC CLIO, 2003), 204.

78. Christine Noelle, *State and Tribe in Early Afghanistan: The Reign of Amir Dost Muhammad Khan (1826-1863)* (Surrey, England: Curzon, 1997), 36.

79. Nabi Misdaq, *Afghanistan: Political Frailty and Foreign Interference* (London: Routledge, 2006), 48–49; M. Hassan Kakar, *A Political and Diplomatic History of Afghanistan, 1863-1901* (Boston: Brill, 2006), 1.

Kakar names Dost Mohammed's son, Sher Ali Khan, and his grandson, AbdurRahman Khan, as the other two "giants."

80. For a useful overview of this context see Kaushik Roy, "Introduction: Armies, Warfare and Society in Colonial India," in his edited collection, *War and Society in Colonial India* (Oxford: Oxford University Press, 2006) and Montstuart Elphinstone's *An Account of the Kingdom of Caubul and its Dependencies in Persia, Tartary and India* (London: Longman, Hurst, Rees, Orme, and Brown, 1815).

81. Henry Havelock, *Narrative of the War in Affghanistan in 1838-39*, 2 vols. (Henry Colburn Publishers, 1840); Jill Casid, *Sowing Empire: Landscape And Colonization* (Minneapolis: University of Minnesota Press, 2004).

82. Alex Marshall, *The Russian General Staff and Asia, 1800-1917* (New York: Routledge, 2006), 139. Even before British troops withdrew from Kandahar in 1881, he was looking to establish his authority beyond the territorial limits (Pishin) that London envisioned for him. See D. Singhal, *India and Afghanistan, 1876-1907: A Study in Diplomatic Relations* (St. Lucia: University of Queensland Press, 1963), 87.

83. Forbes, *Afghan Wars*, 327. In fact, between 1880 and 1896 the new emir faced no fewer than forty uprisings, which he quelled by a combination of "peaceful penetration" and military suppression. See Kakar, *Political and Diplomatic History of Afghanistan*, chaps. 4 and 5. It was perhaps Abdur Rahman's success that led Lord Curzon to imagine that the Afghans might lead a "Moslem nexus of States north of India, sworn-in and paid-up as sentinels of the Raj." See John Gallagher, *The Decline, Revival and Fall of the British Empire*, 91.

84. Forbes, *Afghan Wars*, 324.

85. H. Woosnam Mills cited in Charles Allen, *God's Terrorists: The Wahhabi Cult and the Hidden Roots of Modern Jihad* (Little Brown, 2006), 228.

86. Keith Jeffery, *The British Army and the Crisis of Empire, 1918-22* (Manchester, 1984). 96, 97. Jeffery cites A. J. Balfour in a letter to the Cabinet (September 6, 1905) from Denis Judd, *Balfour and the British Empire: A Study in Imperial Evolution 1874-1932* (New York: St, Martin's Press, 1968), 61.

87. Tonio Andrade, *Lost Colony: The Untold Story of China's First Great Victory over the West* (Princeton, NJ: Princeton University Press, 2011), 17.

88. John Ouchterlony, *The Chinese War; An Account of all the Operations of the British Forces from the Commencement to the Treaty of Nanking* (Praeger, 1972), 33. Originally published in 1844.

89. Ouchterlony, *Chinese War*, 190.

90. Yuan Wei, *Chinese Account of the Opium War*, translated by Edward Harper Parker (Shanghai: Kelly and Walsh, Ltd., 1888), 15.

91. Wei, *Chinese Account*, 15, 17.

92. See Robert Bickers, *The Scramble for China: Foreign Devils in the Qing Empire, 1832-1914* (London: Allen Lane, 2011), 82–84.

93. Wei, *Chinese Account,* 17, 31, and 28–29: "The English were at first rather awed at Yang's military reputation, and not knowing what our dispositions were, sent some white foreigners to Phoenix Hill with peace proposals."

94. Ouchterlony, *Chinese War*, 190–91.

95. Ouchterlony, *Chinese War*, 191–92.

96. The phrase is an echo of Bickers; see his *The Scramble for China*.

97. Jenny Sharpe, *Allegories of Empire: The Figure of Woman in the Colonial Text* (University of Minnesota Press, 1993); Mahasweta Devi, *The Queen of Jhansi* (Calcutta: Seagull, 2000), 107.

98. Cited in Christopher Herbert, *War of No Pity: The Indian Mutiny and Victorian Trauma* (Princeton, NJ: Princeton University Press, 2008), 253.

99. See Alex Tickell, *Terrorism, Insurgency, and Indian-English literature, 1830–1947* (London: Routledge, 2012) and Shaswati Majumdar, *Insurgent Sepoys: Europe Views the Revolt of 1857* (London: Routledge, 2011).

100. Saul David, *The Indian Mutiny: 1857* (New York: Viking, 2002), 231, 258.

101. David, *Indian Mutiny*, 233.

102. Caesar Caine, ed., *Barracks and Battlefields in India* (London: C. H. Kelly, 1891), 106.

103. David, *Indian Mutiny*, 343.

104. Herbert, *War of No Pity*, 45.

105. Tickell, *Terrorism, Insurgency*, 4.

106. Richard Gott, *Britain's Empire: Resistance, Repression and Revolt* (London: Verso, 2012).

107. Richard Price, *Making Empire: Colonial Encounters and the Creation of Imperial Rule in Nineteenth-Century Africa* (Cambridge: Cambridge University Press, 2008), 3.

108. For a study of the pre–Zulu War context, see Clifton Crais, *White Supremacy and Black Resistance in Pre-Industrial South Africa: The Making of the Colonial Order in the Eastern Cape, 1770-1865* (Cambridge: Cambridge University Press, 1992), 143.

109. Bakhshish Sing Nijjar, *Anglo-Sikh Wars, 1845-49* (New Delhi: K. B. Publications, 1976), 10.

110. Nijjar, *Anglo-Sikh Wars*, 22, 40, 54, 55, 66.

111. Immanuel Ness, ed., *International Encyclopedia of Revolution and Protest: 1500 to the Present* (New York: Wiley-Blackwell, 2009), vol. 6: "Santal Rebellion," 2970–71; Stan Lourduswamy, *Jharkandi's Claim for Self-Rule: Its Historical Foundations and Present Legitimacy* (New Delhi: Indian Social Institute, 1997), 7.

112. W. W. Hunter, *The Annals of Rural Bengal* (London: Smith, Elder, 1868), 248.

113. C. E. Buckland, *Bengal under the Lieutenant-governors: Being a Narrative of the Principal Events and Public Measures during their Periods of Office, from 1854 to 1898*, vol. 1 (Calcutta: S.K. Lahiri and Co., 1901), 13–14.

114. Kalikinkar Datta, *The Santal Insurrection of 1855-57* (Calcutta: University of Calcutta, 1988), 58, 60, 62.

115. C. A. Bayly, *Indian Society and the Making of the British Empire* (Cambridge: Cambridge University Press, 1988), 170.

116. See Jennifer Wenzel, *Bulletproof: Afterlives of Anticolonial Prophecy in South Africa and Beyond* (Chicago: University of Chicago Press, 2009), 17. See also David M. Gordon, *Invisible Agents: Spirits in Central African History: Spirits in a Central African History* (Athens: Ohio University Press, 2012).

117. Price, *Making Empire,* 2.

118. Wenzel, *Bulletproof*, 19.

119. John Darwin, *Unfinished Empire: The Global Expansion of Britain* (London: Bloomsbury, 2012), 135.

120. James Belich, *I Shall Not Die: Titikowaru's War, New Zealand 1868-9* (Wellington: Allen Unwin, 1989), 2; James Cowan, *The New Zealand*

Wars: A History of the Maori Campaigns and the Pioneering Period, vol. 1 (Wellington: R. E. Owen, 1922-23), 85, 86.

121. Tony Ballantyne, "War, Knowledge and the Crisis of Empire," in his *Webs of Empire: Locating New Zealand's Colonial Past* (Wellington: Bridget Williams, 2012), 165–66.

122. Damon Ieremia Salesa, *Racial Crossings: Race, Intermarriage and the Victorian British Empire* (New York: Oxford, 2011), 176, 227, 228.

123. Ballantyne, "War, Knowledge and the Crisis," 166.

124. Salesa, *Racial Crossings*, 227.

125. Belich, *I Shall Not Die*, 94 and 89, respectively.

126. James Belich, *The Victorian Interpretation of Racial Conflict: The Maori, the British and the New Zealand Wars* (Montreal: McGill University Press, 1986), 291.

127. Belich, *Victorian Interpretation*, 311–13. There is no denying the impact of British victory, however "fictive," on Maori futures. As Tom Brooking writes, the wars of Rangatiratanga accelerated the loss of Maori land, pushed them to the margins of British settlement and encouraged the myth that "good race relations characterized the New Zealand experience." See his *The History of New Zealand* (Westport, CT: Greenwood Press, 2004), 58–60.

128. Angela Wanhalla, "Interracial Sexual Violence in 1860s New Zealand," *New Zealand Journal of History* 45, 1 (2011): 79–80.

129. Ivor Wilks, *Asante in the Nineteenth Century: The Structure and Evolution of a Political Order* (Cambridge: Cambridge University Press, 1975), esp. 169. Wilks actually calls MacCarthy's assistants "script-writers."

130. Wilks, *Asante*, 170.

131. Wilks, *Asante*, 173, 175, 180–81.

132. Lloyd, *Drums of Kumasi,* 201.

133. Wilks, *Asante*, 183, 185.

134. A. J. Smithers, *The Kaffir Wars, 1779-1877* (London: Leo Cooper, 1972), 226.

135. Smithers, *Kaffir Wars,* 246, 248–49, 254.

136. Lloyd, *Drums*, 76.

137. Lloyd, *Drums*, 97, 152.

138. John Young, *They Fell Like Stones: Battles and Casualties of the Zulu War, 1879* (London: Greenhill Publishers, 1992), 40.

139. Jeff Guy, *The Destruction of the Zulu Kingdom: The Civil War in Zululand, 1879-1884* (Pietermaritzburg: University of Natal Press, 1994; first published in 1979), 207; Adrian Preston, ed., *The South African Journal of Sir Garnet Wolseley, 1879-1880* (Cape Town: A. A. Balkema, 1973), 89.

140. Guy, *Destruction*, xxi.

141. This was especially true of Lord Chelmsford, of whom Punch opined, "Strange official mistake in geography—to have placed Chelmsford in Africa." *Punch, or the London Charivari,* vol. 76, March 15, 1879, quoted in Guy, *Destruction*, 13. For an excellent discussion of Victorian generals and the press, see Streets, *Martial Races,* chap. 4.

142. "To Mate in Three Moves," *Funny Folks*, February 8, 1879, 44. Thanks to T. J. Tallie for this reference. John Young, *They Fell Like Stones: Battles and Casualties of the Zulu War, 1879* (Greenhill Books, 1992), 209. Fortescue is quoted in Smithers, *Kaffir Wars*, 228.

143. C. E. Callwell, *Small Wars: Their Principles and Practice* (London: printed for H. M. Stationery Office by Harrison and Sons, 1899), chap. 17, especially 1–2.

144. Stuart was Captain of the Natal field artillery. See James Stuart, *A History of the Zulu Rebellion, 1906, and of DinZulu's Arrest, Trial and Expatriation* (London: Macmillan, 1913), chap. 4, "Zulu Military System and Connected Customs (with a Note on the Rebel Organization, 1906)."

145. Callwell, *Small Wars*, 26–27.

146. Callwell, *Small Wars*, 205, 443.

147. Callwell, *Small Wars*, 1.

148. James L. Hevia calls it "a world history from a technomilitary point of view." See his "Small Wars and Counterinsurgency" in John D. Kelly, Beatrice Jauregi, Sean T. Mitchell and Jeremy Walton, eds., *Anthropology and Global Counterinsurgency* (Chicago: University of Chicago, 2010), 171.

149. See for example the *Small Wars Journal*, http://smallwarsjournal. com and its blog: http://smallwarsjournal.com/blog/recent. Accessed February 15, 2015.

150. See "The Advance of the Soudan," *The Graphic*, September 18, 1897.

151. See David Levering Lewis, *The Race to Fashoda: Colonialism and African Resistance* (New York: Henry Holt, 1995).

152. Richard Toye, "'The Riddle of the Frontier': Winston Churchill, the Malakand Field Force and the Rhetoric of Imperial Expansion," *Historical Research* 84 (2011): 493–512.

153. (Henry) Spenser Wilkinson, "Lord Roberts in Afghanistan," *National Review* 28 (1897): 844.

154. "There must be something very much amiss with leadership when a compact force leaves camp in the morning, and returns by driblets, disheartened and severely punished; when the general is lost for the night, and having had to fight hard with only an incongruous remnant of his command for his own life, and those of his men, is saved by good fortune rather than by good guidance." *Saturday Review of Politics, Literature, Science and Art*, April 23, 1898, 562.

155. The quote is from a review of Elliott-Lockhart and Dunmore, *A Frontier Campaign* (see FN 19, above) in *The Outlook in Politics, Life, Letters and the Arts* 1, 14 (May 7, 1898): 436.

156. Charles Townshend, *Desert Hell: The British Invasion of Mesopotamia* (Cambridge, MA: Harvard University Press, 2011), 144.

157. Townshend, *Desert Hell*, 157–191.

158. Thanks to Jean Allman for encouraging me to raise this question.

159. See Ashwini Tambe, *Codes of Misconduct: Regulating Prostitution in Late Colonial Bombay* (Minneapolis: University of Minnesota Press, 2009) and Tambe and Harald Fischer-Tiné, eds., *The Limits of British Colonial Control in South Asia: Spaces of Disorder in the Indian Ocean Region* (New York: Routledge, 2009).

160. Churchill, *Malakand*, 9. See James C. Scott, *The Art of Not Being Governed: An Anarchist History of Upland Southeast Asia* (New Haven, CT: Yale University Press, 2009).

161. I am grateful to Dane Kennedy for helping me develop this point.

162. Elliott Evans Mills, *The Decline and Fall of the British Empire: A Brief Account of the Causes which Resulted in the Destruction of our Late Ally, Together with a Comparison between the British and Roman Empires; Appointed for Use in the National Schools of Japan* (Bocario Press, 1905), 48, 22, 2.

163. See John Darwin, *Unfinished Empire: The Global Expansion of Britain* (Bloomsbury, 2012), chap. 5, "Resorting to War," esp. 134–36.

164. See Elaine Freedgood, *Victorian Writing about Risk: Imagining a Safe England in a Dangerous World* (Cambridge: Cambridge University Press, 2000).

165. Speech delivered to the Manchester Free Trade League, 1904, quoted in Frank Trentmann, *Free Trade Nation: Commerce, Consumption and Civil Society in Modern Britain* (Oxford: Oxford University Press, 2008) 134.

Chapter 2

1. P. J. Cain and A. J. Hopkins, "Gentlemanly Capitalism and British Expansion Overseas I: The Old Colonial System, 1688-1850," *Economic History Review*, New Series 39, 4 (1986): 521.

2. T. H. Breen, *The Marketplace of Revolution: How Consumer Politics Shaped American Independence* (New York: Oxford University Press, 2005), 20.

3. William Fox, *An Address to the People of Great Britain On the Propriety of Abstaining from West India Sugar and Rum,* 10th ed. (London, Printer, Philadelphia: Daniel Lawrence, 1792), 4.

4. Fox, *Address*, 4.

5. *An Address Intended to have been delivered at a meeting of the inhabitants of Ipswich, on Friday, February 17th, for the purpose of Considering the Propriety of Petitioning Parliament for an abolition of the Slave Trade* (Printed by G. Jermyn, Bookseller, 1792) http://gallery.nen.gov.uk/gallery1318-abolition.html.

6. Clare Midgley, *Women against Slavery: The British Campaigns 1780-1870* (London: Routledge, 1994), 35, 83.

7. For an example of the racism of "white sugar" economic activity in twentieth-century Australia, see Stefanie Affeldt, "'White Sugar' against 'Yellow Peril': Consuming for National Identity and Racial Purity," http://www.academia.edu/648968/_White_Sugar_Against_Yellow_Peril_Consuming_for_National_Identity_and_Racial_Purity. Accessed April 15, 2015.

8. Louis E. Wilson, "The 'Bloodless Conquest' in Southeastern Ghana: The Huza and Territorial Expansion of the Krobo in the 19th Century,"

International Journal of African Historical Studies 23, 2 (1990): 276; and Freda Wolfson, "A Price Agreement on the Gold Coast: The Krobo Oil Boycott, 1858-1866," *Economic History Review*, New Series 6, 1 (1953): 70.

9. Wolfson, "Price Agreement," 72. For a more detailed account of the boycott with some minor corrections to Wolfson's history, see Louis E. Wilson, *The Krobo People of Ghana to 1892: A Political and Social History* (Athens: Ohio University Press, 1991).

10. John Miles, "Rival Protest in the Gold Coast: The Cocoa Hold-ups, 1908-38," in *The Imperial Impact: Studies in the Economic History of India and Africa*, ed. Clive Dewey and A. G. Hopkins (London: Althone Press, 1978), 160.

11. R. F. Foster, *Modern Ireland 1600-1972* (London: Allen Lane, 1990), 406.

12. Maggie Land Blanck, "Captain Boycott," http://maggieblanck.com/Mayopages/Boycott.html. Accessed May 16, 2015.

13. Foster, *Modern* Ireland, 406. See also Janet McL. Côté, *Fanny and Anna Parnell: Ireland's Patriot Sisters* (London: Macmillan, 1991), 151–52.

14. Charles C. Boycott, "The State of Ireland," *Times* (London), October 18, 1880, 6. Times Digital Archive, June 3, 2014.

15. Janet K. TeBrake, "Irish Peasant Women in Revolt: The Land League Years," *Irish Historical Studies* 28, 109 (1992): 77.

16. Jonathan Bardon, *A History of Ireland in 250 Episodes: A Sweeping Single Narrative of Irish History from the End of the Ice Age to the Peace Settlement in Northern Ireland* (Dublin: Gill and Macmillan, 2008), episode 197.

17. Frank Welsh, *A History of Hong Kong* (New York: Harper Collins, 1993), 371–73.

18. See Welsh, *History of Hong Kong*, 371.

19. Steven Tsang, *A Modern History of Hong Kong* (I. B. Taurus, 2004), 95.

20. Sources of resentment included the 1882 Chinese Exclusion Act and the 1894 American Exclusion Treaty. See Jung-Fan Tsai, *Hong Kong in Chinese History: Community and Social Unrest in the British Colony, 1842-1913* (New York: Columbia University Press, 1993), 182–83. Thanks to Poshek Fu for this reference.

21. Tsai, *Hong King*, 196.

22. Tsai, *Hong Kong*, 90. Tsai identifies this as the "triangular relationship between government, elite and populace."

23. Tsai, *Hong Kong*, 230, 233.

24. Nikki R. Keddie, *Modern Iran: Roots of Revolution* (New Haven, CT: Yale, 2003), 61–62. Thanks to Behrooz Ghamari for pointing me toward this incident.

25. Nancy Y. Reynolds, *City Consumed: Urban Commerce, the Cairo Fire, and the Politics of Decolonization in Egypt* (Redwood City, CA: Stanford University Press, 2012), 79.

26. Sumit Sarkar, *The Swadeshi Movement in Bengal, 1903-1908* (Bombay: People's Publishing House, 1973), 95 and 96–97.

27. Sarkar, *Swadeshi*, 109, 119.

28. Sarkar, *Swadeshi*, 146.

29. Dilip M. Menon, "The Many Spaces and Times of Swadeshi," *Economic and Political Weekly* 47, 42 (2012,), 51.

30. Valentine Chirol, *Indian Unrest* (Light and Life Publishers, 1979), 88.

31. Mohandas K. Gandhi, *Mahatma Gandhi: Essays and Reflections on His Life and Work*, ed. S. Radhakrishnan (Bombay: Jaico Publishing House, 1956). 455, "The Trial Speech." In this speech from 1922, Gandhi said, "Before the British advent, India spun and wove, in her millions of cottages, just the supplement she needed for adding to her meager agricultural resources, This cottage industry, so vital for India's existence, has been ruined by incredibly heartless and inhuman processes."

32. See Lisa Trivedi, *Clothing Gandhi's Nation: Homespun and Modern India* (Bloomington: Indiana University Press, 2007), chap. 1. Discussions of clothing and nation in Egypt at this time were as intense but on occasion, a little more irreverent. See Wilson Chacko Jacob, *Working out Egypt: Effendi Masculinity and Subject Formation in Colonial Modernity, 1870-1940* (Durham NC: Duke University Press, 2011), chap. 7.

33. Trivedi, *Clothing*, 128, 133. Trivedi notes, "The Gandhi topi taught non-cooperators the ease with which they could transform their bodies from sites marked by colonial rule to sites that threatened the imperial habitus.

34. Quoted in Suruchi Thapar-Bjökert, *Women in the Indian National Movement: Unseen Faces and Unheard Voices, 1930-42* (New Delhi: Sage, 2006), 108.

35. Trivedi, *Clothing*, 144–45.

36. Trivedi, *Clothing*, 146.

37. Michele Micheletti, *Political Virtue and Shopping: Individuals, Consumerism and Collective Action* (New York: Palgrave, 2003).

38. Reynolds, *City Consumed*, 84–85.

39. Reynolds, *City Consumed*, 84–85.

40. William Beinart and Colin Bundy, "The Union, the Nation and the Talking Crow: The Ideology and Tactics of the Independent ICU in East London," in Beinart and Bundy, eds., *Hidden Struggles in Rural South Africa: Politics and Popular Movements in the Transkei and Eastern Cape*, 1890-1930 (London: James Currey, 1987), 292.

41. Thanks to Aziz Rana for this latter insight. See his *The Two Faces of American Freedom* (Cambridge, MA: Harvard University Press, 2010), 23.

42. A.A. Boahen, ed, *General History of Africa*, vol. 7 [Africa Under Colonial Domination, 1880-1935] (UNESCO/ James Currey, 1990).

43. Audrey Wipper, *Rural Rebels: A Study of Two Protest Movements in Kenya* (Oxford University Press, 1977), 45–51.

44. Cynthia Brantley, "Mekatalili and the Role of Women in Giriama Resistance," in Donald Crummey, ed., *Banditry, Rebellion and Social Protest in Africa* (London: James Currey, 1986), 343.

45. Cynthia Brantley, *The Giriama and Colonial Resistance in Kenya, 1800-1920* (Berkeley: University of California Press, 1981), 86–88.

46. Quoted in Leigh Brownmiller and Terisa E. Turner, "Subsistence Trade versus World Trade: Gendered Class Struggle in Kenya, 1992-2002," *Canadian Woman Studies* 21/22, 4/1 (2002): 171. See also Leigh Brownmiller, *Land, Food, Freedom: Struggles for the Gendered Commons in Kenya, 1870-2007* (Africa World Press, 2009), 55–60.

47. Letter by Julius Nyerere to the editor of *Africa South*, October-December 1959: http://www.anc.org.za/show.php?id= 6901&t=Boycotts. Accessed May 16, 2015. Earlier that year, Nyerere had helped to launch the Boycott South Africa Movement (renamed the Anti-Apartheid Movement in 1960).

48. See, for example, Tracy Carson, "'There's More to It Than Slurp and Burp': The Fatti's and Moni's Strike and the Use of Boycotts in Mass Resistance in Cape Town," in William Beinart and Marcelle

C. Dawson, eds., *Popular Politics and Resistance Movements in South Africa* (Johannesburg: Wits University Press, 2010), 52–75.

49. Quoted in Peter Fryer, *Staying Power: The History of Black People in Britain* (London: Pluto Press, 1984), 310.

50. Jacqueline Jenkinson, *Black 1919: Riots, Racism and Resistance in Imperial Britain* (Liverpool: Liverpool University Press, 2009), 7.

51. Jenkinson, *Black 1919*, 8.

52. K. L. Tuteja, "Jallianwala Bagh: A Critical Juncture in the Indian National Movement," *Social Scientist* 25, 1/2 (1997): 39.

53. Tuteja, "Jallianwala Bagh," 39.

54. Jennifer Burtner and Quetzil E. Casteneda, "Tourism as 'A Force for World Peace': The Politics of Tourism, Tourism as Governmentality, and the Tourism Boycott of Guatemala," *Journal of Tourism and Peace Research* 1, 2 (2010): 1–21.

55. David Hardiman calls it a "Forgotten Massacre: Motilal Tejawat and His Movement among the Bhils 1921-22," in his *Histories for the Subordinated* (Calcutta: Seagull, 2007), 29–58. Gandhi distanced himself from the movement, fearing its "resort to arms." (35–36).

56. Chitra Joshi, *Lost Worlds: Indian Labour and Its Forgotten Histories* (New Delhi: Permanent Black, 2003), 179, 180.

57. In at least one sense, Kanpur was distinctive for the size of its industrial workforce and the concentration of laborers in big mills (as opposed to the scalar range of workplaces in other Indian cities). See Nandini Gooptu, *The Politics of the Urban Poor in Early Twentieth-Century India* (Cambridge, 2005), 48–49.

58. Joshi, *Lost Worlds*, 185, 196–97.

59. Joshi, *Lost Worlds*, 197.

60. They got raises of between 15 percent and 30 percent as opposed to the 17 percent to 35 percent they struck for, but they did secure a lift on the ban of the Seamen's Union. See Steve Tsang, *A Modern History of Hong Kong* (I. B. Tauris, 2004), 88–89.

61. Charles Van Onselen, *Chibaro: African Mine Labor in South Rhodesia, 1900-1933* (London: Pluto Press, 1976), 219–20.

62. Sophie Loy-Wilson, "'Liberating' Asia: Strikes and Protest in Sydney and Shanghai, 1920-1939," *History Workshop Journal* 72 (2011): 79.

63. Beinart and Bundy, "The Union," 271.

64. Beinart and Bundy, "The Union," 271–72, 274, 290.

65. Beinart and Bundy, "The Union," 297.

66. Beinart and Bundy, "The Union," 296.

67. George Padmore, *The Life and Struggles of Negro Toilers* (London: International Trade Union Committee of Negro Workers, 1931), 81.

68. Van Onselen, *Chibaro,* 209–10.

69. For the challenges he faced negotiating Garveyite and Communist factions in the ICU see George M. Frederickson, *Black Liberation: A Comparative History of Black Ideologies in the United States and South Africa* (New York: Oxford University Press, 1996) .p. 170.

70. See Helen Bradford, "Lynch Law and Laborers: The ICU in Umvoti; 1927-1928," in William Beinart, Peter Delius and Stanley Trapido, eds., *Putting a Plough to the Ground: Accumulation and Dispossession in Rural Southern Africa 1850-1930* (Ravan Press, 1986), 430.

71. Bradford, "Lynch Law," 430.

72. Cherryl Walker, *Women and Resistance in South Africa* (London: Onyx Press, 1982), 65.

73. Walker, *Women and Resistance*, 41.

74. Beinart and Bundy, "The Union," 304–5.

75. I take seriously the call to resist collapsing anticolonial and national intentions and even ascribing nationalist consciousness too liberally—that is to say, without properly historicizing. For a similar caution, see Wenzel, *Bulletproof*, 80–81.

76. Beinart and Bundy, "The Union," 273; see also Bradford, "Lynch Law," 420–28.

77. Beinart and Bundy, "The Union," 293, 292.

78. Janaki Nair, "Representing Labour in Old Mysore: Kolar Gold Fields Strike of 1930," *Economic and Political Weekly* 25, 30 (1990): PE73–86.

79. John Newsinger, *Rebel City: Larkin, Connolly and the Dublin Labour Movement* (London: Merlin, 2004) 120.

80. Rob Turrell, "The 1875 Black Flag Revolt on the Kimberley Diamond Fields," *Journal of Southern African Studies* 7, 2 (1981): 194–235; and I.

B. Sutton, "The Diggers' Revolt in Griqualand West, 1875," *International Journal of African Historical Studies* 12, 1 (1979): 40.

81. Stuart Svensen, *The Shearers' War: The Story of the 1891 Shearers' Strike* (St. Lucia: University of Queensland Press, 1989), 4–34.

82. Svensen, *Shearers' War*. 33–34.

83. Svensen, *Shearers' War*, 131.

84. Svensen, *Shearer's War*, 183, 171. Lawson referred to the protests against the miners' licenses/taxes on gold miners at the Eureka Stockade at Ballarat in 1854. See Donald Denoon and Philippa Mein-Smith, *A History of Australia, New Zealand and the Pacific*, with Marivic Wyndham (London: Blackwell, 2000), 145.

85. Svensen, *Shearers' War*, 186–87.

86. Erik Olssen, *The Red Feds: Revolutionary Industrial Unionism and the New Zealand Federation of Labour, 1908-14* (Auckland, NZ: Oxford University Press, 1988), 1–15.

87. Newsinger, *Rebel City*, 15.

88. Frances Steele, *Oceania under Steam: Sea Transport and the Cultures of Colonialism, c.1870-1914* (Manchester: Manchester University Press, 2011), esp. 100–105.

89. Steele, *Oceania*, 196.

90. Deep Kanta Lahiri Choudhury, "India's First Virtual Community and the Telegraph General Strike of 1908," *International Review of Social History* 48, Supplement S11 (2003): 45–71.

91. Choudhury, "India's First," 67.

92. Choudhury, "India's First," 68.

93. "Socializm bez pochty, telegrafa [. . .]—pusteishaya fraza." (Vladimir Il'ich Lenin, *Sochineniya*, vol. 27, 278). Marx is quoted in John Tully, *The Devil's Milk: A Social History of Rubber* (New York: Monthly Review Press, 2011), 123.

94. V. B. Karnik, *Strikes in India* (Bombay: Manaktalas, 1967) 3.

95. Karnik, *Strikes*, 5,7 and 6, 7.

96. Valerian DeSousa, "Strategies of Control: The Case of British India," *Sociological Viewpoints*, 24 (2008): 72. For pay withholding, see Gooptu, *Politics of the Urban Poor*, 55.

97. Karnik, *Strikes*, 12, 41; the Pal quote is from *Bande Mataram*.

98. Jan Breman, "The Study of Industrial Labour in Post-colonial India: The Formal Sector: An Introductory Review," in Jonathan Parry, Jan Breman, Karin Kapadia, eds., *The Worlds of Indian Industrial Labor* (London: Sage 1999), 8.

99. Keletso E. Atkins, *The Moon Is Dead! Give Us Our Money! The Cultural Origins of an African Work Ethic, Natal, South Africa, 1843-1900* (London: Heinemann, 1993), 142.

100. Georges Kristoffel Lieten, *Colonialism, Class, and Nation: The Confrontation in Bombay around 1930* (Calcutta: K. P. Bagchi, 1984), 62, 69.

101. Visakha Kumari Jayawardena, *The Rise of the Labor Movement in Ceylon* (Durham, NC: Duke University Press, 1972), 95.

102. Jayawardena, *Rise*, 122.

103. Jayawardena, *Rise*, 125, 126.

104. Rajnarayan Chandavarkar, *Imperial Power and Popular Politics: Class, Resistance and the State in India, 1850-1950* (Cambridge: Cambridge University Press, 1998), 154.

105. Chandvarkar, *Imperial Power*, 218.

106. B. W. Higman, *Plantation Jamaica, 1750-1850: Capital and Control in a Colonial Economy* (Kingston: University of the West Indies Press, 2005), 197.

107. Maurice St. Pierre, *Anatomy of Resistance: Anti-Colonialism in Guyana, 1823-1966* (Macmillan, 1999), 15–17.

108. Catherine Hall states unequivocally that "the rebellion and its aftermath played a crucial part in the recognition in Britain that slavery could not survive as a system." Catherine Hall, *Civilizing Subjects Colony and Metropole in the English Imagination 1830-1867* (Chicago: University of Chicago Press, 2002), 106.

109. Thomas Holt, *The Problem of Freedom: Race, Labor, and Politics in Jamaica and Britain, 1832-1938* (Baltimore, MD: Johns Hopkins University Press, 1992), 117, 116.

110. John Dryden, "Pas de Six Ans!," in Anthony de Verteuil, ed., *Seven Slaves and Slavery: Trinidad 1777–1838* (Port of Spain, 1992), 371–79.

111. Higman, *Plantation Jamaica*, 236, 240.

112. Walton Look Lai, *Indentured Labor, Caribbean Sugar: Chinese and Indian migrants to the British West Indies, 1838-1918* (Baltimore, MD: Johns Hopkins University Press, 1993), 11.

113. Look Lai, *Indentured Labor*, 101.

114. I borrow this term from David R. Roediger and Elizabeth D. Esch, *The Production of Difference: Race and the Management of Labor in US History* (Oxford University Press, 2012), chap. 5 (where they use it to refer to the shop floor). See also Daniel Nelson, *Managers and Workers: Origins of the Twentieth-Century Factory System in the United States, 1880–1920* (Madison: University of Wisconsin Press, 1996), chap. 3, "The Foreman's Empire."

115. Clem Seecharan, *Bechu: 'Bound Coolie' Radical in British Guiana 1894-1901* (Kingston: University of the West Indies Press, 1999), 8.

116. Look Lai, *Indentured Labor*, 145–46.

117. Frank J. Korom, *Hosay Trinidad: Muharram Performances in an Indo-Caribbean Diaspora* (Philadelphia: University of Pennsylvania Press, 2003), 97, 101.

118. Korom, *Hosay*, 116.

119. Madhavi Kale, *Fragments of Empire: Capital, Slavery, and Indian Indentured Labor in the British Caribbean* (Philadelphia: University of Pennsylvania Press, 1998), 152.

120. Asef Bayat, "Un-Civil Society: The Politics of the 'Informal People,'" *Third World Quarterly* 18,1 (1997): 56. By this he means the way that admittedly "disenfranchised groups place a great deal of restraint upon the privileges of the dominant groups, allocating segments of their life chances (including capital, social goods, opportunity, autonomy, and thus, power) to themselves. This tends to involve them in a *collective*, open and highly audible campaign," like a strike, though it also has its "quiet" expressions that are different in degree and kind from mere "survival strategies" (57).

121. Adrian Graves, *Cane and Labour: The Political Economy of the Queensland Sugar Industry, 1862-1906* (Edinburgh: Edinburgh University Press, 1993), 196–97.

122. Graves, *Cane and Labour*, 197–98.

123. I am aided in this observation by the work of Thavolia Glymph in particular. See her *Out of the House of Bondage: The Transformation of the*

Plantation Household (Cambridge: Cambridge University Press, 2008), esp. chap. 3.

124. Michael Adas, "From Foot-Dragging to Flight: The Evasive Histories of Peasant Avoidance Protest in South and South-East Asia," *Journal of Peasant Studies* 13, 2 (1986): 71; Samita Sen, "At the Margins: Women Workers in the Bengal Jute Industry," in Parry, Breman, and Kapadia, *Worlds of Indian Industrial Labor*, 255.

125. Kay Saunders, *Workers in Bondage: The Origins and Bases of Unfree Labour in Queensland, 1824-1916* (Brisbane: University of Queensland Press, 1982), 127.

126. Tracey Banivanua Mar, *Violence and Colonial Dialogue: The Australian-Pacific Indentured Labor Trade* (University of Hawaii Press, 2007), 121.

127. See Ravi Ahuja, "Mobility and Containment: The Voyages of South Asian Seamen, *c*.1900–1960," *International Review of Social History* 51, Supplement S14 (2006), 120–21; Kaushik Ghosh, "A Market for Aboriginality: Primitivism and Race Classification in the Indentured Labour Market of Colonial India," in Gautam Bhadra, Gyan Prakash, and Susie Tharu, eds., *Subaltern Studies X. Writings on South Asian History and Society* (New Delhi, 1999), 8–48; and Roediger and Esch, *The Production of Difference*.

128. Ahuja, "Mobility and Containment," 120.

129. I draw here from Rebecca Ginsburg, "Freedom and the Slave Landscape," *Landscape Journal* 26, 1 (2007): 26–44.

130. Ramaswamy, "Labour Control and Labour Resistance in the Plantations of Colonial Malaya," in E. Valentine Daniel, Henry Bernstein and Tom Brass, eds., *Plantations, Proletarians and Peasants in Colonial Asia* (London: Frank Cass, 1992), 87–105.

131. Graves, *Cane and Labour*, 198 and 200. Graves argues that their absconding was "primarily a resistance of pre-capitalist producers to the unbearable stresses of colonial labor" (200).

132. Michael Adas, "From Foot-dragging to Flight: The Evasive Histories of Peasant Avoidance Protest in South and South-East Asia," *Journal of Peasant Studies* 13, 2 (1986): 64–86.

133. Jayeeta Sharma, "'Lazy' Natives, Coolie Labour, and the Assam Tea Industry," *Modern Asian Studies* 43, 6 (2009): 1291–93.

134. Brij V. Lal, "Kunti's Cry: Indentured Women on Fiji Plantations," *Indian Economic Social History Review* 22, 1 (1985): 64.

135. Graves, *Cane and Labour*, 202; Adas, "From Foot-Dragging to Flight."

136. Claire C. Robertson, *Trouble Showed the Way: Women, Men and Trade in the Nairobi Area, 1890-1990* (Bloomington: Indiana University Press, 1997), 92.

137. Philippa Levine, *Prostitution, Race and Politics: Policing Venereal Disease in the British Empire* (London: Routledge, 2003), 103–4.

138. Thanks to Asef Bayat for asking me to hone this point.

139. Robertson, *Trouble Showed the Way* 93–101. See Marina Carter, *Lakshmi's Legacy: The Testimonies of Indian Women in 19th Century Mauritius* (Editions de l'Ocean Indien, 1994), 149; for Guyana see Gauitra Bahadur, *Coolie Woman: The Odyssey of Indenture* (Chicago: University of Chicago Press, 2013), 32. Teresa Barnes puts it best when she says that "by the 1930s rural patriarchs were angry precisely because in difficult and shifting economic sands, women's labor was absolutely crucial to the survival of men's socio-economic status" and that therefore "it was of prime importance to re-impose control over women." Teresa A. Barnes, *"We Women Worked So Hard: Gender, Urbanization and Social Reproduction in Colonial Harare, Zimbabwe, 1930-1956* (London: Heinemann, 1999), xxxii, 50. See also Luise White, *The Comforts of Home: Prostitution in Colonial Nairobi* (Chicago: University of Chicago Press, 1990), 1–2; Sen, "At the Margins," 254; Ashwini Tambe, *Codes of Misconduct.*

140. Carolyn Clark, "Land and Food, Women and Power, in Nineteenth Century Kikuyu," *Africa* 50, 4 (1980), 367.

141. Luise White, *The Comforts of Home: Prostitution in Colonial Nairobi* (Chicago: University of Chicago Press, 1990), 221.

142. Jean Allman and Victoria Tashjian, *"I Will Not Eat Stone": A Women's History of Colonial Asante* (London: Heinemann, 2000), esp. 141.

143. Julia C. Wells, "The War of Degradation: Black Women's Struggle against Orange Free State Pass Laws, 1913," in Donald E. Crummey, ed., *Banditry, Rebellion and Social Protest in Africa* (London: James Currey, 1986), 258.

144. Cora Presley, cited in Robertson, *Trouble Showed the Way,* 64.

145. Pramod Kumar Srivastava, "Resistance and Repression in India: The Hunger Strike at the Andaman Cellular Jail in 1933," *Crime, History and Societies* 7, 2 (2003): 2–19.

146. Kevin Grant, "The Transcolonial World of Hunger Strikes and Political Fasts, c.1909-1935," in Durba Ghosh and Dane Kennedy, eds., *Decentring Empire: Britain, India, and the Transcolonial World* (New Delhi: Orient Longman, 2006), 243–69.

147. Joseph Lennon, "Fasting for the Public: Irish and Indian Sources of Marion Wallace Dunlop's 1909 Hunger Strike," in Eóin Flannery and Angus Mitchell, eds., *Enemies of Empire: New Perspectives on Imperialism, Literature and Historiography* (Dublin: Four Courts Press, 2007), 19–39.

148. Lennon, "Fasting for the Public." See also Howard Spodek, "On the Origins of Gandhi's Political Methodology: The Heritage of Kathiawad and Gujarat," *Journal of Asian Studies* 30, 2 (1971): 363.

149. Keith Breckenridge, *The Biometric State: The Global Politics of Identification and Surveillance in South Africa, 1850-Present* (Cambridge: Cambridge University Press, 2014), 90–114.

150. David Hardiman, *Gandhi in His Time and Ours: The Global Legacy of His Ideas* (New York: Columbia University Press, 2004), 39–65.

151. James Vernon, *Hunger: A Modern History* (Cambridge, MA: Harvard University Press, 2007), chap. 3, esp. 69.

152. Cain and Hopkins, "Gentlemanly Capitalism," 11–12.

153. Beinart, Delius, and Trapido, *Putting the Plough*, 1, 75; G. Roger Knight, "Sugar and Servility: Themes of Forced Labour, Resistance and Accommodation in mid-Nineteenth Century Java," in Edward A. Alpers, Gwyn Campbell and Michael Salman, eds., *Resisting Bondage in Indian Ocean Africa and Asia* (London: Routledge, 2007), 75.

154. Thanks to Nils Jacobson and David Roediger for helping me to appreciate this point.

155. I borrow here from Dilip Simeon, "Work and Resistance in the Jharia Coalfield," in Parry, Breman, and Kapadia, *Indian Industrial Labor*, 67.

156. Atkins, *Moon Is Dead!*, 107.

157. Ranajit Guha, *Elementary Aspects of Peasant Insurgency in Colonial India* (Delhi: Oxford University Press, 1983). What's more, the

consolidation of communal identities might be as significant a result, if not more so, than anti-imperial ones. See Dipesh Chakrabarty, "Communal Riots and Labour: Bengal's Jute Mill-Hands in the 1890s," *Past and Present* 91, 1 (1981): 140–69.

158. On mill ownership, see Chandavarkar, *Imperial Power and Popular Politics: Class, Resistance and the State* (Cambridge: Cambridge University Press, 1998), 100–142; on Asian ship capital, see Jonathan Hyslop, "Steamship Empire: Asian, African and British Sailors in the Merchant Marine, c.1880-1945," *Journal of Asian and African Studies* 44, 1 (2009): 53; and on public trusts, see Ritu Birla, *Stages of Capital: Law, Culture and Market Governance in late-Colonial India* (Durham, NC: Duke University Press, 2009).

159. See Eiichiro Azuma, *Between Two Empires: Race, History, and Transnationalism in Japanese America* (Oxford University Press, 2005) esp. 65 for the 1913 California Alien Land Law; Harvey Feinberg, "The 1913 Natives Land Act in South Africa: Politics, Race and Segregation in the early 20th Century," *International Journal of African Historical Studies* 26, 1 (1993): 65–109; Maureen Swan, "The 1913 Natal Strike," *Journal of Southern African Studies* 10, 2 (1984): 239–58; Gregory Kealey and Bryan Palmer, *Dreaming of What Might Be: The Knights of Labor in Ontario, 1880-1900* (Cambridge: Cambridge University Press, 1982). For some transnational takes, see Peter J. Coleman, *Progressivism and the World of Reform: New Zealand and the Origins of the American Welfare State* (University of Kansas Press, 1987); Daniel T. Rodgers, *Atlantic Crossings: Social Politics in a Progressive Age* (Cambridge, MA: Harvard University Press, 1998).

160. Joel Benin and Zachary Lockman, *Workers on the Nile: Nationalism, Communism, Islam and the Egyptian Working Class, 1882-1954* (Princeton, NJ: Princeton University Press, 1987), 51–52.

161. Chandavarkar, *Imperial* Power, 7–9, 259.

162. Van Onselen, *Chibaro*, 226. Or, as Jamie Belich it put it with respect the comparative military strength of the Maori against the British, "It is the relative effectiveness of Maori resistance that is the interesting question." Belich, "The Victorian Interpretation of Racial Conflict and the New Zealand Wars: An Approach to the Problem of One-sided Evidence," *Journal of Imperial and Commonwealth History* 15, 2 (1987): 125.

Chapter 3

1. See William H. Sewell, Jr., *Logics of History: Social Theory and Social Transformation* (Chicago: University of Chicago Press, 2005).

2. See Richard Gott, *Britain's Empire: Resistance, Repression and Revolt* (London: Verso, 2012).

3. Dadhabhai Naoroji listed this quote at the front of his book as one of "Britain's Solemn Pledges," *Poverty and Un-British Rule in India* (Swan Sonnenschein, 1901), v.

4. Blair Kling, *The Blue Mutiny: The Indigo Disturbances in Bengal 1859-1862* (Philadelphia: University of Pennsylvania Press, 1966), 125.

5. Kling, *Blue Mutiny.* See also Subhas Bhattacharya, "The Indigo Revolt of Bengal," *Social Scientist* 5, 12 (1977): 13.

6. Geoffrey Oddie, *Missionaries, Rebellion and Proto-Nationalism: James Long of Bengal*, (Surrey: Curzon Press, 1999), 110.

7. Bhattacharya,14–15.

8. Bhattacharya, "Indigo Revolt," 16–17, 15.

9. Kling, *Blue Mutiny*, 109–10.

10. Oddie, *Missionaries*, 112.

11. Kling, *Blue Mutiny*, 198.

12. Sisir Kar, *Bengali Books Proscribed under the Raj*, translated by Sumanta Banerjee (New Delhi: Samskriti, 2009), 317, 319.

13. Buckland, *Bengal under the Lieutenant Governors* (Calcutta: K. Bose, 1902), 192.

14. Kling, *Blue Mutiny*, 201.

15. Bhattacharya, "Indigo Revolt," 13–18.

16. Marina Carter and Crispin Bates, "Empire and Locality: A Global Dimension to the 1857 Indian Uprising," *Journal of Global History* 5, 1 (2010): 52–53.

17. Gad Heuman, *"The Killing Time": The Morant Bay Rebellion in Jamaica* (Knoxville: University of Tennessee Press, 1995),

18. Heuman, *Killing Time*, 3.

19. Heuman, *Killing Time*, 3–24.

20. Catherine Hall, *Civilising Subjects: Colony and Metropole in the English Imagination 1830-1867* (Chicago: University of Chicago Press, 2002), 54–55.

21. Newsinger, *Blood Never Dried,* 31.

22. Heuman, *Killing Time,* 121.

23. By the same token, as Isaac Land has argued, counterinsurgency on the part of British imperial officials was counter-revolution by any other name. See the introduction to his edited collection, *Enemies of Humanity: The Nineteenth Century War on Terror* (Palgrave Macmillan, 2008), 1–19. For a careful use of the ascription of terror in the Irish case, see also Amy E. Martin, *Alter-Nations: Nationalisms, Terror and the State in Nineteenth Century Britain and Ireland* (Columbus: Ohio State University Press), 2012.

24. One eye-witness reported that black troops shot people on the road to Manchioneal in the context of martial law. See Mimi Sheller, *Citizenship from Below: Erotic Agency and Caribbean Freedom* (Durham, NC: Duke University Press, 2012), 122.

25. Heuman, *Killing Time*, 98.

26. Heuman, *Killing Time*, 59.

27. Bridget Brereton, *Law, Justice and Empire: The Colonial Career of John Gorrie, 1829-92* (Kingston: University Press of the West Indies, 1997), 51.

28. Hall, *Civilising Subjects*, 406.

29. Robert J. Stewart, "Reporting Morant Bay: The 1865 Jamaican Insurrection as reported and interpreted in the *New York Herald, Daily Tribune and Times*," in Brian L. Moore and Swithin Wilmot, eds., *Before and After 1865: Education, Politics and Regionalism in the Caribbean* (Kingston: Ian Randle Publishers, 1998), 333–34.

30. Heuman, *Killing Time*, 59–60.

31. Heuman, *Killing Time*, 59–60, 45–46.

32. Heuman, *Killing Time*, 89.

33. Sheller, *Citizenship from Below*, 123.

34. Heuman, *Killing Time*, 95.

35. Heuman, *Killing Time*, xix.

36. Oddie, *Missionaries, Rebellion*, 109.

37. T. W. Moody, *Davitt and Irish Revolution, 1846-82* (Oxford: Clarendon, 1981), 34.

38. Moody, *Davitt*, 36.

39. Some scholars have suggested it even echoed the historicist approach laid out in *England and Ireland*, John Stuart Mill's classic case for such claims; Moody, *Davitt*, 37–38.

40. Anne Kane, *Constructing Irish National Identity: Discourse and Ritual during the Land War, 1879-82* (London: Palgrave Macmillan, 2014), 95.

41. J. O'Connor Power, "The Irish Land Agitation," *Nineteenth Century* 6 (December 1879): 954.

42. TeBrake, "Irish Peasant Women in Revolt," 68.

43. See Brian Jenkins, *The Fenian Problem: Insurgency and Terrorism in a Liberal State, 1858-1874* (Montreal: McGill-Queen's University Press, 2008), 7–9.

44. Anne Kane, *Constructing Irish National Identity: Discourse and Ritual during the Land War, 1879-82* (New York: Palgrave MacMillan, 2011), 1–2.

45. O'Connor Power, "Irish Land Agitation," p. 954.

46. Jenkins, *Fenian Problem*, 331.

47. John Darwin, "Imperialism and the Victorians: The Dynamics of Territorial Expansion," *English Historical Review* 112, 447 (1997): 614–42.

48. See Juan Cole, *Colonialism and Revolution in the Middle East: Social and Cultural Origins of Egypt's 'Urabi Movement* (Princeton, NJ: Princeton University Press, 1993).

49. Cole, *Colonialism and Revolution*, 271.

50. Barbara Harlow and Mia Carter, eds., *Imperialism and Orientalism: A Documentary Sourcebook* (Oxford: Blackwell, 1999), 138.

51. "Thin jurisdictional line" is an echo of Lauren Benton's "jurisdictional net." See *A Search for Sovereignty: Law and Geography in European Empires, 1400-1900* (Cambridge University Press, 2010), 101.

52. Harlow and Carter, eds., *Imperialism and Orientalism*, 139. In fact, Urabi was an obstacle to Cromer's mission: to lead the Egyptians from

bankruptcy to solvency, from solvency to affluence, and from there to British justice. See Thornton, *Imperial Idea*, 79.

53. Alice Moore-Harell, *Egypt's African Empire: Samuel Baker, Charles Gordon and the Creation of Equatoria* (Eastbourne: Sussex Academic Press, 2010), chap. 5.

54. David Robinson, *Muslim Societies in African History* (Cambridge, 2004), 175.

55. "Gordon's Dream: The Martyr Hero of Khartoum," *The Graphic* (Christmas Number, 1887), reproduced in Harlow and Carter, eds., *Archives of Empire*, vol 2,, *The Scramble for Africa* (Durham, NC: Duke University Press, 2003), 624–25. See also Janice Boddy, *Civilizing Women: British Crusades in Colonial Sudan* (Princeton, NJ: Princeton University Press, 2007).

56. P. M. Holt, *The Mahdist State in the Sudan, 1881-1898: A Study of its Origins, Development and Overthrow* (Oxford: Clarendon Press, 1970; originally published in 1898), 224–25.

57. Henry S. L. Alford and W. Dennistoun Sword, *The Egyptian Soudan: Its Loss and Recovery* (Negro Universities Press, 1969; originally published 1898), 291.

58. Though Gladstone did survive censure, by fourteen votes; Dominic Green, *Three Empires on the Nile: The Victorian Jihad, 1869-1899* (New York: Free Press, 2007), 202.

59. Robinson, *Muslim Societies*, 169–70.

60. Lytton Strachey, *Eminent Victorians* (New York: The Modern Library, 1918), 339.

61. Green, *Three Empires*, 199, 205.

62. Green, *Three Empires*, 215.

63. Green, *Three Empires*, 210.

64. Hasan 'Ismat Zilfu, *Karari: The Sudanese Account of the Battle of Omdurman* (London: F. Warne, 1980), 198–99.

65. Gabriel Warburg, *The Sudan under Wingate: Administration in the Anglo-Egyptian Sudan, 1899-1916* (London: Frank Cass, 1971). p. 6.

66. Hassan Ahmed Ibrahim, "Mahdist Risings against the Condominium Government in the Sudan, 1900-1927," *International Journal of African Historical Studies* 12, 3 (1979): 440. Ibrahim calls this

phenomenon "neo-Mahdism." According to Robinson, Sudanese called the Condominium "the Second Turkiyya." (*Muslim Societies*, 179.)

67. Ibrahim, "Madhist Risings," 448.

68. Ibrahmim, "Madhist Risings," 451.

69. Heather J. Sharkey, *Living with Colonialism: Nationalism and Culture in the Anglo-Egyptian Sudan* (Berkeley: University of California, 2003), 106.

70. Shamil Jeppie, "Madhist State, Mahdiyya," in Richard C. Martin, ed., *Encyclopedia of Islam and the Muslim World*, vol. 2 (Macmillan Reference, 2004), 422–24.

71. Thomas Pakenham, *The Scramble for Africa: White Man's Conquest of the Dark Continent from 1876-1912* (New York: Avon Books, 1991), xxi.

72. For an excellent account of this, with primary documents, see Barbara Harlow and Mia Carter, eds., *Imperialism and Orientalism: A Documentary Sourcebook* (Oxford: Blackwell, 1999, 244–330.

73. Viera Pawliková-Vilhanová, *History of Anti-colonial Resistance and Protest in the Kingdoms of Buganda and Bunyoro, 1890-1899* (Prague: Oriental Institute of the Czechoslovak Academy of Sciences, 1988), 118.

74. Pawliková-Vilhanová, *History of Anti-colonial Resistance,* 120.

75. Pawliková-Vilhanová, *History of Anti-colonial Resistance,* 124.

76. Pawliková-Vilhanová, *History of Anti-colonial Resistance,* 226–44.

77. Pawliková-Vilhanová, *History of Anti-colonial Resistance,* 213.

78. Pawliková-Vilhanová, *History of Anti-colonial Resistance,* 228.

79. D. A. Low, *Fabrication of Empire: The British and the Uganda Kingdoms, 1890-1902* (Cambridge: Cambridge University Press, 2009). p. 341.

80. Karen E. Fields, *Revival and Rebellion in Colonial Central Africa* (Princeton, NJ: Princeton, 1985) p. 28.

81. Low, *Fabrication*, esp. 341.

82. See Terence O. Ranger, *Bulawayo Burning: the Social History of a Southern African City, 1893-1960* (London: James Currey, 2010).

83. For a variety of reasons, including the increased stakes of African development in the wake of Indian independence, the Shangani Reserve was subject to a second stage of colonial occupation in the

postwar period. See Jocelyn Alexander, JoAnn McGregor and Terence Ranger, *Violence and Memory: One Hundred Years in the 'Dark Forests' of Matabeleland* (London: James Currey, 2000), chap. 3.

84. Enocent Msindo, *Ethnicity in Zimbabwe: Transformations in Kalanga and Ndebele Societies, 1860-1990* (Rochester, 2012), esp. 97. John Iliffe argues that "to rebel against a colonial government was more difficult than to resist initial conquest" because rebellion had to be covertly organized "on a larger scale" if it were to succeed. John Iliffe, *Africans: The History of a Continent* (Cambridge: Cambridge University Press, 1995), 195.

85. Terence O. Ranger, *Revolt in Southern Rhodesia, 1896-97: A Study in African Resistance* (Chicago: Northwestern University Press, 1967), 127.

86. See John Darwin on Zululand in *Unfinished Empire*, 141–47.

87. Shula Marks, *Reluctant Rebellion: The 1906-8 Disturbances in Natal* (Oxford: Clarendon, 1970), 16.

88. Marks, *Reluctant Rebellion*, 144. She borrows here from E. Brookes and C. de B. Webb, *A History of Natal* (Natal, 1965).

89. William Beinart, "The Anatomy of a Rural Scare: East Griqualand in the 1890s," in Beinart and Bundy, *Hidden Struggles in Rural South Africa* (London: James Currey, 1986), 46–77.

90. See Ben MacLennan, *A Proper Degree of Terror: John Graham and the Cape's Eastern Frontier* (Johannesburg: Ravan Press, 1986).

91. Jeff Guy, *Remembering the Rebellion: The Zulu Uprising of 1906* (Durban: UKZN Press, 2006), 41.

92. Marks, *Reluctant Rebellion*, 26.

93. See Marc Matera, Misty Bastian and Susan Kingsley Kent, *The Women's War of 1929: Gender and Violence in Colonial Nigeria* (New York: Palgrave, 2012).

94. Matera et al., *The Women's War*, esp. chap. 4.

95. "Fenian" was, in fact, the term for Irish revolutionaries in both the US and Britain; John Newsinger, *Blood Never Dried*, 26.

96. Newsinger, *Blood Never Dried*, 29, 40–41.

97. John Newsinger, *Fenianism in Mid-Victorian Britain* (London: Palgrave Macmillan, 1994), 43.

98. Newsinger, *Blood Never Dried*, 51.

99. For the text of the proclamation see Antoinette Burton, ed., *Politics and Empire in Victorian Britain: A Reader* (New York: Palgrave, 2001), 125.

100. Michael de Nie, *The Eternal Paddy: Irish Identity and the British Press, 1798-1882* (Madison: University of Wisconsin Press, 2004), 162, 163.

101. Paul McMahon, *British Spies and Irish Rebels: British Intelligence and Ireland, 1916-1945* (Rochester, NY: Boydell and Brewer, 2008), 97.

102. See Jenkins, *Fenian Problem*; and Niall Whelehan, *The Dynamiters: Irish Nationalism and Political Violence in the Wider World, 1867-1900* (Cambridge: Cambridge University Press, 2012.

103. Newsinger, *Blood Never Dried* , 48.

104. Phillip Thurmond Smith, *Policing Victorian London: Political Policing, Public Order and the Metropolitan Police* (Westport, CT: Greenwood, 1985), 197.

105. Martin, *Alter-Nations*, 141. See also Whelehan, *Dynamiters*, chapter 5 ("Bridget and the Bomb").

106. K. R. M. Short, *The Dynamite War: Irish-American Bombers in Victorian Britain* (Dublin: Gill and MacMillan, 1979), 1.

107. Short, *Dynamite Wars*, 35.

108. Whelehan, *Dynamiters,* 3.

109. Short, *Dynamite Wars*, 160–61. Robert J.C. Young draws a parallel between this and the 7/7 Tube bombings. See his "Terror Effects" in Elleke Boehmer and Stephen Morton, eds., *Terror and the Postcolonial* (London: Wiley-Blackwell, 2010), 309.

110. McMahon, *British Spies*, 3, 166, 164.

111. Padraic Kenney, "'I Felt a Kind of Pleasure In Seeing Them Treat Us Brutally': The Emergence of the Political Prisoner, 1865–1910," *Comparative Studies in Society and History* 54, 4 (2012): 872.

112. Bernard Porter, *The Origins of the Vigilant State: The London Metropolitan Police Special Branch before the First World War* (London: Weidenfeld and Nicolson, 1987).

113. Robert J. C. Young, "International Anti-Colonialism: The Fenian Invasions of Canada," in Fiona Bateman and Lionel Pilkington, eds., *Studies in Settler Colonialism* (London: Palgrave, 2010), 85–86.

114. Kate O'Malley, *Ireland, India and Empire: Indo-Irish Radical Connections, 1919-64* (Manchester: Manchester University Press, 2008) and Jennifer Regan-Lefebvre, *Cosmopolitan Nationalism in the Victorian Empire: Ireland, India and the Politics of Alfred Webb* (London: Palgrave, 2009).

115. Tickell, *Terrorism,* 136; Rozina Visram, *Asians in Britain: 400 Years of History* (London: Pluto, 2002), esp. 156.

116. Tickell, *Terrorism*, esp. 137.

117. Peter Hopkirk, *Like Hidden Fire: The Plot to Bring Down the British Empire* (New York: Kodansha International, 1994), 45.

118. David Garnett, *The Golden Echo*, 146 (London: Chatto and Windus, 1953), 146.

119. Tickell, *Terrorism*, 81, 143–45, 173.

120. See Christopher Pinney, "The Body and the Bomb: Technologies of Modernity in Colonial India," in Richard Davis, ed., *Picturing the Nation: Iconographies of Modern India* (New Delhi: Orient Longman, 2007), 53.

121. *The Bomb in Bengal: The Rise of Revolutionary Terrorism in India, 1900-1910* (Oxford: Oxford University Press, 1993). An alternative term for *terrorist*, one that has been applied to M. N. Roy, is *insurrectional nationalist*, but this stages the nation more than some Indian revolutionaries, at any rate, intended. The term is from "The Comintern Brahmin: The Untold Story of M. N. Roy": http://vimeopro.com/ekstasy/mnroy-the-comintern-brahmin (Vladimir Leon, dir., 2006); password mnroy. [you need this password to get in] Accessed February 2, 2015. Thanks to Dave Roediger for this reference.

122. Geraldine Forbes, *Women in Modern India* (Cambridge, 1996), esp. 139; Sikata Banerjee, *Muscular Nationalism: Gender, Violence, and Empire in India and Ireland, 1914-2004* (New York: NYU Press, 2012), 101–2. Of Waddedar it was also said, "she is such a quiet girl, speaks so well, I could not imagine she had so much in her." Kalpana Dutt, *Chittagong Armoury Raiders: Reminiscences* (Bombay: People's Publishing House, 1945), 55.

123. See Dutt, *Chittagong Armoury Raiders.*

124. See Senia Pašeta, *Irish Nationalist Women, 1900-1918* (Cambridge: Cambridge University Press, 2013), 136, 169.

125. Heehs, *Bomb in Bengal*, 87. Indian women revolutionaries, for their part, believed in "maximum sacrifice by a minimum number" rather than in building a mass movement. See Suruchi Thapar-Björkert, *Women and the Indian National Movement* (Delhi: Sage, 2006), 129.

126. Peter Heehs, "Foreign Influences on Bengali Revolutionary Terrorism 1902-1908," *Modern Asian Studies* 28, 3 (1994): 533.

127. Amitav Kumar Gupta, "Defying Death: Nationalist Revolutionism in India, 1897-1938" *Social Scientist* 25, (Sept.–Oct. 1997): 8.

128. Maia Ramnath, "Meeting the Rebel Girl: Anticolonial Solidarity and Interracial Romance" in Ali Raza, Franziska Roy and Benjamin Zachariah, eds., *The Internationalist Moment: South Asia, Worlds, and World Views 1917-39* (London: Sage, 2014), 149

129. Geoff Read and Todd Webb, "'The Catholic Mahdi of the North West': Louis Riel and the Metis Resistance in Transatlantic and Imperial Context," *Canadian Historical Review* 93, 2 (2012); Jennifer Reid, *Louis Riel and the Creation of Modern Canada: Mythic Discourse and the Postcolonial State* (University of New Mexico Press, 2008), 171–95. Thomas Flanagan points out that the rebellion was in response not to grievances unanswered but more precisely, a reaction against how those grievances were to be addressed. See his *Louis 'David' Riel: 'Prophet of the New World'* (Toronto: Toronto University Press, 1996; revised edition), 147.

130. Maia Ramnath, *Haj to Utopia: How the Ghadar Movement Charted Global Radicalism and Attempted to Overthrow the British Empire* (Berkeley: University of California Press, 2011), 2.

131. Ramnath, *Haj,* 2, 8, 21.

132. Ramnath *Haj*, 44.

133. See Harish K. Puri, "Revolutionary Organization: A Study of the Ghadar Movement," *Social Scientist* 9, 2–3 (1980): 56, 58. *Ghadar* started in 1913 (Urdu edition in November; Gurmukhi edition in December, and Gujerati edition, in May) and it ends after the war. By 1920, Ghadar leaders were publishing the *Independent Hindustan* (from 1920) in English, rather than Ghadar in vernaculars; see Ramnath, *Haj*. Thanks to Irina Spector-Marks for these details.

134. Ramnath, *Haj*, 41.

135. Heather Streets-Salter, "The Local Was Global: The Singapore Mutiny of 1915," *Journal of World History* 24, 3 (2013): 539–76.

136. Ramnath, *Haj*, 50.

137. Ramnath, *Haj*, 40.

138. Michael Silvestri, *Ireland and India: Nationalism, Empire and Memory* (London: Palgrave, 2009), chapter 2.

139. See Ramnath, *Haj*, chaps. 2 and 3.

140. Harald Fischer-Tiné makes a case for 1905 as a nodal point, rather than WWI. See his "Indian Nationalism and the 'World Forces': Transnational and Diasporic Dimensions of the Indian Freedom Movement on the Eve of the First World War," *Journal of Global History* 2, 3 (2007): 325–44.

141. Streets-Salter, "Local was Global." For US reverberations and contexts see Seema Sohi, "Race, Surveillance, and Indian Anticolonialism in the Transnational Western U.S.-Canadian Borderlands," *Journal of American History* 98, 2 (2011): 420–436. For the role of Canada and especially its enterprising agent from the Vancouver Immigration Department, see Richard Popplewell, "The Surveillance of Indian 'Seditionists' in North America, 1905-1915," in Christopher Andrew and Jeremy Noakes, eds., *Intelligence and International Relations, 1900-1945* (Exeter: University of Exeter Press, 1987), esp. 58.

142. Ramnath, *Haj*, 62.

143. Bernard Porter, *Plots and Paranoia: A History of Political Espionage in Britain, 1790-1988* (London: Unwin Hyman, 1989), 142.

144. See Roger Casement cited in Peter de Rosa, *Rebels: The Irish Rising of 1916* (Fawcett, 1990), 495; Bruce Nelson, *Irish Nationalists and the Making of the Irish Race* (Princeton, NJ: Princeton University Press, 2012), 181.

145. From his 1921 speech to the Northern Ireland Parliament; cited in Keith Jeffery, *The British Army and the Crisis of Empire, 1918-1922* (Manchester: Manchester University Press, 1984), 75; and Sikata Banerjee, *Muscular Nationalism*, 87.

146. Suchetana Chattopadhyay, "The Myth of the Outside: From Whitehall to Elysium Row, 1917-1921," *Twentieth Century Communism: A Journal of International History* 6 (2014): 114.

147. O'Malley, *Ireland, India and Empire*, 42–43.

148. O'Malley, *Ireland, India and Empire*, 53. See also Éamon de Valera, *India and Ireland* (New York: Friends of Freedom for India, 1920).

149. Toby Dodge, *Inventing Iraq: The Failure of Nation-Building and a History Denied* (New York: Columbia University Press, 2003), xxxiii and chap. 1.

150. Shompa Lahiri, *Indian Mobilities in the West, 1900-1947: Gender, Performance, Embodiment* (London: Palgrave, 2010), 69–71.

151. Ramnath, *Haj*, chap.5. For more on the university recruitment pathways see Hari Vasudevan and Anjan Saker, "Colonial Dominance and Indigenous Response," in Jayanta Kumar Ray, ed., *Aspects of India's International Relations, 1700 to 2000: South Asia and the World* (New Delhi: Pearson, 2007), 39. For indications of how central a role Afghanistan had played in regional/global instabilities before the war, see Suhash Chakravarty, *Anatomy of the Raj: Russian Consular Reports* (Bombay: People's Publishing House, 1981), 354.

152. Vijay Prashad, *The Darker Nations: A People's History of the Third World* (New Press, 2007), 22.

153. Jonathan Schneer, *London 1900: The Imperial Metropolis* (New Haven, CT: Yale University Press, 2001), esp. 23.

154. Marika Sherwood, *Origins of Pan-Africanism: Henry Sylvester Williams, Africa and the African Diaspora* (London: Routledge, 2011), 79.

155. C. L. R. James, *A History of Pan-African Revolt*, with an introduction by Robin D. G. Kelley (Chicago: Charles Kerr, 2012). Thanks to Dave Roediger for bringing this edition to my attention. An "imperial pan-Africanist," Henry Sylvester Williams had an empire-wide view of political and labor questions, owing in his case in part to the time he spent in the Cape Colony in 1903–4. See J. R. Hooker, *Henry Sylvester Williams: Imperial Pan–Africanist* (London: Rex Collings Ltd, 1975), esp. 64; and Sherwood, *Origins*, chap. 10.

156. Minkah Makalani, *In the Cause of Freedom: Radical Black Internationalism from Harlem to London, 1917-1939* (Chapel Hill: University of North Carolina Press, 2011), 134.

157. Abu Yusuf Alam, *Khilafat Movement and The Muslims of Bengal* (Kolkata: Raktakarabee, 2007), 35.

158. Alam, *Khilafat*, 51.

159. Alam, *Khilafat*, 97; (f. Gandhi's hesitancy).

160. Alam, *Khilafat,* 98.

161. Alam, Khilafat, 101, 103; Hailey is quoted in Imran Ali, *The Punjab under Imperialism, 1885-1947* (Princeton, NJ: Princeton University Press, 1988), 105.

162. Gaul Minault, *The Khilafat Movement: Religious Symbolism and Political Mobilization in India* (Columbia, 1982), 169.

163. Rajat Ray, "Revolutionaries, Pan-Islamists and Bolsheviks: Maulana Abul Kalam Azad and the Political Underworld of Calcutta, 1905-1925," in Mushirul Hasan, ed., *Communal and Pan-Islamic Trends in Colonial India* (Delhi: Manohar, 1985), 101–110.

164. Sandeep Chawla, "The Palestinian Issue in Indian Politics in the 1920s" in Hasan, *Communal and Pan-Islamic Trends*, 44–51.

165. Chawla, "Palestinian Issue," 51.

166. M. Naeem Qureshi, *Pan-Islamism in British Indian Politics: A Study of the Khilafat Movement, 1918-1924* (London: Brill, 1999), 49.

167. Ayesha Jalal, *Partisans of Allah: Jihad in South Asia* (Cambridge, MA: Harvard University Press, 2008), 118.

168. These were considered "predatory hordes" who were "backed by a stream of wily tribesmen from the northwestern frontier." As Jalal goes on to note, "a sense of injustice, coupled with disdain for an immoral and tyrannical English government, was also already widespread, even before the annexation of Awadh inflamed the soldiers of the Bengal army" and fueled the onset of mutiny Jalal, *Partisans*, 118.

169. Jalal, *Partisans*, 121.

170. W. W. Hunter, *The Indian Musalmans: Are They Bound in Conscience to Rebel against the Queen?* (London: Trübner and Co., 1871).

171. Hunter, *Indian Musalmans*, 146.

172. See Faisal Devji, *Landscapes of the Jihad: Militancy, Morality, Modernity* (Ithaca, NY: Cornell University Press, 2005), 37.

173. Thomas Carlyle, "How the Irish Land System Breeds Disaffection," *Fraser's Magazine* 77 (1868): 265.

174. Nikki R. Keddie, *An Islamic Response to Imperialism; Political and Religious Writings of Sayyid Jamāl ad-Dīn "al-Afghānī* (Berkeley: University of California Press, 1968), 20.

175. A ratcheting up in the coordination of colonial intelligence would not happen until the 1880s, with the development of an intelligence

department; see William Beaver, *Under Every Leaf: How Britain Played the Greater Game from Afghanistan to Africa* (Biteback, 2012), esp. chap. 5.

176. Keddie, *Islamic Response*, 24–25.

177. Keddie, *Islamic Response*, 30–31.

178. Keddie, *Modern Iran*, 63.

179. Seema Alavi, "'Fugitive Mullahs and Outlawed Fanatics': Indian Muslims in 19th c. Trans-Asiatic Imperial Rivalries" *Modern Asian Studies* 45, 6 (2011): 1137–78.

180. See Siobhan Lambert-Hurley, *Muslim Women, Reform and Princely Patronage: Nawab Sultan Jahan Begam of Bhopal* (London: Routledge, 2007) and Charlotte Weber, "Between Nationalism and Feminism: The Eastern Women's Congresses of 1930 and 1932," *Journal of Middle East Women's Studies* 4, 1 (2008): 83–106.

181. Siobhan Lambert-Hurley, *Muslim Women, Reform and Princely Patronage* (Routledge. 2007), 33–34; and "Princes, Paramountcy and the Politics of Muslim Identity: The Begam of Bhopal on the Indian National Stage, 1901-26," *South Asia* 26, 2 (2003): 165–91.

182. Alavi, "Fugitive Mullahs," 1340–41.

183. Pankaj Mishra, *From the Ruins of Empire: The Intellectuals Who Remade Asia* (New York: Farrar, Strauss and Giroux, 2012), 49.

184. Mushirul Hasan, "The Khilafat Movement: A Reappraisal," in his edited collection, *Communal and Pan-Islamic Trends in Colonial India* (Delhi: Manohar 1985), 5.

185. C. Sankaran Nair, *Gandhi and Anarchy* (Nair Foundation, 2000); first published 1922.

186. See entry for Bhicco Batlivala at "Making Britain," http://www.open.ac.uk/researchprojects/makingbritain/content/bhicoo-batlivala. Accessed May 16, 2015.

187. See Shompa Lahiri, *Indian Mobilities in the West, 1900-47* (London: Palgrave Macmillan, 2010), 71–76, esp. 76. For an expert treatment of Naidu that was just coming out as this book went to press, see Elleke Boehmer, *Indian Arrivals, 1870-1915: Networks of British Empire* (Oxford: Oxford University Press, 2015).

188. Fields, *Revival and Rebellion*, 4, 6, 32, 168, 181–82, 200.

189. Martin Kolinsky, *Law, Order and Riots in Mandatory Palestine, 1928-35* (New York: St. Martin's, 1993), 19–30.

190. Kolinsky, *Law, Order and Riots*, 69.

191. Matthew Hughes, "The Banality of Brutality: British Armed Forces and the Repression of the Armed Revolt in Palestine, 1936-39," *English Historical Review* 124, 507 (2009): and "The Practice and Theory of British Counterinsurgency: The Histories of the Atrocities at the Palestinian Villages of al-Bassa and Halhul, 1938-39," *Small Wars and Insurgencies* 3–4 (2009): 528.

192. Ted Swedenburg, *Memories of Revolt: The 1936-1939 Rebellion and the Palestinian National Past* (Minnesota, 1995), 1–2, 78, 104.

193. As Matthew Hughes also notes,

> The British by the 1930s had ruled out full martial law in situations of 'sub-wars,' excepting in the most extreme cases, the reference here usually being to the 'Indian Mutiny' of 1857, but after the Arab capture of the Old City of Jerusalem in October 1938, the army effectively took over Jerusalem and then all of Palestine. In fact, since late 1937, the army had been in charge with the 'full power of search and arrest, independent of the police, and the right to shoot and kill any man attempting to escape search or ignoring challenges. Grenades may be used during searches of caves, wells, etc. Since November [1937] co-operating aircraft have been "bombed-up," and pilots instructed to machine gun or bomb "armed parties." There was *de facto* if not *de jure* martial law from late 1937 or early 1938. (Hughes, "Banality," 318–19)

194. Swedenburg, *Memories of Revolt*, 177–79.

195. Swedenburg, *Memories*; and Ellen Fleischmann, *The Nation and Its 'New' Women: The Palestinian Women's Movement, 1920-1948* (Berkeley: University of California, 2003), 122–28

196. Hughes, "Practice and Theory," 533.

197. Georgina Sinclair, "'Get into a Crack Force and Earn £20 a Month and All Found . . .': The Influence of the Palestinian Police upon Colonial Policing 1922-1948," *European Review of History* 13, 1 (2006): 49–65.

198. For an emphasis on intellectual anti-imperialism, see Mishra, *From the Ruins of Empire*.

199. Quoted in Edward Said, *Orientalism* (New York: Vintage, 1979), 33.

200. This paradox, especially with respect to British intelligence in India, is outlined in Richard J. Popplewell, *Intelligence and Imperial*

Defence: British Intelligence and the Defence of the Indian Empire, 1904-1924 (London: Frank Cass, 1995), chap. 1.

201. I draw here on Elaine Freedgood's luminous study, *Victorian Writing about Risk: Imagining a Safe England in a Dangerous World*. (Cambridge: Cambridge University Press, 2000).

202. Jasbir Puar, *Terrorist Assemblages: Homonationalism in Queer Times* (Durham, NC: Duke University Press, 2007).

Chapter 4

1. Simon Winchester, "Amid the tears and cheers, a full stop to Britain's colonial experience in Northern Ireland," *Guardian*, June 15, 2010.

2. Winchester, "Amid the tears and cheers."

3. Even allowing for the uneven histories of the relationship of the Irish to whiteness that colleagues David Roediger and James Barrett have so deftly chronicled, this is one difference that race continues to make. Whether they wish to be or not, the Irish are becoming postcolonial white in contradistinction to other postcolonial "others"—Indians, Pakistanis, Jamaicans, and, more circuitously, Poles as well. See their "Inbetween Peoples: Race, Nationality and the 'New Immigrant' Working Class," *Journal of American Ethnic History* 16, 3 (1997): 3–44.

4. Kwasi Karteng, "Echoes of the End of the Raj," Op-Ed, *New York Times*, April 16, 2012.

5. Said, *Culture and Imperialism* (New York: Vintage Books, 1994), 25; Ranajit Guja, *Elementary Aspects of Peasant Insurgency in Colonial India* (Delhi: Oxford University Press, 1983), Epilogue.

6. Frank Furedi, "Creating a Breathing Space: The Political Management of Colonial Emergencies," *Journal of Imperial and Commonwealth History* 21, 3 (2008): 89–106.

7. See Benjamin Grobb-Fitzgibbon, *Imperial Endgame: Britain's Dirty Wars and the End of Empire* (London: Palgrave, 2011).

8. See, for example, Christopher Shackle and Javeed Majeed, eds., *Hali's Musaddas: The Ebb and Flow of Islam* (Oxford: Oxford University Press, 1997), 9. The *Musaddas* is an epic poem by one of the leading nineteenth-century Urdu poets, first published in 1879, about historical cycles of progress and decline in the wake of the trauma of 1857.

For the plot-closure-device schema see Michael Rothberg, "Progress, Progression, Procession: William Kettridge and the Narratology of Transitional Justice," *Narrative* 20, 1 (2012): 7.

9. Alfred W. McCoy, "Fatal Florescence: Europe's Decolonization and America's Decline," in McCoy, Josep M. Fradera and Stephen Jacobson, eds., *Endless Empire: Spain's Retreat, Europe's Eclipse, America's Decline* (Madison: University of Wisconsin Press, 2012), 3–29.

BIBLIOGRAPHY

Adas, Michael. "Contested Hegemony: The Great War and the Afro-Asian Assault on the Civilizing Mission Ideology." *Journal of World History* 15, 1 (2004): 31–63.

Adas, Michael. "From Foot-Dragging to Flight: The Evasive Histories of Peasant Avoidance Protest in South and South-East Asia." *Journal of Peasant Studies* 13, 2 (1986): 64–86.

Ahmed, Rehana, and Sumita Mukherjee, eds. *South Asian Resistances in Britain, 1858-1947*. London: Continuum, 2012.

Ahuja, Ravi. "Mobility and Containment: The Voyages of South Asian Seamen, c.1900–1960." *International Review of Social History* 51, Supplement S14 (2006): 111–41.

Alam, Abu Yusuf. *Khilafat Movement and the Muslims of Bengal*. Kolkata: Raktakarabee, 2007.

Alavi, Seema. "'Fugitive Mullahs and Outlawed Fanatics': Indian Muslims in 19th c. trans-Asiatic Imperial Rivalries." *Modern Asian Studies* 46, 6 (2011): 1337–82.

Alexander, Anne, and David Renton. "Globalization, Imperialism and Popular Resistance in Egypt, 1880-2000." In Leo Zeileg, ed., *Class Struggle and Resistance in Africa*. Cheltenham, Oxford: New Clarion Press, 2002, 87–115.

Alexander, Jocelyn, JoAnn McGregor, and Terence Ranger. *Violence and Memory: One Hundred Years in the "Dark Forests" of Matabeleland*. London: James Currey, 2000.

Alford, Henry S. L., and W. Dennistoun Sword. *The Egyptian Soudan; Its Loss and Recovery*. New York: Negro Universities Press, 1969.

Ali, Imran. *The Punjab under Imperialism, 1885-1947*. Princeton, NJ: Princeton University Press, 1988.

Allman, Jean, and Victoria B. Tashjian. *"I Will Not Eat Stone": A Women's History of Colonial Asante*. London: Heinemann, 2000.

Andrade, Tonio. *Lost Colony: The Untold Story of China's First Great Victory over the West*. Princeton, NJ: Princeton University Press, 2011.

Atkins, Keletso. *The Moon Is Dead! Give Us Our Money! The Cultural Origins of an African Work Ethic, Natal, South Africa, 1843-1900*. London: Heinemann, 1993.

Aydin, Cemil. *The Politics of Anti-Westernism in Asia: Visions of World Order in Pan-Islamic and Pan-Asian Thought*. New York: Columbia University Press, 2007.

Azuma, Eichirro. *Between Two Empires: Race, History and Transnationalism in Japanese America*. New York: Oxford University Press, 2005.

Bahadur, Gaiutra. *Coolie Woman: The Odyssey of Indenture*. Chicago: University of Chicago Press, 2014.

Ballantyne, Tony. "War, Knowledge and the Crisis of Empire." In his *Webs of Empire: Locating New Zealand's Colonial Past*. Wellington: Bridget Williams Books, 2012, 161–78.

Banerjee, Sikata. *Muscular Nationalism: Gender, Violence and Empire in India and Ireland, 1914-2004*. New York: New York University Press, 2012.

Barnes, Teresa A. *"We Women Worked So Hard": Gender, Urbanization and Social Reproduction in Colonial Harare, Zimbabwe, 1930-1956*. London: Heinemann, 1999.

Barthorp, Michael. *The North-West Frontier: British India and Afghanistan; A Pictorial History 1839-1947*. Dorset: Blandford Press, 1982.

Banivanua Mar, Tracey. *Violence and Colonial Dialogue: The Australian-Pacific Indentured Labor Trade*. Honolulu: University of Hawaii Press, 2007.

Barrett, James R. and David Roediger. "Inbetween Peoples: Race and the 'New Immigrant' Working Class." *Journal of American Ethnic History* 16, 3 (1997): 3–44.

Bayat, Asef. "Un-Civil Society: The Politics of 'Informal People.'" *Third World Quarterly* 18, 1 (1997): 53–72.

Bayly, C. A. *Indian Society and the Making of the British Empire*. Cambridge, 1988.

Beaver, William. *Under Every Leaf: How Britain Played the Greater Game from Afghanistan to Africa*. Biteback, 2012.

Beinart, William, and Colin Bundy, eds. *Hidden Struggles in Rural South Africa: Politics and Popular Movements in the Transkei and Eastern Cape*, 1890-1930. London: James Curry, 1987.

Beinin, Joel, and Zachary Lockman. *Workers on the Nile: Nationalism, Communism, Islam and the Egyptian Working Class, 1882-1954*. Princeton, NJ: Princeton University Press, 1987.

Belich, James. *I Shall Not Die: Titikowaru's War, New Zealand 1868-9*. Wellington: Allen and Unwin, 1989.

Belich, James. *The Victorian Interpretation of Racial Conflict: The Maori, the British and the New Zealand Wars*. Montreal: McGill-Queens University Press, 1986.

Benton, Lauren. *A Search for Sovereignty: Law and Geography in European Empires, 1400-1900*. Cambridge University Press, 2010.

Bhattacharya, Subhas. "The Indigo Revolt of Bengal." *Social Scientist* 5, 12 (1977): 13–23.

Bickers, Robert. *The Scramble for China: Foreign Devils in the Qing Empire, 1832-1914*. Allen Lane, 2011.

Birla, Ritu. *Stages of Capital: Law, Culture, and Market Governance in Late Colonial India*. Durham, NC: Duke University Press, 2009.

Blackhawk, Ned. *Violence over the Land: Indians and Empires in the Early American West*. Cambridge, MA: Harvard University Press, 2006.

Boddy, Janice. *Civilizing Women: British Crusades in Colonial Sudan*. Princeton, NJ: Princeton University Press 2007.

Boehmer, Elleke and Stephen Morton, eds., *Terror and the Postcolonial*. London: Wiley-Blackwell, 2010.

Boyce, George. *Decolonisation and the British Empire, 1775-1997*. London: St. Martins Press, 1999.

Bradford, Helen. "Lynch Law and Labourers: The ICU in Umvoti, 1927-1928." In William Beinart, Peter Delius, and Stanley Trapido, eds., *Putting a Plough to the Ground: Accumulation and Dispossession in Rural South Africa 1850-1930*. Johannesburg: Ravan Press, 1986, 420–49.

Brantley, Cynthia. *The Giriama and Colonial Resistance in Kenya, 1800-1920*. Berkeley: University of California Press, 1981.

Brantley, Cynthia. "Mekatilili and the Role of Women in Giriama Resistance." In Donald Crummey, ed., *Banditry, Rebellion, and Social Protest in Africa*. London: James Currey, 1986.

Breen, T. H. *The Marketplace of Revolution: How Consumer Politics Shaped American Independence*. New York: Oxford University Press, 2005.

Breman, Jan. ""The Study of Industrial Labour in Post-Colonial India: The Formal Sector; An Introductory Review." In Jonathan P. Parry, Jan Breman, Karin Kapadia, eds. *The Worlds of Indian Industrial Labor*. Delhi: New Sage Publications, 1999, 1–42.

Brereton, Bridget. *Law, Justice, and Empire: The Colonial Career of John Gorrie, 1829-92*. Kingston: University Press of the West Indies, 1997.

Brooking, Tom. *The History of New Zealand*. Westport, CT: Greenwood, 2004.

Brownhill, Leigh S. *Land, Food, Freedom: Struggles for the Gendered Commons in Kenya, 1870-2007*. Trenton, NJ: Africa World Press, 2009.

Brownhill, Leigh S., and Terisa E. Turner, "Subsistence Trade versus World Trade: Gendered Class Struggle in Kenya, 1992-2002." *Canadian Woman Studies* 21/22, 4/1 (2002): 169–77.

Buckland, C. E. *Bengal under the Lieutenant-Governors: Being a Narrative of the Principal Events and Public Measures during Their Periods of Office, from 1854 to 1898*. Calcutta: S. K. Lahiri and Co., 1901.

Burton, Antoinette. *Burdens of History: British Feminists, Indian Women and Imperial Culture, 1865-1915*. Chapel Hill: University of North Carolina Press, 1994.

Burton, Antoinette. "On the First Anglo-Afghan War, 1839-42: Spectacle of Disaster." http://www.branchcollective.org/?ps_articles= antoinette-burton-on-the-first-anglo-afghan-war-1839-4 2-spectacle-of-disaster.

Burton, Antoinette, ed. *The First Anglo-Afghan Wars: A Reader*. Durham, NC: Duke University Press, 2014.

Cain, P. J., and A. J. Hopkins. "Gentlemanly Capitalism and British Expansion Overseas I. The Old Colonial System, 1688-1850." *Economic History Review* 39, 4 (1986): 501–25.

Cain, P. J., and A. J. Hopkins. "Gentlemanly Capitalism and British Expansion Overseas II: New Imperialism, 1850-1945." *Economic History Review*, New Series 40, 4 (1987): 1–26.

Caine, Caesar, ed. *Barracks and Battlefields in India*. London: C. H. Kelly, 1891.

Callwell, Charles Edward. *Small Wars: Their Principles and Practice*. 3rd ed. London: H. M. Stationery Office, 1906.

Carter, Marina. *Lakshmi's Legacy: The Testimonies of Indian Women in 19th-Century Mauritius*. Rose-Hill, Mauritius: Editions de l'Ocean Indien, 1994.

Carter, Marina, and Crispin Bates. "Empire and Locality: A Global Dimension to the 1857 Indian Uprising." *Journal of Global History* 5, 1 (2010): 51–73.

Casid, Jill H. *Sowing Empire: Landscape and Colonization*. Minneapolis: University of Minnesota Press, 2004.

Cell, John. "The Imperial Conscience." In Peter Marsh, ed., *The Conscience of the Victorian State*. New York: Syracuse University Press, 1979, 173–213.

Chakravarty, Suhash. *Anatomy of the Raj: Russian Consular Reports*. New Delhi: People's Publishing House, 1981.

Chandavarkar, Rajnarayan. *Imperial Power and Popular Politics: Class, Resistance and the State in India, c.1850-1950*. Cambridge; Cambridge University Press, 1998.

Chirol, Valentine. *Indian Unrest*. New Delhi: Light and Life Publishers, 1979.

Choudhury, Deep Kanta Lahiri. "India's First Virtual Community and the Telegraph General Strike of 1908." *International Review of Social History* 48, Supplement S11 (2003): 45–71.

Churchill, Winston. *My Early Life: 1874-1904*. New York: Charles Scribner's Sons, 1930.

Churchill, Winston. *The Story of the Malakand Field Force: An Episode of Frontier War*. London: Leo Cooper, 1989.

Claeys, Gregory. *Imperial Sceptics: British Critics of Empire, 1850-1920*. Cambridge: Cambridge University Press, 2010.

Clark, Carolyn M. "Land and Food, Women and Power, in Nineteenth Century Kikuyu." *Africa* 50, 4 (1980): 357–70.

Clements, Frank A. *Conflict in Afghanistan: A Historical Encyclopedia*. Santa Barbara, CA: ABC CLIO, 2003.

Cole, Juan Ricardo. *Colonialism and Revolution in the Middle East: Social and Cultural Origins of Egypt's 'Urabi Movement*. Princeton, NJ: Princeton University Press, 1993.

Coleman, Peter J. *Progressivism and the World of Reform: New Zealand and the Origins of the American Welfare State*. Manhattan, KS: University of Kansas Press, 1987.

Comaroff, John L. "Colonialism, Culture and the Law: A Foreword." *Law and Social Inquiry* 26, 2 (2001): 305–14.

Cooper, Frederick, and Ann Laura Stoler, eds. *Tensions of Empire: Colonial Cultures in a Bourgeois World*. Berkeley: University of California Press, 1997.

Côté, Janet McL. *Fanny and Anna Parnell: Ireland's Patriot Sisters*. New York: St. Martin's Press, 1991.

Cowan, James. *The New Zealand Wars: A History of the Maori Campaigns and the Pioneering Period*. 2 vols. Wellington: R. E. Owen, 1922–23.

Crais, Clifton C. *White Supremacy and Black Resistance in Pre-Industrial South Africa: The Making of the Colonial Order in the Eastern Cape, 1770-1865*. Cambridge: Cambridge University Press, 1992.

Daniel, E. Valentine. *Fluid Signs: Being a Person in the Tamil Way*. Berkeley: University of California Press, 1987.

Darwin, John. *The Empire Project: The Rise and Fall of the British World System, 1830-1970*. Cambridge: Cambridge University Press, 2009.

Darwin, John. "Imperialism and the Victorians: The Dynamics of Territorial Expansion." *English Historical Review* 112, 447 (1997): 614–42.

Darwin, John. *Unfinished Empire: The Global Expansion of Britain*. London: Bloomsbury, 2012.

Datta, Kalikinkar. *The Santal Insurrection of 1855-57*. Kolkata, West Bengal: University of Calcutta, 1988.

David, Saul. *The Indian Mutiny: 1857* New York: Viking, 2002.

de Nie, Michael. *The Eternal Paddy: Irish Identity and the British Press, 1798-1882*. Madison: University of Wisconsin Press, 2004.

De Rosa, Peter. *Rebels: The Irish Rising of 1916*. New York: Fawcett, 1990.

de Verteuil, Anthony, ed. *Seven Slaves and Slavery: Trinidad 1777–1838*. Port of Spain, 1992.

Denoon, Donald. *A Grand Illusion: The Failure of Imperial Policy in the Transvaal Colony during the Period of Reconstruction, 1900-1905*. London: Longman, 1973.

Denoon, Donald, and Philippa Mein-Smith. *A History of Australia, New Zealand and the Pacific*. With Marivic Wyndham. Blackwell, 2000.

Devi, Mahasweta. *The Queen of Jhansi*. Calcutta: Seagull Calcutta, 2000.

Devji, Faisal. *Landscapes of the Jihad: Militancy, Morality, Modernity*. Ithaca, NY: Cornell University Press, 2005.

Dirks, Nicholas B. "History as the Sign of the Modern." *Public Culture* 2, 2 (1990): 25–32.

Dodge, Toby. *Inventing Iraq: The Failure of Nation-Building and a History Denied*. New York: Columbia University Press, 2003.

Dutt, Kalpana. *Chittagong Armoury Raiders: Reminiscences*. Bombay: People's Publishing House, 1945.

Edwards, David B. "Mad Mullahs and Englishmen: Discourse in the Colonial Encounter." In Fernando Coronil and Julie Skurksi, eds.

States of Violence, Ann Arbor: University of Michigan Press, 2006, 153–78.

Elbourne, Elizabeth. "Broken Alliance: Debating Six Nations Land Claims in 1822." *Cultural and Social History* 9, 4 (2012): 497–525.

Elliott-Lockhart, Percy Clare., and Edward M. Dunmore, Earl of Alexander. *A Frontier Campaign: A Narrative of the Operations of the Malakand and Buner Field Forces, 1897-1898*. London: Methuen and Co.,, 1898.

Elphinstone, Montstuart. *An Account of the Kingdom of Cabul and Its Dependencies in Persia, Tartary, and India*. London: Longman, Hurst, Rees, Orme, and Brown, 1815.

Engels, Dagmar, and Shula Marks, eds. *Contesting Colonial Hegemony: State and Society in Africa and India*. London: I. B. Tauris, 1994.

Epstein, James. *Scandal of Colonial Rule: Power and Subversion in the British Atlantic during the Age of Revolution*. Cambridge, 2012.

Ewans, Martin. *Conflict in Afghanistan: Studies in Asymmetric Warfare*. London: Routledge, 2005.

Feinberg, Harvey M. "The 1913 Natives Land Act in South Africa: Politics, Race and Segregation in the early 20th Century." *International Journal of African Historical Studies* 26, 1 (1993): 65–109.

Fields, Karen E. *Revival and Rebellion in Colonial Central Africa*. Princeton, NJ: Princeton University Press 1985.

Fischer-Tiné, Harald. "Indian Nationalism and the 'World Forces': Transnational and Diasporic Dimensions of the Indian Freedom Movement on the Eve of the First World War." *Journal of Global History* 2, 3 (2007): 325–44.

Flanagan, Thomas. *Louis 'David' Reil: 'Prophet of the New World.'* Toronto: University of Toronto Press, 1996 (revised edition).

Fleischmann, Ellen. *The Nation and Its 'New' Women: The Palestinian Women's Movement, 1920-1948*. Berkeley: University of California Press, 2003.

Forbes, Archibald. *The Afghan Wars, 1839-1842 and 1878-80*. London: Seeley and Co., 1896.

Forbes, Geraldine. *Women in Modern India*. Cambridge: Cambridge University Press, 1996.

Foster, R. F. *Modern Ireland 1600-1972*. London: Allen Lane, 1990.

Fox, William. *An Address to the People of Great Britain On the Propriety of Abstaining from West India Sugar and Rum*. London, Printer, Philadelphia: Daniel Lawrence, 1792.

Freedgood, Elaine. *Victorian Writing about Risk: Imagining a Safe England in a Dangerous World*. Cambridge: Cambridge University Press, 2000.

Fryer, Peter. *Staying Power: The History of Black People in Britain.* London: Pluto, 1984.

Furedi, Frank. "Creating a Breathing Space: The Political Management of Colonial Emergencies." *Journal of Imperial and Commonwealth History* 21, 3 (2008): 89–106.

Galbraith, John S. "The 'Turbulent Frontier' as a Factor in British Expansion." *Comparative Studies in Society and History* 2, 2 (1960): 150–68.

Gallagher, John. *The Decline, Revival and Fall of the British Empire: The Ford Lectures and other Essays.* Edited by Anil Seal. Cambridge: Cambridge University Press, 1982.

Garnett, David. *The Golden Echo.* London: Chatto and Windus, 1953.

Ghosh, Kaushik. "A Market for Aboriginality: Primitivism and Race Classification in the Indentured Labour Market of Colonial India." In G. Bhadra, G. Prakash, and S. Tharu, eds. *Subaltern Studies X: Writings on South Asian History and Society.* New Delhi: Oxford University Press, 1999, 8–48.

Ginsburg, Rebecca. "Freedom and the Slave Landscape." *Landscape Journal* 26 (2007): 26–44.

Gooptu, Nandini. *The Politics of the Urban Poor in Early Twentieth-Century India.* Cambridge: Cambridge University Press, 2005.

Gordon, David M. *Invisible Agents: Spirits in Central African History.* Athens: Ohio University Press, 2012.

Gott, Richard. *Britain's Empire: Resistance, Repression and Revolt.* London: Verso, 2012.

Graeber, David. "On Cosmopolitanism and (Vernacular) Democratic Creativity: Or, There Never was a West," in Pnina Werbner, ed., *Anthropology and the New Cosmopolitanism.* New York: Berg, 2008, 281–306.

Grant, Kevin. "The Transcolonial World of Hunger Strikes and Political Fasts, c.1909-1935." In Durba Ghosh and Dane Kennedy, eds. *Decentering Empire: Britain, India, and the Transcolonial World.* Hyderabad: Orient Longman, 2006, 243–69.

Graves, Adrian. *Cane and Labour: The Political Economy of the Queensland Sugar Industry, 1862-1906.* Edinburgh: Edinburgh University Press, 1993.

Green, Dominic. *Three Empires on the Nile: The Victorian Jihad, 1869-1899.* New York: Free Press, 2007.

Grewal, Inderpal, and Caren Caplan, eds. *Scattered Hegemonies: Postmo-dernity and Transnational Feminist Practices*. Minneapolis: University of Minnesota Press, 1994.

Grobb-Fitzgibbon, Benjamin. *Imperial Endgame: Britain's Dirty Wars and the End of Empire*. London: Palgrave, 2011.

Guha, Ranajit. *Elementary Aspects of Peasant Insurgency in Colonial India*. Delhi: Oxford University Press, 1983.

Guha, Ranajit. ed. *The Small Voice of History: Collected Essays*. Delhi: Permanent Black, 2009.

Gupta, Hari Ram. *Panjab, Central Asia and the First Afghan War, Based on Mohan Lal's Observations*. Chandigarh: Panjab University, 1940.

Guy, Jeff. *The Destruction of the Zulu Kingdom: The Civil War in Zululand, 1879-1884*. Durban: University of Natal Press, 1994; first edition, 1979.

Guy, Jeff. *Remembering the Rebellion: The Zulu Uprising of 1906*. Durban: UKZN Press, 2006.

Hall, Catherine. *Civilizing Subjects: Colony and Metropole in the English Imagination 1830-1867*. Chicago: University of Chicago Press, 2002.

Hall, Catherine. *Macaulay and Son: Architects of Imperial Britain*. New Haven, CT: Yale University Press, 2012.

Hardiman, David. *The Coming of the Devi: Adivasi Assertion in Western India*. Dehli: Oxford University Press, 1987.

Hardiman, David. *Gandhi in His Time and Ours: The Global Legacy of his Ideas*. New York: Columbia University Press, 2004, 39–65.

Hardiman, David. *Histories for the Subordinated*. Calcutta: Seagull, 2007.

Harlow, Barbara, and Mia Carter, eds. *Imperialism and Orientalism: A Documentary Sourcebook*. Blackwell, 1999.

Hasan, Mushirul, ed. *Communal and Pan-Islamic Trends in Colonial India*. New Delhi: Manohar, 1985.

Havelock, Henry. *Narrative of the War in Affghanistan in 1838-39*. 2 vols. London: Henry Colburn Publishers, 1840.

Heehs, Peter. *The Bomb in Bengal: The Rise of Revolutionary Terrorism in India, 1900-1910*. New Delhi: Oxford University Press, 1993.

Hemmings, Clare. *Why Stories Matter: The Political Grammar of Feminist Theory*. Durham, NC: Duke University Press, 2011.

Herbert, Christopher. *War of No Pity: The Indian Mutiny and Victorian Trauma*. Princeton, NJ: Princeton University Press, 2008.

Heuman, Gad. 'The Killing Time': The Morant Bay Rebellion in Jamaica. Knoxville: University of Tennessee Press, 1995.

Hevia, James L. "Small Wars and Counterinsurgency." In John D. Kelly, Beatrice Jauregi, Sean T. Mitchell and Jeremy Walton, eds., Anthropology and Global Counterinsurgency. Chicago: University of Chicago Press, 2010, 169–77.

Higman, B. W. Plantation Jamaica, 1750-1850: Capital and Control in a Colonial Economy. Kingston: University of the West Indies Press, 2005.

Holt, P. M. The Mahdist State in the Sudan, 1881-1898: A Study of Its Origins, Development and Overthrow. Clarendon Press, 1970; originally published in 1898.

Holt, Thomas. The Problem of Freedom: Race, Labor, and Politics in Jamaica and Britain, 1832-1938. Baltimore, MD: Johns Hopkins University Press, 1991.

Hooker, J. R. Henry Sylvester Williams: Imperial Pan–Africanist. London: Rex Collings Ltd, 1975.

Hopkirk, Peter. Like Hidden Fire: The Plot to Bring Down the British Empire. New York: Kodansha International, 1994.

Hughes, Matthew. "The Banality of Brutality: British Armed Forces and the Repression of the Armed Revolt in Palestine, 1936-39." English Historical Review 124, 507 (2009): 313–54.

Hughes, Matthew. "The Practice and Theory of British Counterinsurgency: The Histories of the Atrocities of the Palestinian Villages at al-Bassa and Halhul, 1938-39." Small Wars and Insurgencies 3–4 (2009): 528–50.

Hunter, W. W. The Annals of Rural Bengal. London: Smith, Elder, 1868.

Hunter, W. W. The Indian Musalmans: Are They Bound in Conscience to Rebel against the Queen? London: Trubner and Co., 1872.

Hyslop, Jonathan. "Steamship Empire: Asian, African and British Sailors in the Merchant Marine, c.1880-1945." Journal of Asian and African Studies 44, 1 (2009): 49–67.

Ibrahim, Hassan Ahmed. "Mahdist Risings against the Condominium Government in the Sudan, 1900-1927." International Journal of African Historical Studies 12, 3 (1979): 440–471.

Ileto, Reynaldo C. "Outlines of a Non-Linear Emplotment of Philippine History." In Lim Teck Ghee, ed., Reflections on Development in Southeast Asia. Singapore: ASEAN, 1988, 130–59.

Iliffe, John. Africans: The History of a Continent. Cambridge: Cambridge University Press, 1995.

Jacob, Wilson Chacko. *Working out Egypt: Effendi Masculinity and Subject Formation in Colonial Modernity, 1870-1940*. Durham, NC: Duke University Press, 2011.

Jalal, Ayesha. *Partisans of Allah: Jihad in South Asia*. Cambridge, MA: Harvard University Press, 2008.

James, C. L. R. *A History of Pan-African Revolt*. With an introduction by Robin D. G. Kelley. Chicago: Charles Kerr, 2012.

Jayawardena, Kumari. *Perpetual Ferment: Popular Revolts in Sri Lanka in the 18th and 19th Centuries*. Colombo: Social Scientists' Association, 2010.

Jayawardena, Kumari. *The Rise of the Labor Movement in Ceylon*. Durham: Duke University Press, 1972.

Jeffery, Keith. *The British Army and the Crisis of Empire, 1918-22*. Manchester: Manchester University Press, 1984.

Jenkins, Brian. *The Fenian Problem: Insurgency and Terrorism in a Liberal State, 1858-1874*. Montreal: McGill-Queen's University Press, 2008.

Jenkinson, Jacqueline. *Black 1919: Riots, Racism and Resistance in Imperial Britain*. Liverpool: Liverpool University Press, 2009.

Joshi, Chitra. *Lost Worlds: Indian Labour and Its Forgotten Histories*. Delhi: Permanent Black, 2003.

Kakar, M. Hassan. *A Political and Diplomatic History of Afghanistan, 1863-1901*. Boston: Brill, 2006.

Kale, Madhavi. *Fragments of Empire: Capital, Slavery, and Indian Indentured Labor in the British Caribbean*. Philadelphia: University of Pennsylvania Press, 1994.

Kane, Anne. *Constructing Irish National Identity: Discourse and Ritual during the Land War, 1879-82*. New York: Palgrave MacMillan, 2011.

Karnik, V. B. *Strikes in India*. Bombay: Manaktalas, 1967.

Kealey, Gregory, and Bryan Palmer. *Dreaming of What Might Be: The Knights of Labor in Ontario, 1880-1900*. Cambridge: Cambridge University Press, 1982.

Keddie, Nikki R. *An Islamic Response to Imperialism; Political and Religious Writings of Sayyid Jamāl ad-Dīn "al-Afghānī*. Berkeley: University of California Press, 1968.

Keddie, Nikki R. *Modern Iran: Roots and Results of Revolution*. New Haven, CT: Yale University Press, 2003.

Kelly, John D., Beatrice Jauregi, Sean T. Mitchell and Jeremy Walton, eds. *Anthropology and Global Counterinsurgency*. Chicago: University of Chicago, 2010.

Kennedy, Dane. "The Great Arch of Empire." In Martin Hewitt, ed., *The Victorian World*. New York: Routledge, 2012, 57–72.

Kennedy, Dane. *The Last Blank Spaces: Exploring Africa and Australia*. Cambridge, MA: Harvard University Press, 2013.

Kling, Blair. *The Blue Mutiny: The Indigo Disturbances in Bengal 1859-1862*. Philadelphia: University of Pennsylvania Press, 1966.

Knight, G. Roger. "Sugar and Servility: Themes of Forced Labour, Resistance and Accommodation in mid-Nineteenth Century Java" In Edward A. Alpers, Gwyn Campbell, and Michael Salman, eds., *Resisting Bondage in Indian Ocean Africa and Asia*. London: Routledge, 2007, 69–81.

Koditschek, Theodore. *Liberalism, Imperialism, and the Historical Imagination: Nineteenth Century Visions of a Greater Britain*. Cambridge: Cambridge University Press, 2011.

Kolinsky, Martin. *Law, Order and Riots in Mandatory Palestine, 1928-35*. London: St. Martin's Press, 1993.

Kolsky, Elizabeth. *Colonial Justice in British India*. Cambridge: Cambridge University Press, 2010.

Korom, Frank J. *Hosay Trinidad: Muharram Performances in an Indo-Caribbean Diaspora*. Philadelphia: University of Pennsylvania Press, 2003.

Lahiri, Shompa. *Indian Mobilities in the West, 1900-1947: Gender, Performance, Embodiment*. London: Palgrave, 2010.

Lake, Marilyn. "'The Day Will Come': Charles H. Pearson's *National Life and Character: A Forecast*." In Antoinette Burton and Isabel Hofmeyr, eds., *Ten Books That Shaped the British Empire: Creating an Imperial Commons*. Durham, NC: Duke University Press, 2014, 90–111.

Lal, Brij V. "Kunti's Cry: Indentured Women on Fiji Plantations." *Indian Economic Social History Review* 22, 1 (1985): 55–71.

Lambert-Hurley, Siobhan. *Muslim Women, Reform and Princely Patronage*. London: Routledge, 2007.

Lambert-Hurley, Siobhan. "Princes, Paramountcy and the Politics of Muslim Identity: The Begam of Bhopal on the Indian National Stage, 1901-26." *South Asia* 26, 2 (2003): 165–91.

Land, Isaac, ed. *Enemies of Humanity: The Nineteenth Century War on Terror*. New York: Palgrave Macmillan, 2008.

Lazarus, Neil. *The Postcolonial Unconscious*. Cambridge: Cambridge University Press, 2011.

Lennon, Joseph. "Fasting for the Public: Irish and Indian Sources of Marion Wallace Dunlop's 1909 Hunger Strike." In Eion Flannery and Angus Mitchell, eds., *Enemies of Empire: New Perspectives on Imperialism, Literature and Historiography*. Dublin: Four Courts Press, 2007, 19–39.

Levine, Philippa. *Prostitution, Race and Politics: Policing Venereal Disease in the British Empire*. New York: Routledge, 2003.

Lewis, David Levering. *The Race to Fashoda: Colonialism and African Resistance*. New York: Henry Holt, 1995.

Lieten, Georges Kristofel. *Colonialism, Class, and Nation: The Confrontation in Bombay around 1930*. Calcutta: K. P. Bagchi, 1984.

Lloyd, Alan, *The Drums of Kumasi: The Story of the Ashanti Wars*. London: Longman's, 1964.

Loewen, Arley, and Josette McMichael, eds. *Images of Afghanistan: Exploring Afghan Culture through Art and Literature*. Karachi: Oxford University Press, 2010.

Look Lai, Walton. *Indentured Labor, Caribbean Sugar: Chinese and Indian Migrants to the British West Indies, 1838-1918*. Baltimore, MD: Johns Hopkins University Press, 1993.

Lourduswamy, Stan. *Jharkandi's Claim for Self-Rule: Its Historical Foundations and Present Legitimacy*. New Delhi: Indian Social Institute, 1997.

Low, D. A. *Fabrication of Empire: The British and the Uganda Kingdoms, 1890-1902*. Cambridge: Cambridge University Press, 2009.

Loy-Wilson, Sophie. "'Liberating' Asia: Strikes and Protest in Sydney and Shanghai, 1920-1939." *History Workshop Journal* 72, 1 (2011): 75–102.

Lynn, John. *Battle: A History of Combat and Culture*. Boulder, CO: Westview, 2003.

Maclennan, Ben. *A Proper Degree of Terror: John Graham and the Cape's Eastern Frontier*. Johannesburg: Ravan Press, 1986.

Macrory, Patrick. *Signal Catastrophe: The Story of the Disastrous Retreat from Kabul, 1842*. London: Hodder and Stoughton, 1966.

Makalani, Minkah. *In the Cause of Freedom: Radical Black Internationalism form Harlem to London, 1917-1939*. Chapel Hill: University of North Carolina Press, 2011.

Mandel, Robert. "Defining Postwar Victory." In Jan Angstrom and Isabelle Duyvesteyn, eds. *Understanding Victory and Defeat in Contemporary War*. New York: Routledge, 2007, 13–45.

Mann, Gregory. *Native Sons: West African Veterans and France in the Twentieth Century*. Durham, NC: Duke University Press, 2006.

Marks, Shula. *Reluctant Rebellion: The 1906-8 Disturbances in Natal*. Oxford: Clarendon, 1970.

Marshall, Alex. *The Russian General Staff and Asia, 1800-1917*. New York: Routledge, 2006.

Martin, Amy E. *Alter-Nations: Nationalisms, Terror and the State in Nineteenth Century Britain and Ireland*. Columbus: Ohio State University Press, 2012.

Matera, Marc, Misty Bastian, and Susan Kingsley Kent. *The Women's War of 1929: Gender and Violence in Colonial Nigeria*. New York: Palgrave, 2012.

Mazumdar, Shaswati. *Insurgent Sepoys: Europe Views the Revolt of 1857*. London: Routledge, 2011.

McCormick, Thomas J. *America's Half-Century: United States Foreign Policy in the Cold War and After*. Baltimore, MD: Johns Hopkins University Press, 1989.

McCoy, Alfred. "Fatal Florescence: Europe's Decolonization and America's Decline," in McCoy, Josep M. Fradera and Stephen Jacobson, eds., *Endless Empire: Spain's Retreat, Europe's Eclipse, America's Decline*. Madison: University of Wisconsin Press, 2012, 3–29.

McMahon A. H., and A. D. G. Ramsay, *Report on the Tribes of Dir, Swat and Bajour Together with the Utman-Khel and Sam Ranizai*. Peshawar: Saeed Book Bank 1981; originally published in 1901.

McMahon, Paul. *British Spies and Irish Rebels: British Intelligence and Ireland, 1916-1945*. Rochester, NY: Boydell and Brewer Press, 2008.

Menon, Dilip M. "The Many Spaces and Times of Swadeshi." *Economic and Political Weekly* 48, 42 (2012): 44–52.

Midgley, Clare. *Women against Slavery: The British Campaigns 1780-1870*. London: Routledge, 1994.

Miles, John. "Rival Protest in the Gold Coast: The Cocoa Hold-ups, 1908-38." In Clive Dewey and A. G. Hopkins, eds. *The Imperial Impact: Studies in the Economic History of Africa and India*. London: Althone Press, 1978, 152–70.

Mills, Elliott Evans. *The Decline and Fall of the British Empire: A Brief Account of the Causes which Resulted in the Destruction of Our Late Ally, Together with a Comparison between the British and Roman Empires; Appointed for Use in the National Schools of Japan*. Oxford: Alden and Co., Ltd., Bocario Press, 1905.

Minault Gail. *The Khilafat Movement: Religious Symbolism and Political Mobilization in India*. New York: Columbia University Press, 1982.

Misdaq, Nabi. *Afghanistan: Political Frailty and Foreign Interference*. London: Routledge, 2006.

Moody, T. W. *Davitt and Irish Revolution, 1846-82*. Oxford: Clarendon, 1981.

Moore-Harell, Alice. *Egypt's African Empire: Samuel Baker, Charles Gordon and the Creation of Equatoria*.Brighton: Sussex Academic Press, 2010.

Msindo, Enocent. *Ethnicity in Zimbabwe: Transformations in Kalanga and Ndebele Societies, 1860-1990*. Rochester, Rochester, NY: University of Rochester Press, 2012.

Mukherjee, Meenakshi. *The Perishable Empire: Essays on Indian Writing in English*. Oxford: Oxford University Press, 2000.

Nair, C. Sankaran. *Gandhi and Anarchy*. Nair Foundation, 2000; first published in 1922.

Nelson, Bruce. *Irish Nationalists and the Making of the Irish Race*. Princeton, NJ: Princeton University Press 2012.

Ness, Immanuel, ed. *International Encyclopedia of Revolution and Protest: 1500 to the Present*. New York: Wiley-Blackwell, 2009.

Newsinger, John. *The Blood Never Dried: A People's History of the British Empire*, London: Bookmarks Publications, Ltd.,2006.

Newsinger, John. *Fenianism in Mid-Victorian Britain*. London: Palgrave Macmillan, 1994.

Newsinger, John. *Rebel City: Larkin, Connolly and the Dublin Labour Movement*. London: Merlin Press, 2004.

Nijjar, Bakshish Sing. *Anglo-Sikh Wars, 1845-49*. New Delhi: K. B. Publications.

Noelle, Christine. *State and Tribe in Early Afghanistan: The Reign of Amir Dost Muhammad Khan (1826-1863)*. Surrey, UK: Curzon Press, 1997.

Norris, J. A. *The First Afghan War, 1838-1842*. Cambridge University Press, 1967.

Oddie, Geoffrey. *Missionaries, Rebellion and Proto-Nationalism: James Long of Bengal, 1814-87*. Surrey: Curzon Press, 1999.

Olssen, Erik. *The Red Feds: Revolutionary Industrial Unionism and the New Zealand Federation of Labour, 1908-14*. Auckland: Oxford University Press, 1988.

O'Malley, Kate. *Ireland, India and Empire: Indo-Irish Radical Connections, 1919-64*. Manchester: Manchester University Press, 2008.

Ouchterlony, John. *The Chinese War; An Account of All the Operations of the British Forces from the Commencement to the Treaty of Nanking*. New York: Praeger, 1972; originally published in 1844.

Padmore, George. *The Life and Struggles of Negro Toilers*. London: International Trade Union Committee of Negro Workers, 1931.

Pakenham, Thomas. *The Scramble for Africa: White Man's Conquest of the Dark Continent from 1876-1912*. New York: Avon Books, 1992.

Pašeta, Senia. *Irish Nationalist Women, 1900-1918*. Cambridge: Cambridge University Press, 2013.

Pawliková-Vilhanová, Viera. *History of Anti-Colonial Resistance and Protest in the Kingdoms of Buganda and Bunyoro, 1890-1899*. Prague: Oriental Institute of the Czechoslovak Academy of Sciences, 1988.

Popplewell, Richard J. *Intelligence and Imperial Defence: British Intelligence and the Defence of the Indian Empire, 1904-1924*. London: Frank Cass, 1995.

Popplewell, Richard J. "The Surveillance of Indian 'Seditionists' in North America, 1905-1915." In Christopher Andrew and Jeremy Noakes, eds., *Intelligence and International Relations, 1900-1945*. Exeter: University of Exeter Press, 1987, 49–76.

Porter, Bernard. *The Origins of the Vigilant State: The London Metropolitan Police Special Branch before the First World War*. London: Weidenfeld and Nicolson, 1987.

Porter, Bernard. *Plots and Paranoia: A History of Political Espionage in Britain, 1790-1988*. London: Unwin Hyman, 1989.

Prashad, Vijay. *The Darker Nations: A People's History of the Third World*. New York: New Press, 2007.

Preston, Adrian, ed., *The South African Journal of Sir Garnet Wolseley, 1879-1880*. Cape Town: A. A. Balkema, 1973.

Price, Richard. *Making Empire: Colonial Encounters and the Creation of Imperial Rule in Nineteenth-Century Africa*. Cambridge: Cambridge University Press, 2008.

Puar, Jasbir K.. *Terrorist Assemblages: Homonationalism in Queer Times*. Durham, NC: Duke University Press, 2007.

Puri, Harish K. "Revolutionary Organization: A Study of the Ghadar Movement." *Social Scientist* 9, 2–3 (1980): 53–66.

Qureshi, M. Naeem. *Pan-Islamism in British Indian Politics: A Study of the Khilafat Movement, 1918-1924*. Leiden: Brill, 1999.

Radhakrishnan, S., ed. *Mahatma Gandhi: Essays and Reflections on His Life and Work*. Bombay: Jaico Publishing House, 1956.

Ramaswamy, P. "Labour Control and Labour Resistance in the Plantations of Colonial Malaya." In E. Valentine Daniel, Henry Bernstein, and Tom Brass, eds. *Plantations, Peasants and Proletarians in Colonial Asia*. London: Frank Cass, 1992, 87–105.

Ramnath, Maia. *Haj to Utopia: How the Ghadar Movement Charted Global Radicalism and Attempted to Overthrow the British Empire*. Berkeley: University of California Press, 2011.

Rana, Aziz. *The Two Faces of American Freedom*. Cambridge, MA: Harvard University Press, 2010.

Ranger, Terence O. *Bulawayo Burning: the Social History of a Southern African City, 1893-1960*. London: James Currey, 2010.

Ranger, Terence O. *Revolt in Southern Rhodesia, 1896-97: A Study in African Resistance*. Evanston: Northwestern University Press, 1967.

Raza, Ali, Franziska Roy and Benjamin Zachariah, eds., *The Internationalist Moment: South Asia, Worlds, and World Views 1917-39*. London: Sage, 2014.

Read, Geoff, and Todd Webb, "'The Catholic Mahdi of the North West': Louis Riel and the Metis Resistance in Transatlantic and Imperial Context." *Canadian Historical Review* 93, 2 (2012): 171–95.

Regan-Lefebvre, Jennifer. *Cosmopolitan Nationalism in the Victorian Empire: Ireland, India and the Politics of Alfred Webb*. London: Palgrave 2009.

Reid, Jennifer. *Louis Riel and the Creation of Modern Canada: Mythic Discourse and the Postcolonial State*. Albuquerque: University of New Mexico Press, 2008.

Reynolds, Nancy Y. *City Consumed: Urban Commerce, the Cairo Fire, and the Politics of Decolonization in Egypt*. Redwood City, CA: Stanford University Press, 2012.

Richards, D. S. *The Savage Frontier: A History of the Anglo-Afghan Wars*. London: Macmillan, 1990.

Robb, George C. *British Culture and the First World War*. New York: Palgrave, 2002.

Robbins, Bruce. *Perpetual War: Cosmopolitanism from the Viewpoint of Violence*. Durham, NC: Duke University Press, 2012.

Roberston, Claire C. *Trouble Showed the Way: Women, Men and Trade in the Nairobi Area, 1890-1990*. Bloomington: Indiana University Press, 1997.

Robinson, David. *Muslim Societies in African History*. Cambridge: Cambridge University Press, 2004.

Robinson, Paul. *Military Honour and the Conduct of War*. London: Routledge, 2006.

Rodgers, Daniel T. *Atlantic Crossings: Social Politics in a Progressive Age*. Cambridge, MA: Harvard University Press, 1998.

Roediger, David R., and Elizabeth D. Esch. *The Production of Difference: Race and the Management of Labor in US History*. Oxford: Oxford University Press, 2012.

Roy, Kaushik, ed. *War and Society in Colonial India*. New Delhi: Oxford University Press, 2006.

Saha, Jonathan. *Law, Disorder and the Colonial State: Corruption in Burma c.1900*. London: Palgrave Macmillan, 2013.

Said, Edward. *Culture and Imperialism*. New York: Vintage Books, 1994.

Said, Edward. *Orientalism*. New York: Vintage Books, 1979.

Salesa, Damon Ieremia. *Racial Crossings: Race, Intermarriage and the Victorian British Empire*. New York: Oxford University Press, 2011.

Salesa, Damon Ieremia. "Samoa's Half-Castes and Some Frontiers of Comparison." In Ann L. Stoler, ed., *Haunted by Empire: Geographies of Intimacy in North American History*. Durham, NC: Duke University Press, 2006, 71–93.

Sanderson, Edgar. *The British Empire in the Nineteenth Century: Its Progress and Expansion at Home and Abroad; comprising a description and history of the British colonies and dependencies*, vol. 4. London: Blackie and Son, 1897.

Sandoval, Chela. *Methodology of the Oppressed* Minneapolis: University of Minnesota Press, 2000.

Sarkar, Sumit. *The Swadeshi Movement in Bengal, 1903-1908*. New Delhi: People's Publishing House, 1973.

Saunders, Kay. *Workers in Bondage: The Origins and Bases of Unfree Labour in Queensland, 1824-1916*. St. Lucia: University of Queensland Press, 1982.

Schneer, Jonathan. *London 1900: The Imperial Metropolis*. New Haven, CT: Yale University Press, 2001.

Schofield, Victoria. *Afghan Frontier: Feuding and Fighting in Central Asia*. London: I. B. Tauris, 2003.

Scott, James C. *The Art of Not Being Governed: An Anarchist History of Upland Southeast Asia*. New Haven, CT: Yale University Press, 2009.

Seecharan, Clem. *Bechu: "Bound Coolie" Radical in British Guiana, 1894-1901*. Kingston: University of the West Indies Press, 1999.

Seigel, Micol. "World History's Narrative Problem." *Hispanic American Historical Review* 84, 3 (2004): 431–46.

Sen, Samita. "At the Margins: Women Workers in the Bengal Jute Industry." In Jonathan Parry, Jan Breman, and Karin Kapadia, eds., *The Worlds of Indian Industrial Labor*, New Delhi: Sage, 1999, 239–70.

Sewell, William H., Jr. *Logics of History: Social Theory and Social Transformation*. Chicago: University of Chicago Press, 2005.

Sharkey, Heather J. *Living with Colonialism: Nationalism and Culture in the Anglo-Egyptian Sudan*. Berkeley: University of California Press, 2003.

Sharma, Jayeeta. "'Lazy' Natives, Coolie Labour, and the Assam Tea Industry." *Modern Asian Studies* 43, 6 (2009): 1287–324.

Sharpe, Jenny. *Allegories of Empire: The Figure of Woman in the Colonial Text*. Minneapolis: University of Minnesota Press, 1993.

Sheller, Mimi. *Citizenship from Below: Erotic Agency and Caribbean Freedom*. Durham, NC: Duke University Press, 2012.

Sherwood, Marika. *Origins of Pan-Africanism: Henry Sylvester Williams, Africa and the African Diaspora*. London: Routledge, 2011.

Short, K. R. M. *The Dynamite War: Irish-American Bombers in Victorian Britain*. Dublin: Gill and Macmillan, 1979.

Silvestri, Michael. *Ireland and India: Nationalism, Empire and Memory*. London: Palgrave, 2009.

Simeon, Dilip. "Work and Resistance in the Jharia Coalfield." In Jonathan P. Parry, Jan Breman, and Karin Kapadia, eds., *Worlds of Indian Industrial Labor*, 43–76.

Sinclair, Georgina. "'Get into a Crack Force and Earn £20 a Month and all Found . . .': The Influence of the Palestinian Police upon Colonial Policing 1922-1948." *European Review of History* 13, 1 (2006): 49–65.

Singhal, Damodar P. *Indian and Afghanistan, 1876-1907: A Study in Diplomatic Relations*. St. Lucia: University of Queensland Press, 1963.

Singh, Khushwant. *Ranjit Singh: Maharaja of the Punjab*. New Delhi: Penguin Books, 2009.

Smith, Linda Tuhiwai. *Decolonizing Methodologies: Research and Indigenous Peoples*. London: Zed Books, 1999.

Smith, Philip Thurmond. *Policing Victorian London*. Westport, CT: Greenwood, 1985.

Smithers, A. J. *The Kaffir Wars, 1779-1877*. London: Leo Cooper, 1972.

Sohi, Seema. "Race, Surveillance, and Indian Anticolonialism in the Transnational Western U.S.-Canadian Borderlands." *Journal of American History* 98, 2 (2011): 420–36.

Spodek, Howard. "On the Origins of Gandhi's Political Methodology: The Heritage of Kathiawad and Gujarat." *Journal of Asian Studies* 30, 2 (1971): 361–72.

St. Pierre, Maurice. *Anatomy of Resistance: Anti-Colonialism in Guyana, 1823-1966*. London: Macmillan Education, 1999.

Steele, Frances. *Oceania under Steam: Sea Transport and the Cultures of Colonialism, c.1870-1914*. Manchester: Manchester University Press, 2011.

Steinmetz, George. *The Devil's Handwriting: Precoloniality and the German Colonial State in Qingdao, Samoa and Southwest Africa*. Chicago: University of Chicago Press, 2007.

Stewart, Robert J. "Reporting Morant Bay: The 1865 Jamaican Insurrection as Reported and Interpreted in the *New York Herald, Daily Tribune* and *Times*." In Brian L. Moore and Swithin Wilmot, eds. *Before and after 1865: Education, Politics and Regionalism in the Caribbean*. Kingston: Ian Randle Publishers, 1998, 330–42.

Stoler, Ann Laura. *Race and the Education of Desire: Foucault's History of Sexuality and the Colonial Order of Things*. Durham, NC: Duke University Press, 1995.

Stone, Lawrence. *An Imperial State at War: Britain From 1689-1815*. London: Routledge, 1993.

Streets, Heather. *Martial Races: The Military, Race and Masculinity in British Imperial Culture, 1857-1914*. Manchester: Manchester University Press, 2004.

Streets-Salter, Heather. "The Local was Global: The Singapore Mutiny of 1915." *Journal of World History* 24, 3 (2013): 539–76.

Stuart, James. *A History of the Zulu Rebellion, 1906, and of DinZulu's Arrest, Trial and Expatriation*. London: Macmillan, 1913.

Sutton, I. B. "The Diggers' Revolt in Griqualand West, 1875." *International Journal of African Historical Studies* 12, 1 (1979): 40–61.

Svensen, Stuart. *The Shearers' War: The Story of the 1891 Shearers' Strike*. St. Lucia: University of Queensland Press, 1989.

Swan, Maureen. "The 1913 Natal Indian Strike." *Journal of Southern African Studies* 10, 2 (1984): 239–58.

Swedenburg, Ted. *Memories of Revolt: The 1936-1939 Rebellion and the Palestinian National Past*. Minneapolis: University of Minnesota Press, 1995.

Tambe, Ashwini. *Codes of Misconduct: Regulating Prostitution in Late Colonial Bombay*. Minneapolis: University of Minnesota Press, 2009.

Tambe, Ashwini, and Harald Fischer-Tiné, eds. *The Limits of British Colonial Control in South Asia: Spaces of Disorder in the Indian Ocean Region*. London: Routledge, 2009.

TeBrake, Janet K., "Irish Peasant Women in Revolt: The Land League Years." *Irish Historical Studies* 28, 109 (1992): 63–80.

Thapar-Björkert, Suruchi. *Women in the Indian National Movement*. New Delhi: Sage, 2006.

Thornton, A. P. *The Imperial Idea and Its Enemies: A Study in British Power*. New York: Doubleday, 1957.

Tickell, Alex. *Terrorism, Insurgency, and Indian-English Literature, 1830-1947*. New York: Routledge, 2012.

Townshend, Charles. *Desert Hell: The British Invasion of Mesopotamia*. Cambridge, MA: Harvard University Press. 2011.

Toye, Richard. "'The Riddle of the Frontier': Winston Churchill, the Malakand Field Force and the Rhetoric of Imperial Expansion." *Historical Research* 84 (October 2010): 493–512.

Trentmann, Frank. *Free Trade Nation: Commerce, Consumption and Civil Society in Modern Britain*. Oxford: Oxford University Press, 2008.

Trivedi, Lisa. *Clothing Gandhi's Nation: Homespun and Modern India*. Bloomington: Indiana University Press, 2007.

Tsai, Jung-Fan. *Hong Kong in Chinese History: Community and Social Unrest in the British Colony, 1842-1913*. New York: Columbia University Press, 1993.

Tsang, Steve. *A Modern History of Hong Kong*. London: I. B. Taurus, 1994.

Tsing, Anna Lowenhaupt. *Friction: An Ethnography of Global Connection*. Princeton, NJ: Princeton University Press, 2005.

Turrell, Rob. "The 1875 Black Flag Revolt on the Kimberley Diamond Fields." *Journal of Southern African Studies* 7, 2 (1981): 194–235.

Tuteja, K. L. "Jallianwala Bagh: A Critical Juncture in the Indian National Movement." *Social Scientist* 25, Jan.–Feb. (1997): 25–61.

Van Onselen, Charles. *Chibaro: African Mine Labor in South Rhodesia, 1900-1933*. London: Pluto Press, 1976.

Vernon, James. *Hunger: A Modern History*. Cambridge, MA: Harvard University Press, 2007.

Visram, Rozina. *Asians in Britain: 400 years of History*. London: Pluto Press, 2002

Walker, Cherryl. *Women and Resistance in South Africa*. London: Onyx Press, 1982.

Wanhalla, Angela. "Interracial Sexual Violence in 1860s New Zealand." *New Zealand Journal of History* 45, 1 (2011): 71–84.

Warburg, Gabriel. *The Sudan under Wingate: Administration in the Anglo-Egyptian Sudan, 1899-1916*. London: Frank Cass, 1971.

Warrior, Robert. "Native Critics in the World: Edward Said and Nationalism." In Craig Womack, Jace Weaver, and Robert Warrior, eds., *American Indian Literary Nationalism*. Albuquerque: University of New Mexico Press, 2006, 179–223.

Weber, Charlotte. "Between Nationalism and Feminism: The Eastern Women's Congresses of 1930 and 1932." *Journal of Middle East Women's Studies* 4, 1 (2008): 83–106.

Wei, Yuan. *Chinese Account of the Opium War*. Translated by Edward Harper Parker. Shanghai: Kelly and Walsh, 1888.

Wells, Julia C. "The War of Degradation: Black Women's Struggle against Orange Free State Pass Laws, 1913." In Donald E. Crummey, ed., *Banditry, Rebellion and Social Protest in Africa*. London: James Currey, 1986, 253–70.

Welsh, Frank. *A History of Hong Kong*. New York: Harper Collins, 1993.

Wenzel, Jennifer. *Bulletproof: Afterlives of Anticolonial Prophecy in South Africa and Beyond*. Chicago: University of Chicago Press, 2009.

Whelehan, Niall. *The Dynamiters: Irish Nationalism and Political Violence in the Wider World, 1867-1900*. Cambridge: Cambridge University Press, 2012.

White, Luise. *The Comforts of Home: Prostitution in Colonial Nairobi*. Chicago: University of Chicago Press, 1990.

Wilks, Ivor. *Asante in the Nineteenth Century: The Structure and Evolution of a Political Order*. Cambridge: Cambridge University Press, 1975.

Wilson, Louis E. "The 'Bloodless Conquest' in Southeastern Ghana: The Huza and Territorial Expansion of the Krobo in the 19th Century." *International Journal of African Historical Studies* 23, 2 (1990): 269–97.

Wilson, Louis E. *The Krobo People of Ghana to 1892: A Political and Social History*. Athens: Ohio University Press, 1991.

Wipper, Audrey. *Rural Rebels: A Study of Two Protest Movements in Kenya*. Nairobi: Oxford University Press, 1977.

Wolfson, Freda. "A Price Agreement on the Gold Coast-The Krobo Oil Boycott, 1858-1866." *Economic History Review,* New Series 6, 1 (1953): 68–77.

Yang, Anand. *The Limited Raj: Agrarian Relations in Colonial India, Saran District, 1793-1920*. Berkeley: University of California Press 1989.

Young, John. *They Fell Like Stones: Battles and Casualties of the Zulu War, 1879*. London: Greenhill, 1991.

Young, Robert J. C. "Colonial Anti-Colonialism: The Fenian Invasions of Canada." In Fiona Bateman and Lionel Pilkington, eds. *Studies in Settler Colonialism*. Palgrave, 2010, 75–89.

Zilfu, Ismat Hasan. *Karari: The Sudanese Account of the Battle of Omdurman*. London: F. Warne, 1980.

INDEX

Abdul Hamid II, Sultan, 199
Abdur Rahman Khan (amir
  of Afghanistan): control
  of Afghanistan, 52;
  extraterritorial authority
  of, 233n82; support for
  tribesmen, 40; uprisings
  against, 233n83
Abolition Act (Great Britain,
  1833), 128
abolitionist movement: use of
  boycott, 91–93; working
  class in, 92–93
Abu Hamd, Sultan, 206
Ad-din, Nasir (shah of
  Iran): assassination of, 207
Afghani, Jamal ad-Din, al-, 205–7;
  threat to imperial security,
  208–9; visit to Britain, 206
Afghanistan: contemporary
  wars in, 217; independence
  for, 53; role in imperial
  insecurity, 262n151;
  strategic importance of, 27;
  terrain of, 51–52

Afghans: anticolonialism
  of, 205–6; Churchill's
  characterization of,
  46; conflation with
  terrain, 51–52; guerrilla
  tactics of, 51
Afghan War, First (1839–42), 47
Afghan War, Second (1878–80),
  47, 76; failure of, 81
Afghan War, Third, 53
Africa: British protectorates of,
  172, 173, 174; collective
  counteraggression in, 174;
  Congress of Berlin on,
  169–70; development of,
  256n83; imperial capital in,
  169, 172; imperial insecurity
  in, 175–76, 177; indirect rule
  in, 210; political economy of,
  210; resource extraction in,
  172; Scramble for, 162–177;
  transportation networks of,
  168; ungovernability of, 174;
  white settlement in, 163
Africa, central: rebellions in, 210

293

of, 17, 219; anti-state challenges of, 147; appreciation of history, 14; collective action by, 142; disruption of empire, 6, 14, 88; economic disruptions by, 87–107; economic power of, 88; histories of, 221; incomplete control over, 215; labor disruptions by, 88, 89; market relations of, 88; mixed-race, 9; modes of protest, 89; preemptive postures of, 14– 15; production of instability, 220; radical, 195–96; relationship with colonizers, 12; resistance by, 13, 141; under settler sovereignty, 147; shaping of empire, 11; skepticism among, 15, 142, 144; understanding of empire, 8; use of imperial tools, 15; white settlers, 9. *See also* indigenous peoples

Combined Diggers Association, 118

commerce, British imperial, 3, 11. *See also* marketplace

communal identity, consolidation of, 251n157

Congreve Rocket, 72

consumption: in anticolonial politics, 99–100; in anticolonial struggles, 102–3; unpredictable, 142; withholding of, 106–7; women's role in, 92

Contagious Diseases Acts, 136

Coomasie, march to, 178

Costello, Lieutenant: at Malakand, 33

Cotton, Sir Willoughby, 49

counterinsurgency, British, 59–61, 212–14, 253n23; in Palestine, 265n193

Cowper, William: "Negro's Complaint," 91

Craddock, George, 156

Cromer, Evelyn Baring, Lord, 165, 254n52

Ctesiphon, battle of (1915), 82

Cullen, Paul, 179

Cumann na mBan (Irish feminist organization), 189, 194

Curry, J. C., 126

Curzon, Lord, 233n83; partition of Bengal, 100

Cutt, Michael Madhusudan, 152

Dacca Anushilan Samiti, 202

Dandi salt march, 102

Daniels, Leo, 109

Darfur, rebellion in, 165

Darwin, John, 11; *The Empire Project*, 226n26

Das, Bina: assassination attempt by, 189

Das, Hem Chandra: biblio-bomb of, 189

Das, Kalyani, 189

Das, Nafar, 148

Das, Taraknath, 191

Davitt, Michael, 158

Dayal, Har, 192

Deane, Major: at Malakand, 32, 229n21

peace: challenges to, 21; by fire, 42–45
Pease, Elizabeth, 92
Persians, interest in Herat, 48
Peshawar: British raids on, 45; Dost Mohammed's interest in, 48
plantations: abusive systems of, 157; anticolonialism on, 132; desertion from, 132, 135; labor resistance on, 127–33; labor shortages on, 129, 132; legal actions against, 133; micro aggressions on, 136; modes of resistance on, 132–33; racial hierarchies on, 135; regional mixes on, 131; retaliation against owners, 127; suicide on, 135–36; tea, 135; tenant rents in, 153; uprisings on, 127–28; violence against workers on, 129–31, 133; women's defiance on, 135; worker agency on, 134–35. *See also* indigo cultivation; sugar industry
Pollock, Sir George, 50
Popplewell, Richard J., 265n200
power, British imperial: in Africa, 168; anglophone, 218; challenges to, 1, 89; checks on, 12; cooptation of, 9; discontinuous, 22; global, 22; impediments to, 11; inevitability of, 13; limits of, 9, 47, 79; modern, 21; newspaper accounts

of, 178; protests against, 9; public perceptions of, 218; rise-and-fall narratives of, 4; shifting relations of, 17; uneven, 21; vulnerabilities of, 14
Power, J. O'Connor, 161–62
print culture, Islamic, 200
prisons, hunger strikes in, 138
progress, British imperial, 3; injustices of, 15
prostitution, regulation of, 136–37
protest: consumer, 92; Russian traditions of, 138. *See also* hartal; insurgency; labor protest; resistance
protest, colonial: economic, 87–107, 145–46; and end of empire, 93; instability in, 98; in Ireland, 94–96; modes of, 89; political consequences of, 92; power of, 9; small-scale, 89, 90–107
Punjab, British control of, 64, 65

Qassam, Shaykh Izz al-Din, al-, death of, 211, 212
Qing dynasty, conflict with British, 54–55
Quakers, boycott of sugar, 91–93, 110

race riots (Tyneside, 1919), 108
races, fraternization among, 144
racial superiority, imperial belief in, 15, 29, 81, 214, 217
radicalism, 17; in United States, 190